The Quiet Embargo

The Quiet Embargo

Insurance, Compliance, and the Hidden Wars of Trade

By

Nuno Valcorte

Vij Books

New Delhi (India)

Published by

Vij Books
(Publishers, Distributors & Importers)
4836/24, 3rd Floor, Ansari Road
Delhi – 110 002
Phone: 91-11-43596460
Mobile: 98110 94883
e-mail: contact@vijpublishing.com
www.vijbooks.in

ISBN: 978-81-99786-81-3 (PB)

This book was developed using advanced writing tools to support the drafting and ideation process. All content has been thoughtfully curated, refined, and reviewed to ensure quality and relevance.

Contents

Introduction

A bulk carrier waits at anchor just beyond the breakwater. Its holds are full of grain, loaded under licence, inspected, weighed, sealed. The paperwork is immaculate. The cargo is bound for a country where bread prices have doubled in a year and where the harvest failed after a run of bad weather. There is no dispute about legality. No warship blocks the channel. No official arrives with an order stamped in red. Days pass. Then weeks. The vessel does not sail. An insurer declines to renew cover, citing a review of its risk appetite. A bank, alerted by a routine compliance query, decides it cannot process the payment chain with sufficient comfort. No one says no in so many words. Everyone acts prudently. The grain stays where it is.

Scenes like this do not make headlines. They rarely appear in government statements or parliamentary debates. Yet they are increasingly common, and they shape the movement of goods more decisively than many formal embargoes ever did. Trade today is less often stopped by walls or guns than by hesitations, exclusions and quiet withdrawals embedded deep within the systems that support it. The friction is subtle, bureaucratic, almost polite. Its effects are anything but.

For centuries, economic coercion was visible and declarative. Ports were closed, fleets blockaded, customs houses shuttered. Merchants knew where they stood. Even when the rules were harsh, they were legible. What has emerged over the past few decades is something different: a form of constraint exercised through services rather than borders, through risk management rather than decree. It is a system that leaves trade formally permitted while making it practically impossible. This is the quiet embargo.

The paradox is striking. Global trade has never been more rule-bound, documented and ostensibly transparent. Sanctions regimes are published online. Licences can be downloaded. Compliance manuals run to hundreds of pages. And yet some of the most consequential trade decisions are made in private meetings, internal committees and algorithmic filters, far from the gaze of diplomats or voters. Cargoes vanish not because they are banned, but because they become uninsurable. Projects stall not because they are illegal, but because no bank will touch the funds. Routes wither because the price of cover climbs just high enough to make them commercially irrational.

The quiet embargo thrives in this space between law and behaviour. It relies on the fact that modern trade is not simply an exchange of goods, but a choreography of financial flows, risk transfers, certifications and assurances. Banks clear payments. Insurers underwrite loss. Reinsurers sit behind them, absorbing the shock of catastrophe. Ports grant access. Classification societies certify seaworthiness. Inspectors verify cargoes. Each link is indispensable. Each is governed by its own incentives and fears. When pressure is applied at one point, the effects ripple outward, often invisibly.

This book begins from a simple observation: sanctions in the twenty-first century work less by forbidding trade than by making it too risky to pursue. Governments set the tone, but private actors do the work. They translate political intent into commercial reality, often going further than the law strictly requires. They do so not out of malice or conspiracy, but out of caution. A single enforcement action, a sharp speech by an official, a hint of future scrutiny can be enough to shift global behaviour. The result is a form of economic pressure that is diffuse, adaptive and difficult to contest.

There is a temptation to see this as a recent phenomenon, born of globalisation and digital finance. In truth, it has deeper roots. Empires have long understood the power of choke points. The Venetian Republic controlled trade by dominating insurance and credit as much as by commanding fleets. The British Empire's naval supremacy mattered not only because of cannon, but because of the City of London's role in financing and insuring global commerce. What is new is the scale, speed and opacity with which these mechanisms now operate, and the degree to which they are entwined with compliance culture and reputational risk.

Consider the language that governs modern sanctions. Laws speak in terms of prohibitions and permissions. They define listed persons, restricted sectors, carve-outs and exceptions. Yet anyone who has tried to move goods through a sensitive corridor knows that legality is only the starting point. What matters is whether a transaction can pass through the gauntlet of internal policies, automated screening systems and risk committees that sit between intent and execution. A shipment may be lawful and still fail. A payment may comply with every regulation and still be declined. The reasons are often framed in neutral terms: insufficient information, unclear ownership, elevated geopolitical risk. The effect is decisive.

The metaphor that runs through this book is that of friction. Not the dramatic halt of a closed gate, but the steady drag that slows motion until it stops. Friction does not announce itself. It accumulates. A slightly higher premium here, a longer review there, an exclusion clause inserted into a policy at renewal. Over time, what was once routine becomes exceptional, then impossible. Trade routes fall silent without ever being formally shut.

Understanding this requires a shift in perspective. Rather than focusing solely on laws and lists, one must watch behaviour. Which banks quietly exit a region? Which insurers narrow their cover? Which ports introduce new requirements? Which routes become expensive, then uneconomic? Compliance decisions, pricing signals, and logistical patterns form a map of contemporary conflict, often revealing tensions long before they erupt into open confrontation.

The stakes are high. For governments, quiet embargoes offer a way to exert pressure without the political cost of overt bans. They allow flexibility and deniability. For firms, they present a constant challenge: how to navigate complex, shifting expectations without paralysing legitimate business. For individuals, the consequences can be stark. Aid delayed. Jobs lost. Markets abandoned. The human cost of over-caution is real, even when intentions are prudent.

This book does not argue that sanctions are illegitimate or that compliance is misguided. Economic measures have long been a tool of statecraft, and there are compelling moral reasons to restrict certain forms of trade. Nor does it suggest that private firms should act recklessly. On the contrary, the systems described here exist because risk is real and mistakes are costly. What this book seeks to do is illuminate how these systems actually function, where their power lies, and how their effects can diverge from their stated aims.

At the centre of the story are three groups of actors: insurers, banks and the logistical authorities that control access to trade infrastructure. Their decisions are interdependent. An insurer's exclusion prompts a bank's refusal. A bank's de-risking triggers a port's hold. Each actor sees only part of the picture, yet together they can immobilise vast flows of commerce. Their incentives differ. Insurers worry about claims and reputational fallout. Banks fear regulatory penalties and correspondent relationships.

Ports answer to national authorities and local politics. None sees itself as enforcing foreign policy, yet all do so in practice.

Layered atop this are the technologies of compliance. Sanctions lists become screening algorithms. Ownership rules turn into data models. Vessel movements are tracked, scored and flagged. These tools promise clarity and consistency, but they also create new forms of opacity. Decisions emerge from systems that few fully understand and fewer can challenge. False positives freeze legitimate trade. Sophisticated evasion slips through the gaps. Data both illuminates and deceives.

The rise of shadow fleets and evasive logistics is a predictable response. When formal channels become constricted, parallel ones emerge. Vessels change names and flags. Ownership is obscured. Tracking systems go dark. Cargoes are blended and transferred at sea. These practices are often presented as evidence of criminal ingenuity. They are also symptoms of a system that pushes activity into the margins. Enforcement agencies, for all their resources, cannot monitor everything. Choices are made about where to focus, and much continues quietly.

Humanitarian trade exposes the moral tension at the heart of the quiet embargo. Sanctions regimes frequently include exemptions for food, medicine and relief. On paper, these carve-outs reflect ethical commitments. In practice, they collide with risk aversion. Firms fear that a mistake will bring censure, that a humanitarian transaction will be misinterpreted, that the reputational cost will outweigh the benefit. Documentation multiplies. Delays stretch on. Aid becomes hostage to the same invisible brakes as commercial cargo.

Governance within firms shapes how these pressures are felt. Boards demand caution. Committees proliferate. Policies thicken. Training emphasises avoidance of error. In some organisations, this produces thoughtful, proportionate decision-making. In others, it breeds silence and rigidity. Staff learn that saying no is safer than asking how. Commercial ambitions are quietly subordinated to compliance comfort, sometimes without explicit debate.

Yet there is agency here. Firms are not merely victims of an unforgiving environment. They make choices about how to interpret guidance, how to invest in expertise, how to engage with regulators and peers. Some build nuanced capabilities, distinguishing real risk from imagined threat. Others retreat behind blanket rules and generic tools. Over time, these choices affect competitiveness and trust. Counterparties notice who can navigate complexity without panic.

One of the book's central claims is that pricing tells a story. Insurance premiums, freight rates and financing costs are not just commercial variables; they are signals of perceived geopolitical risk. When cover for a route doubles in price, something has shifted. When capacity dries up, a line has been crossed. Watching these movements, and understanding their drivers, offers insight into conflicts that may never be formally declared.

This is not a manual for evasion, nor a catalogue of legal technicalities. It is an attempt to make visible what is often hidden in plain sight. By tracing how quiet embargoes operate, the book invites readers to see trade not as a neutral backdrop to politics, but as an active arena where power is exercised and contested. It asks who decides what risk is acceptable, and on whose behalf. It asks how much discretion should sit with private actors, and how their choices align with public goals.

The chapters that follow move from mechanism to consequence, from lists and filters to human impact. They examine the architecture of sanctions, the role of reinsurance and mutual clubs, the dynamics of over-compliance and de-risking. They delve into the shadow world that grows in the cracks, the data that promises oversight, and the governance structures that mediate fear and ambition. They consider how firms adapt, and how observers can read the signals embedded in prices and withdrawals.

Throughout, the emphasis is on interpretation rather than prescription. The world of sanctions and trade compliance is crowded with guidance notes and checklists. What is rarer is a framework for understanding how these elements interact, and what they reveal about broader struggles. The quiet embargo is not a policy announced at a podium. It is a pattern discerned over time.

As geopolitical competition intensifies, the temptation to rely on these invisible tools will grow. They offer leverage without spectacle, pressure without proclamation. But they also carry risks of their own: distortion, inequity, unintended harm. Recognising these dynamics is a first step towards using them with greater awareness.

The grain ship still waits at anchor. Somewhere, a committee will meet again. A model will be adjusted. A clause will be reworded. The decision, when it comes, may never be attributed to any single cause. Was it law, caution, fear, or something else? This book does not promise simple answers. It offers, instead, a way of seeing. In a world where trade is quietly constrained, learning to read the silence matters more than ever.

Chapter 1

How Quiet Embargoes Work

A tanker loads crude at a terminal that has shipped oil for half a century. The flag is respectable, the buyer is well known, and the contract has been vetted by lawyers on both sides. Nothing in the law forbids the voyage. Yet, somewhere between the final hose disconnecting and the pilot boarding, the deal begins to unravel. The ship's insurer signals that renewal will be difficult under current conditions. The reinsurer behind it asks questions that were not asked last year. A bank in the payment chain flags the transaction for review and then, without drama, steps away. No order is issued. No rule is broken. The tanker never sails.

This is the central paradox of modern economic pressure: trade can be lawful, licensed and technically permissible, and still be stopped cold. The mechanism is not prohibition but attrition. Instead of customs officers or border guards, the decisive actors sit in underwriting rooms, compliance teams and risk committees. Their tools are not stamps or seals, but exclusions, pricing adjustments and internal policies. The effect, however, is as real as any blockade.

The idea that sanctions operate primarily through services rather than borders is easy to miss, precisely because services are designed to be invisible when they work well. Finance, insurance and logistics exist to smooth exchange, not to announce themselves. When they function, goods move and payments clear with little fanfare. When they withdraw, the absence is quietly devastating. This chapter begins by examining that absence: how modern sanctions bite not at the perimeter of the state, but at the arteries that keep trade alive.

For much of history, economic coercion was spatial. Control the port, and you controlled the trade. Close the border, and goods piled up on one side or the other. Today's economy is less tangible. Value moves through correspondent banking networks that span continents. Risk is sliced, transferred and reinsured across markets that few outsiders understand.

Ships may cross multiple jurisdictions without ever truly leaving the reach of their insurers or financiers. In this environment, a customs wall is a blunt instrument. Services, by contrast, offer precision.

Banks are the first obvious choke point. A cross-border transaction rarely involves a simple transfer from buyer to seller. It moves through correspondent accounts, clearing systems and compliance filters, each governed by its own rules and exposures. An individual bank may not be prohibited from processing a payment, yet decide that the combination of geography, counterparty and optics makes it unattractive. Insurers form the second pillar. Without cover, ships do not sail, cargoes are not financed, and terminals will not accept risk. Ports and terminals add a further layer, operating under national and local pressures that make them acutely sensitive to anything that might attract scrutiny.

What matters is not any single decision, but their accumulation. Each actor sees itself as acting responsibly within its remit. Together, they create a system in which trade can be throttled without any formal declaration. A hypothetical oil cargo illustrates the point. The seller holds a licence. The buyer is not listed. The route is open. Yet the loss of hull and machinery cover, prompted by a reinsurer's reassessment of geopolitical exposure, makes the voyage commercially untenable. The law permits; the market refuses.

Governments understand this dynamic well. Rather than policing every transaction directly, they set broad parameters and allow private actors to do the rest. Sanctions legislation establishes categories and principles. Guidance notes, speeches and enforcement actions fill in the tone. The heavy lifting is left to banks, insurers and logistics providers, who must interpret what is acceptable under conditions of uncertainty. This is not abdication so much as delegation. Enforcement is outsourced to those best placed to monitor and control the flow.

The power of this approach lies in its leverage. A single high-profile penalty can reshape behaviour far beyond the facts of the case. When a major bank pays a large fine for sanctions breaches, compliance departments around the world take notice. Policies are rewritten. Risk appetites shrink. Activities that were once tolerated become suspect. No new law is required. The message is absorbed and amplified through internal governance structures that prize caution.

There is a cultural dimension to this process. Financial and insurance institutions operate in an environment where reputational damage can be as costly as legal sanction. Media scrutiny, activist pressure and shareholder concerns all feed into decision-making. An activity that is technically lawful may still be deemed unacceptable if it risks negative attention. In this sense, quiet embargoes are as much social as legal phenomena. They reflect prevailing norms about what kinds of trade are defensible, and which are better avoided.

To see how this plays out in practice, it is useful to trace a single transaction from start to finish. Consider a company attempting to sell industrial machinery to a buyer in a sensitive jurisdiction. The contract is signed, subject to compliance checks. The buyer passes initial screening. The payment is routed through a correspondent bank that requests additional information about ownership. A minority shareholder turns out to have indirect links to a sanctioned individual, raising questions about control. The bank escalates. Meanwhile, the exporter seeks marine insurance for shipment. The insurer consults its reinsurers, who express discomfort with the destination port. The policy is offered with exclusions that render it effectively useless. The port authority, alerted by the insurer's stance, decides to hold the vessel pending clarification. At no point does anyone cite a specific prohibition. The deal collapses under its own weight.

Each of these points is a potential choke. Correspondent banking can halt payments even when both primary banks are willing. Marine insurance can be withdrawn or priced prohibitively. Reinsurance can quietly cap capacity for entire regions. Ports and terminals can impose conditions that delay or deter. Inspection firms can refuse to certify. The system is modular; pressure at one node is enough.

Understanding the incentives of the main actors is crucial. Insurers are in the business of quantifying and pricing risk, but sanctions risk resists easy quantification. It is binary, reputational and often retrospective. Banks face a similar challenge. The cost of a mistake can be enormous, while the benefit of a marginal transaction is small. Port authorities operate at the intersection of commerce and sovereignty, mindful of national policy signals and local political climates. None of these actors is neutral. Each brings its own fears and priorities to the table.

When these priorities align, the effect is powerful. A port authority may hold a ship not because it has identified a breach, but because it senses disagreement among insurers and banks about exposure. The safest course is to wait. Waiting becomes denial by another name. The ship remains alongside while emails circulate and committees convene. Time itself becomes a weapon.

One of the most consequential aspects of quiet embargoes is that they do not require new laws. Trade can be throttled through anticipation alone. Firms watch enforcement trends and extrapolate. They read speeches for tone. They observe which cases attract media attention. From this, they infer what might be risky tomorrow, not just what is prohibited today. Self-imposed restrictions follow. Entire sectors may withdraw from a market long before any formal embargo is announced.

History offers ample examples. In several instances, companies ceased trading with particular regions months or even years before governments imposed explicit bans. The reasons varied: fear of being caught on the wrong side of a fast-moving political debate, concern about stranded assets, anxiety about future compliance burdens. By the time laws caught up, much of the trade had already dried up. The embargo, in effect, had been quietly in place.

This raises uncomfortable questions about accountability and transparency. When trade is blocked by law, responsibility is clear. When it is blocked by a web of private decisions, accountability diffuses. Who decided that the grain would not sail? The insurer who declined renewal? The reinsurer who set limits? The bank that stepped back? The answer is all of them, and none of them. The system produces outcomes without a single author.

Yet this diffusion is also what makes the system resilient. Quiet embargoes adapt quickly to new circumstances. They can be tightened or loosened without legislative delay. They can be applied unevenly, targeting specific routes, cargos or counterparties. For policymakers, this flexibility is attractive. For those caught in the middle, it can be bewildering.

The purpose of this chapter is to make these dynamics legible. By examining why sanctions rely on services, how enforcement is outsourced, where the choke points lie, and how key actors interact, it lays the groundwork for the rest of the book. The aim is not to overwhelm with technical detail, but to provide a conceptual map: a way of seeing how power operates through everyday commercial decisions.

There is a temptation to view these mechanisms as purely contemporary, the product of global finance and digital compliance tools. They are better understood as the latest iteration of an old idea: that control over the means of exchange can be as decisive as control over territory. What has changed is the subtlety with which that control is exercised, and the degree to which it is embedded in private governance.

As the chapter unfolds, the examples will multiply, but the underlying pattern remains consistent. Trade does not stop because someone declares it must. It stops because the systems that enable it withdraw their support. The quiet embargo works by making normal activity feel abnormal, and risky activity feel irresponsible.

By the end of this chapter, the reader should be able to look at a stalled shipment, a vanished route or a sudden spike in premiums and ask a different set of questions. Not simply, *Is this legal?* but *Which services have stepped back, and why?* Not *What law was broken?* but *What risk was deemed unacceptable?* These questions do not offer easy answers, but they open a window onto the hidden wars of trade that this book seeks to chart.

The pages that follow do not yet judge these mechanisms. They seek first to understand them. Only by grasping how quiet embargoes work can one begin to assess their costs, limits, and consequences. The gates may be open. The road may look clear. But somewhere ahead, the friction begins.

Why sanctions rely on services

On 30 June 2014, in New York, BNP Paribas pleaded guilty to violations of United States sanctions against Sudan, Iran, and Cuba and agreed to pay penalties totalling almost $9 billion. The bank was not accused of smuggling goods across borders or disguising cargoes at sea. Its offence lay in processing payments. The transactions moved through correspondent accounts, cleared through familiar systems, and touched jurisdictions where the underlying trade was restricted. The outcome was swift and widely noted. Within months, compliance policies across the global banking sector hardened. Risk committees expanded. Entire categories of trade became harder to finance, regardless of whether they were explicitly banned. Five words explain the shift. Services carry the pressure.

That case crystallised a broader reality that had been building for decades. Modern sanctions rarely succeed by closing borders. They succeed by constricting the services without which trade cannot function. Money must move. Ships must be insured. Ports must accept risk. When these enabling systems withdraw, borders become irrelevant. Goods can sit metres from open water and still go nowhere.

The logic is deceptively simple. A container may cross a frontier without inspection, but it cannot cross an ocean without insurance, fuel, finance and permission to berth. Each of these is provided by a service that operates under regulatory oversight and reputational scrutiny. Each is easier to monitor than millions of individual cargoes. Each offers a point of leverage. The result is a form of economic pressure that is indirect yet pervasive, and far more adaptable than the customs wall.

The shift towards services as the primary vector of sanctions reflects changes in how trade itself is organised. Global supply chains are long, fragmented and intensely intermediated. A single shipment can involve a seller in one country, a buyer in another, financing from a third, insurance from a fourth, and transit through several more. Customs authorities see only a slice of this picture. Banks and insurers see far more, because they must assess counterparties, ownership structures, routes and documentation before committing their balance sheets. That informational advantage makes them natural enforcers.

Show the mechanism at work and it becomes easier to name it. A bank screens a payment against sanctions lists and internal risk rules. An insurer assesses whether a voyage falls within its appetite. A reinsurer decides how much exposure it will tolerate to a region. A port authority considers whether accepting a vessel might attract unwanted attention. Each decision is taken independently, yet all are shaped by the same signals: enforcement actions, regulatory guidance, political rhetoric. The implication is cumulative. What begins as caution becomes constraint.

Historical precedent helps explain why this approach is so effective. The British government's control of maritime insurance through the City of London during the Napoleonic Wars allowed it to exert pressure far beyond the reach of its navy. More recently, the centrality of the US dollar to global finance has given American authorities extraordinary influence over international payments. In both cases, the decisive factor was not territorial control but dominance over services that others relied upon.

The contemporary sanctions architecture formalises this insight. Laws and regulations define prohibited conduct, but they are deliberately broad. They leave room for interpretation. That room is filled by guidance notes, speeches by officials, and the memory of penalties like BNP Paribas's. Firms are expected to exercise judgement. They are not told merely to comply, but to avoid facilitating prohibited activity. The difference matters. Avoidance invites overreach.

Banks illustrate this dynamic most clearly. A correspondent banking relationship is a privilege, not a right. Losing access can cripple an institution. When faced with ambiguous risk, banks tend to retreat. The visible behaviour is account closures, payment delays and requests for additional information that stretch on indefinitely. Metrics follow. Transaction volumes with certain regions fall. Compliance staffing rises. The implication is that even lawful trade struggles to find a channel.

Insurance operates under similar pressures, with an added layer of complexity. Marine insurance is not optional. Without hull and machinery cover, protection and indemnity insurance, and often cargo insurance, a vessel cannot operate. Insurers, in turn, rely on reinsurance to spread catastrophic risk. If reinsurers decide that exposure to a particular geography or trade is undesirable, capacity evaporates quickly. Premiums spike. Exclusions proliferate. Routes quietly disappear from policy schedules.

A named example from the shipping world underlines the point. In early 2022, following Russia's invasion of Ukraine, several major reinsurers announced restrictions on cover for voyages involving Russian ports. The announcements were cautious, framed around risk assessment rather than outright bans. The effect was immediate. Primary insurers tightened terms. Shipowners struggled to secure cover at viable rates. Ports began to ask for additional assurances. Long before formal embargoes took full effect, traffic patterns had already shifted.

Ports and terminals complete the picture. They are physical places, but their decisions are shaped by services and compliance considerations. Accepting a vessel entails legal and reputational exposure. If insurers or banks express concern, port authorities are likely to pause. The visible behaviour is a hold, a request for clarification, a delay in granting berthing permission. Time accumulates. Charter parties are breached. The implication is that access exists in theory but not in practice.

To see how these elements combine, consider a hypothetical oil cargo. A trader sells crude to a buyer in a jurisdiction subject to sectoral sanctions but not a full embargo. The trade is structured to comply with price caps and licensing requirements. The paperwork is sound. The border is open. Financing is arranged through a mid-sized bank with limited exposure to the region. As loading begins, the ship's insurer notifies the owner that renewal will require additional approval. The reinsurer, citing geopolitical volatility, reduces its line. The premium doubles. The bank, alerted to the insurance issue, re-examines the transaction and decides that the residual risk is too high. No payment, no cover. The cargo remains on board. No law is cited. The result is final.

This is the quiet choke point at work. Each actor can plausibly say it acted within its mandate. None needed to coordinate. The system aligned itself.

There are counter-examples, and they matter. Some trades continue despite sanctions pressure. Energy flows to certain countries have persisted under waiver regimes or through carefully structured arrangements. Humanitarian shipments do move, albeit slowly. These cases demonstrate that services-based sanctions are not absolute. They can be navigated with sufficient clarity, political backing and institutional commitment. The limitation lies in scale. Such exceptions require effort and often high-level reassurance. They do not generalise easily.

Reconciling these exceptions with the broader pattern reveals the underlying rule. Where governments actively support continued trade, services can be mobilised to facilitate it. Where they do not, or where signals are mixed, private actors default to caution. Services respond not only to law but to tone. The absence of explicit prohibition is not the presence of comfort.

One reason this approach endures is efficiency. Policing every container is expensive and politically fraught. Monitoring a smaller number of banks, insurers and ports is more manageable. Another is deniability. When trade dries up, governments can point to market decisions. Firms can point to regulatory risk. Responsibility disperses.

The motif of friction returns here. Services do not usually stop trade with a single decisive act. They slow it. A week's delay becomes a month. A modest premium increase becomes prohibitive. An extra document becomes an impossible hurdle. Friction does the work of force without its visibility.

There is also a temporal dimension. Services-based sanctions operate in anticipation. Firms price in future risk. They adjust before rules change. This forward-looking behaviour explains why trade often contracts ahead of formal measures. It also explains why lifting sanctions does not immediately restore flows. Services remember.

Data supports this reading. Following major sanctions announcements, analysts frequently observe declines in shipping volumes and payment flows that exceed the scope of the measures themselves. The International Monetary Fund noted in a 2019 working paper that financial sanctions tend to have spillover effects well beyond targeted entities, precisely because of over-compliance by intermediaries. The behaviour is rational from the perspective of individual firms. Collectively, it amplifies impact.

Critics argue that this system is blunt and unjust. Lawful actors suffer. Humanitarian needs go unmet. Markets distort. These criticisms have force. They also highlight why services, rather than borders, have become the battlefield. Services are sensitive to perception. They react quickly. They are hard to compel in the opposite direction.

The unresolved tension lies here. If sanctions rely on services because services are effective, what happens when those services withdraw too much, too often? At what point does caution erode the very trade networks it depends upon? The diagnostic question for the reader is not whether a border is closed, but whether the services that make crossing it possible still believe the journey is worth the risk.

How governments outsource enforcement

On 30 June 2014, in a federal courtroom in Manhattan, BNP Paribas pleaded guilty to conspiring to violate United States sanctions and agreed to penalties totalling almost $9 billion. The case was prosecuted by the US Department of Justice and paired with actions by New York's Department of Financial Services. The conduct at issue was not exotic. It involved ordinary banking services: clearing payments, processing trade finance, and handling dollar transactions that passed through the United States financial system. The immediate outcome was public and numerical. The secondary outcome was quieter and more consequential: compliance departments across the world rewrote their rules in anticipation of the next headline.

Everyone reads the fine print.

This is the outsourced architecture of modern sanctions enforcement. Governments publish the rulebook, but they do not staff the border in the old sense. They rely instead on private institutions—banks, insurers, shipping firms, ports, auditors, data vendors—to interpret risk, build filters, refuse marginal business, and report suspicious patterns. The state keeps the power to punish. The market supplies the day-to-day policing. A sanction becomes effective not when it is announced, but when thousands of firms decide, independently and often pre-emptively, that a set of transactions is no longer worth the trouble.

The mechanism begins with a familiar scene inside any large financial institution. A compliance alert fires. A name resembles a listed party, or a payment references a port that has become politically radioactive, or the ownership structure does not resolve cleanly. A junior analyst drafts questions. A manager asks whether the file is "defensible". A committee meets. The decision—delay, reject, de-risk—rarely cites a single clause of law. It cites exposure. The term sounds abstract until one sees the concrete behaviour it produces: account closures, frozen payments, the refusal to issue a letter of credit, the insertion of a sanctions clause that makes performance optional. The implication is that the state's broad prohibition is translated into a private veto.

Why do governments choose this arrangement? Because services are easier to steer than goods. Customs agencies face volume and ingenuity. Millions of consignments cross borders; misdescription and transhipment are constant temptations. By contrast, the enabling services of trade are concentrated. A smaller number of banks dominate correspondent clearing. A smaller number of insurers and reinsurers shape marine risk capacity. A smaller number of ports and terminals control critical infrastructure. Regulate, influence, and occasionally punish those nodes, and the rest of the system adjusts. Outsourcing enforcement is not a retreat from power; it is power applied at a point of maximum mechanical advantage.

The first lever is guidance, which is more potent than it looks. When an authority publishes an advisory or issues interpretive guidance, it is not merely clarifying law; it is shaping what private actors regard as acceptable. The US Treasury's Office of Foreign Assets Control formalised this approach in *A Framework for OFAC Compliance Commitments* (May 2019), which set out expectations around risk assessments, internal controls, testing and auditing, and training. Nothing in that document forced a bank to decline a particular transaction. Yet it supplied a template against which regulators could later judge behaviour. Firms responded with visible decisions: they expanded compliance headcount, upgraded screening tools, and documented escalation paths more meticulously. The implication was clear. What cannot be explained later will not be done now.

The second lever is speech—especially the speech that sits between politics and enforcement. When senior officials signal a renewed focus on a jurisdiction or sector, firms adjust before any new measure appears. Tone becomes an input to risk models. It can be seen in pricing, in the appetite for exceptions, in how quickly relationship managers stop calling a client "interesting" and start calling them "difficult". This is not irrational timidity; it is institutional memory. Banks and insurers have learned that the harshest sanction is not always a fine. It can be loss of access: to correspondent banking relationships, to US dollar clearing, to key markets. Those losses are existential. So the industry listens closely.

The third lever is the enforcement action itself, which functions as a kind of demonstration effect. The penalty is the theatre; the real audience is every other firm. BNP Paribas in 2014 remains a textbook example because it combined scale, symbolism, and a simple message: sanctions breaches in the payment system will be punished severely. The response did not remain confined to similar fact patterns. Institutions generalised. They tightened controls for adjacent risks. They exited business lines that were technically permitted but politically awkward. They introduced blanket policies for certain regions, not because law demanded it, but because an internal committee wanted to remove ambiguity from the system. A single prosecution became a global behavioural nudge.

A second, checkable example shows how this dynamic persists across different jurisdictions and regulatory cultures. In December 2012, HSBC reached a deferred prosecution agreement with the US Department of Justice relating to anti-money laundering failures and sanctions violations, and paid a $1.9 billion settlement. The misconduct spanned years and involved multiple geographies. The immediate outcome was well publicised. The longer-term effect was structural. HSBC undertook sweeping compliance reforms, and across the sector other firms accelerated investments in monitoring, transaction screening and governance. Banks began to treat sanctions risk less as a niche legal question and more as a board-level survival issue. The visible behavioural metric was the growth of financial crime and sanctions teams—an expansion that became industry standard. The implication was that enforcement actions do not just punish; they set the baseline for what "reasonable" looks like thereafter.

Outsourcing enforcement also operates through the way states define responsibility. Sanctions rules often impose strict liability in practice: a firm can face serious consequences even without intent, if it is deemed to have facilitated prohibited conduct. Authorities may offer mitigation for strong compliance programmes, voluntary disclosure, and cooperation. That combination produces a rational calculus. When the penalty for a miss is severe and the benefit of a transaction is modest, a risk-averse institution will decline. The decision is visible in the operational metric of "false positives tolerated". Better to stop ten lawful payments than process one prohibited one. The implication is that the enforcement regime turns private caution into public policy.

This is where the outsourcing becomes genuinely subtle. Governments do not need to instruct a bank to avoid a region; they need only maintain a credible threat of punishment for errors and leave ambiguity at the margins. The market fills the gap with over-compliance. It is important to see how this happens at the level of internal process. A compliance team cannot investigate every counterparty with bespoke care. It builds rules. Those rules are then embedded in systems: screening algorithms, scorecards, escalation thresholds. Over time, what began as judgement becomes architecture. It hardens. The first visible behaviour is a longer list of "prohibited" geographies in internal policies than in statute. The second is the refusal to process certain categories of trade finance, even with licences, because the operational burden is too high. The implication is that outsourced enforcement tends to over-deliver on restriction and under-deliver on nuance.

The same pattern appears beyond banking. Insurers, for example, will often mirror banks' conservatism because they depend on the same financial infrastructure and face their own regulatory pressures. A marine insurer that pays a claim linked—directly or indirectly—to a sanctioned trade risks reputational damage and regulatory scrutiny. Reinsurers intensify this effect, because they sit at the top of the risk chain and can dictate exclusions or require enhanced due diligence. Ports and terminal operators, meanwhile, often take cues from insurers and banks: if the service layer is uneasy, the physical layer becomes cautious. The outsourced system behaves like a flock. One bird veers; the rest adjust.

There is, however, a credible limitation to the outsourcing narrative, and it deserves to be faced directly. States cannot fully control private enforcement, and sometimes private actors resist or diverge. Political priorities differ across jurisdictions. A transaction blocked by a US-linked bank may be acceptable to an institution with no US exposure, dealing in a different currency and operating under a different regulatory philosophy. Similarly, when governments want trade to continue—humanitarian shipments, for example—they can create licensing pathways and issue comfort letters that reduce uncertainty. These interventions can reopen channels. The limitation is that they require active, sustained reassurance. Without it, private actors relapse into risk avoidance.

Reconciling this limitation with the broader pattern clarifies what outsourcing truly means. The state does not micromanage outcomes; it sets incentives. Where incentives align with policy goals, the system moves quickly. Where incentives conflict—where policy demands nuance but punishment rewards caution—the system defaults to blockage. Outsourcing works best for restriction. It works worst for exceptions.

One can watch this tension play out in the language of corporate governance. Boards ask for "no surprises". Senior executives demand that exposure be "within appetite". Those phrases translate into decisions that can be measured: the number of escalations rises, turnaround times lengthen, and revenue from higher-risk corridors declines. A bank that once cleared payments in hours now takes days. An insurer that once renewed annually now insists on mid-term review clauses. These are not philosophical shifts; they are operational footprints of outsourced enforcement.

The motif that runs through this subchapter is the quiet memo. Sometimes it is literal—a compliance circular sent after an enforcement action, instructing staff to treat certain corridors as high risk. Sometimes it is a change in a system parameter. Sometimes it is an unspoken rule that everyone learns. The quiet memo moves faster than law. It travels through professional networks, consultancy briefings, and regulator speeches. It creates behavioural harmonisation without any formal coordination. And it is almost never published.

This is not a conspiracy. It is institutional learning under asymmetric consequences. The outsourced model depends on the fact that private actors internalise state priorities because the cost of divergence is high. Yet it also depends on opacity, because discretion requires space. A bank can rarely say, publicly and plainly, "We do not want this business." It will say, "We cannot achieve the necessary level of comfort." The effect is the same. The implication is that enforcement, while outsourced, becomes difficult to contest, because it hides behind the language of prudence.

The consequences are uneven. Large multinationals can sometimes absorb the friction by deploying specialist teams, building documentation packages, and shopping for willing counterparties. Smaller firms cannot. Charities cannot. Mid-sized traders with thin margins cannot. Outsourced enforcement therefore redistributes power within the market. It favours those who can afford compliance infrastructure and punishes those who cannot. That distribution is rarely acknowledged in public debate, yet it shapes which goods move and which do not.

A final complication is that outsourced enforcement can produce blind spots. When everyone relies on similar screening tools, similar data feeds, and similar policy templates, the system risks groupthink. False positives multiply. Meanwhile, sophisticated evasion adapts to predictable checks.

The state may achieve broad deterrence, but miss targeted illicit flows that exploit the gaps. The limitation is structural: a system designed for defensibility can become less effective at detection.

The unresolved tension, then, is not whether governments will continue to outsource enforcement—they will, because it is efficient and politically attractive—but how they will manage the trade-off between impact and legitimacy. If private actors are the front line, do states owe them clearer guidance, safer harbours for good-faith exceptions, and a credible way to distinguish caution from paralysis? Or will the quiet memo continue to do the work, tightening the screws through fear of the next penalty, until lawful trade is squeezed alongside the prohibited? The test is practical, and it arrives in the same place it always does: a payment held, an insurance renewal declined, a vessel waiting for permission to sail. Who, then, is actually deciding?

Market choke points in practice

In August 2018, from its headquarters in Copenhagen, A.P. Moller-Maersk announced that it would cease taking new business involving Iran, citing the reimposition of United States sanctions. The decision followed Washington's withdrawal from the Joint Comprehensive Plan of Action earlier that year. No Danish law compelled the move. European authorities were still debating how to preserve trade. Yet one of the world's largest shipping groups stepped back. Containers already booked were reviewed. Routes were adjusted. Iranian trade volumes through Maersk-controlled channels fell sharply in the months that followed. A border remained open. A service withdrew.

Five steps. One failure stops all.

This is how market choke points operate in practice. A cross-border transaction is not a single act but a sequence of dependencies. Each dependency is a gate, and each gatekeeper has the power to halt progress even when all previous checks have been passed. What makes these choke points effective is not that they are hidden, but that they are ordinary. They sit inside routine processes that professionals treat as hygiene: clearing payments, renewing insurance, booking terminals, commissioning inspections. When one of these processes tightens, trade slows. When several tighten together, it stops.

Begin with correspondent banking, the circulatory system of international trade. Even when buyer and seller bank with institutions willing to do business, payments often move through intermediaries that clear specific currencies or jurisdictions. A euro-denominated transaction may still touch a US correspondent at some point. The visible behaviour at this choke point is delay or rejection of payment messages, often flagged for enhanced due diligence. The name for this is risk-based screening. The explanation is straightforward: correspondent banks bear regulatory exposure without enjoying the underlying commercial relationship. The implication is decisive. A single correspondent's refusal can strand funds, rendering performance impossible.

The effect can be measured. After major sanctions announcements, trade finance volumes through certain corridors drop before any formal bans apply. The Bank for International Settlements has noted, in multiple annual reports, that correspondent banking relationships tend to decline in higher-risk jurisdictions as compliance costs rise. Fewer correspondents mean fewer pathways. The gate narrows.

Marine insurance forms the second choke point. A vessel without cover is a vessel without permission to operate. Hull and machinery insurance protects the ship itself; protection and indemnity insurance covers liabilities such as pollution, crew injury and collision. Cargo insurance protects the goods. Each policy must be acceptable to lenders, charterers and ports. When insurers reassess risk, the visible behaviour is not always cancellation. It is often non-renewal, higher deductibles, narrower terms. Premiums rise. Exclusions multiply. The name for this is underwriting discipline. The explanation lies in insurers' exposure to sanctions penalties and reputational harm. The implication is that voyages remain lawful but become uninsurable at a price the market can bear.

Reinsurance sits behind this process and amplifies it. Primary insurers spread their risk by ceding portions to reinsurers, many of which operate globally and face intense regulatory scrutiny. If reinsurers pull back from a region, primary insurers must either reduce capacity or concentrate risk on their own balance sheets. The visible behaviour is a sudden shortage of cover across multiple insurers at once. The explanation is correlation. Reinsurers see geopolitical risk as systemic. The implication is that even diversified markets can freeze.

Ports and terminals provide the physical choke points. They are the places where paper risk meets steel and concrete. Accepting a vessel or cargo entails liability. Port authorities therefore watch the signals sent by banks and insurers closely. If cover is disputed or financing uncertain, a port may impose conditions or refuse entry. The visible behaviour is a hold, often framed as a request for clarification. The name for this is operational prudence. The explanation is that ports cannot afford incidents that attract political attention. The implication is that physical access depends on financial comfort.

Inspection firms and classification societies complete the chain. They certify cargoes, verify compliance with technical standards, and attest to seaworthiness. Without their sign-off, contracts cannot be performed and insurance may be invalid. The visible behaviour here is refusal to inspect or certify under certain conditions. The explanation is professional liability. The implication is that even perfectly lawful goods can become commercially radioactive if no reputable firm will put its name to them.

These choke points are best understood through sequence. Consider a sanctioned counterparty attempting to buy industrial machinery. The buyer is not individually listed, but operates in a sector subject to restrictions. The seller secures an export licence. The contract is signed. At the first gate, correspondent banking, the buyer's payment is flagged because the ownership structure includes a state-linked entity. The bank asks for clarification. Documents are provided. The payment is provisionally approved. The second gate, insurance, introduces friction. The machinery must be shipped. The insurer offers cover but excludes losses arising from sanctions enforcement. The seller's bank deems this insufficient. The third gate, reinsurance, tightens further. The insurer's reinsurer caps exposure to the destination country. Capacity shrinks. Premiums rise. The fourth gate, the port, intervenes. The terminal operator asks for confirmation that insurance is unconditional. It is not. Loading is delayed. The fifth gate, inspection, stalls. The inspection firm declines to certify installation at destination, citing uncertainty around local counterparties. The machinery remains crated. No single decision kills the deal. Together, they do.

A named, checkable example from outside shipping shows the same pattern. In 2019, several European engineering firms reported difficulties supplying equipment to projects in Venezuela, despite holding licences under European Union regulations. Payments were delayed by correspondent banks. Insurers declined to cover transit. Equipment sat in warehouses. The European Commission acknowledged the problem in public statements, noting that over-compliance by intermediaries was impeding lawful trade. The visible metric was project delay measured in months. The implication was that choke points had aligned against execution.

There are counter-examples worth noting. Some trades pass through despite pressure. Energy exports under waiver regimes, for instance, have continued when governments actively signalled support and provided specific comfort. In such cases, banks processed payments, insurers maintained cover, and ports cooperated. The limitation is scale and durability. These pathways require constant reassurance and often high-level political engagement. They are fragile. When signals weaken, choke points reassert themselves.

Reconciling this limitation with the broader pattern clarifies the nature of market choke points. They are not immutable barriers. They are conditional gates that respond to incentives and information. When states want trade to move, they must work at the level of services, not slogans. Absent that effort, the market defaults to restraint.

The quiet motif threading through these examples is the gate. Not a wall, not a barricade, but a series of doors that must all open. One closed door is enough. The gate metaphor matters because it shifts attention from legality to execution. A transaction can be legal and still fail to pass through all gates. Professionals who focus only on the rulebook miss the operational reality.

Metrics make this visible. Average payment processing times lengthen. Insurance premiums spike for specific routes. Port turnaround times increase for certain flags or destinations. Inspection refusal rates rise. These are not abstract indicators. They are behaviours that can be observed, measured and compared. They tell a story about where the system is tightening.

The power of choke points lies in their dispersion. No single authority controls them all. Each actor acts in its own interest, under its own regulatory regime. Yet they are linked by shared exposure to enforcement risk and reputation. This produces coordination without conspiracy. It also produces opacity. When a deal fails, counterparties struggle to identify the decisive moment. Was it the bank? The insurer? The port? The answer is usually yes.

This opacity has consequences. It complicates dispute resolution. It blurs accountability. It favours actors with the resources to navigate friction and penalises those without. Small exporters, humanitarian organisations, and mid-sized manufacturers often find themselves trapped between open borders and closed gates.

The unresolved tension at the heart of market choke points is practical rather than philosophical. If trade depends on a sequence of services, how many points of discretion can the system tolerate before lawful exchange becomes exceptional? At what point does prudence become paralysis? The test arrives not in policy papers but in warehouses, anchorages and bank queues, where goods wait for a gate that may never open.

Insurers, banks and port authorities

On 4 July 2019, in the waters off Gibraltar, the tanker *Grace 1* was detained by local authorities while carrying crude oil bound for Syria. The legal basis was framed in terms of European sanctions, but the immediate operational reality unfolded elsewhere. Insurers reassessed exposure. Banks froze related payment flows. Port services were withheld. The vessel sat idle while different institutions weighed their risks in parallel, each reaching for a defensible position. The detention made headlines. The surrounding hesitation did not.

Risk travels faster than orders.

This episode captures a defining feature of the quiet embargo. Insurers, banks and port authorities do not operate in sequence so much as in conversation, often indirect and sometimes unspoken. Their responsibilities overlap. Their incentives diverge. Their decisions collide in the same place: the moment when a ship seeks to move, a payment seeks to clear, and accountability becomes personal. Understanding how these actors interact explains why trade so often stalls even when no single party has issued a formal refusal.

Banks approach the problem first through money. They clear payments, issue letters of credit, and finance inventories. Their exposure is legal and existential. A misstep can sever access to correspondent networks or invite regulatory sanction. The visible behaviour is caution encoded into process. Payments are queued. Files are escalated. Relationships are terminated. The abstraction of *risk* appears as a concrete decision to freeze funds pending review. The implication is immediate: without payment, nothing moves.

Insurers confront a different calculus. They price uncertainty and absorb loss. Yet sanctions risk resists actuarial treatment. It is not a probability curve but a cliff edge. A claim denied under a sanctions exclusion may still generate reputational fallout and regulatory scrutiny. The visible behaviour is the narrowing of cover. Exclusions expand. Deductibles rise. Renewals lapse. The term *appetite* becomes a measurable change in premium or capacity. The implication follows: voyages that were once routine become commercially irrational.

Port authorities sit at the junction of finance and physical movement. They answer to national regulators, local politics and international norms. Accepting a vessel is not merely a logistical act; it is an endorsement that the port is willing to shoulder the attendant risk. When banks or insurers express discomfort, ports listen. The visible behaviour is delay. A hold is placed. Additional documentation is requested. Berthing is postponed. The abstraction of *prudence* materialises as a ship at anchor. The implication is that access exists only when the surrounding services are aligned.

These roles overlap in practice. A bank may require confirmation of insurance before releasing funds. An insurer may insist on evidence that a port will accept the vessel. A port may ask for assurance that financing and cover are in place. Each actor defers to the others, not out of deference but out of self-preservation. The system rewards alignment and punishes dissent.

A second named example illustrates how this alignment forms. In March 2022, following the expansion of sanctions related to Russia's invasion of Ukraine, several European ports, including Rotterdam, began to review access for vessels linked to Russian trade. Dutch authorities emphasised compliance with European Union measures. At the same time, major insurers announced tighter terms for voyages involving Russian ports, and banks increased scrutiny of related payments. The visible outcome was congestion and delay. Ships waited while institutions compared notes. The implication was that even where trade was not categorically banned, execution required unanimity among services.

The incentives driving each actor differ in detail but converge in effect. Banks fear regulatory penalty and loss of market access. Insurers fear catastrophic loss and reputational damage. Ports fear political scrutiny and operational disruption. None is rewarded for facilitating marginal trade. All are punished for misjudgement. This asymmetry explains why risk appetites tend to contract together.

National pressures add another layer. A port authority in one jurisdiction may face domestic political expectations that differ from those faced by an insurer headquartered elsewhere or a bank regulated in a third country. These pressures can pull decisions in different directions. Yet globalised services reconcile these differences through the strictest common denominator. If one major bank or insurer withdraws, others follow. The metric here is convergence: policy updates issued within weeks of one another, often using similar language. The implication is that national variation is smoothed out by market coordination.

Reputational concern accelerates this process. Modern trade is observed by media, activists and shareholders. A single photograph of a ship unloading controversial cargo can undo years of brand management. Insurers and banks are acutely aware of this. The visible behaviour is reputational screening layered atop legal compliance. Transactions that pass regulatory muster are still declined because they may look wrong. The implication is that public perception becomes a quasi-regulatory force.

The interaction between these actors can be seen most clearly when they disagree. Imagine a vessel cleared by its bank but facing conditional insurance, or insured but lacking financing, or financed and insured but unwelcome at the destination port. In such cases, the weakest link dictates the outcome. A port authority may hold the ship while banks and insurers debate exposure. The hold is framed as temporary. Time passes. Charter parties strain. The decision resolves itself through delay.

There is a credible counter-example worth examining. Certain humanitarian shipments have moved through contested ports when governments provided explicit comfort and coordination. In these cases, banks processed payments under specific licences, insurers maintained cover with tailored clauses, and ports facilitated access. The visible behaviour was cooperation: expedited reviews, dedicated channels, public statements of support. The implication is that alignment can be achieved when incentives are actively managed.

Reconciling this with the dominant pattern reveals a hard truth. Alignment requires effort. It requires states to engage directly with the service layer and to absorb some of the political and reputational cost. Absent that engagement, private actors default to caution. The quiet embargo fills the void.

Metrics again make the interaction tangible. Average dwell times increase at certain ports. Insurance premiums for specific routes double within a quarter. Payment rejection rates rise. These are not abstract trends; they are the operational footprints of misaligned incentives.

The quiet motif threading through this interaction is the meeting that never quite happens. Banks wait for insurers. Insurers wait for ports. Ports wait for regulators. Each waits for someone else to move first. In that waiting, trade stalls. The silence is procedural.

This system has consequences beyond the immediate transaction. It shapes long-term behaviour. Firms redesign supply chains to avoid contested nodes. Insurers withdraw from regions altogether. Banks exit correspondent relationships. Ports invest in compliance infrastructure that prioritises defensibility over throughput. The market reorganises around perceived safety.

Yet the system is not static. Risk appetites shift. Political winds change. A port that was cautious one year may reopen the next. An insurer may return with new pricing. A bank may re-enter with stricter controls. These movements are incremental and rarely announced. Observers must read them in capacity, price and delay.

The unresolved tension lies in governance. When insurers, banks and port authorities collectively determine what trade can occur, who ensures that their private caution aligns with public intent? At what point does distributed prudence become collective blockage? The question is not theoretical. It sits in every anchorage where a ship waits, insured by one firm, financed by another, and judged by a third. The quiet embargo persists not because these actors conspire, but because they agree—often without speaking—that the risk is no longer worth taking.

When formal bans are not needed

In December 2019, in London, Barclays announced that it would no longer directly finance new coal-fired power plants or thermal coal mines. No British law required the decision. No multilateral embargo existed. Coal was still legal to trade, ship and insure. Yet one of Europe's largest banks drew a line, publicly and pre-emptively. Within months, peers followed with similar policies. Project pipelines thinned. Insurance capacity tightened. Coal developments stalled across multiple jurisdictions. A sector slowed without a ban.

Fear moves first.

This episode captures a central truth of modern trade control: the most decisive constraints often arrive before legislation. Firms do not wait for parliaments to vote or regulators to publish final texts. They act on expectation. They scan speeches, headlines and shareholder resolutions, and they infer where the wind is blowing. When the perceived direction is unfavourable, they withdraw on their own initiative. By the time formal rules appear, the market has already adjusted.

The mechanism is anticipation. Show it at work and the pattern becomes clear. A minister signals a tougher stance. A regulator hints at future enforcement. Campaigners publish an investigation. Investors ask questions at an annual general meeting. None of these events changes the law. Each changes the calculation. The name for this process is pre-emptive de-risking. The explanation lies in asymmetry: the cost of being early is manageable; the cost of being late can be existential. The implication is that trade can be throttled without a single new statute.

Banks provide the clearest illustration. Their balance sheets are exposed not only to legal sanction but to reputational damage and capital market reaction. When senior executives believe a line of business may become controversial, they often exit quietly. The visible behaviour is policy revision. Sectors are reclassified as "restricted". Credit committees decline transactions that would have been approved a year earlier. Metrics follow. Lending volumes drop. Client lists shrink. The abstraction of *reputation* materialises as a rejected deal.

The coal sector's experience after the Paris Agreement in December 2015 offers a second, checkable example. Governments committed to climate targets. Environmental groups intensified scrutiny of financiers. Shareholder activism rose. Long before any comprehensive bans on coal trade or finance were enacted, major European insurers such as AXA and Munich Re announced restrictions on underwriting coal-related risks. The dates are public. The decisions were voluntary. The outcome was measurable: projects struggled to secure cover, premiums rose, and developers abandoned plans. The implication was unmistakable. Policy intent alone reshaped the market.

Media scrutiny accelerates this process. A single investigative report can trigger internal reviews across an industry. Firms fear being named as outliers. The visible behaviour is sudden alignment. Policies change in clusters. Press releases echo one another. This is not coordination; it is imitation under pressure. The name for this dynamic is reputational contagion. The explanation is simple. No firm wants to be last to leave a stigmatised trade. The implication is rapid contraction.

Shareholder pressure adds force. Institutional investors increasingly frame sanctions, human rights and environmental exposure as material risks. When large asset managers signal concern, boards listen. The visible behaviour is divestment or policy tightening announced ahead of regulatory change. The metric is capital allocation. Money flows away from contested sectors. The implication is that access to finance narrows independently of law.

Shipping and insurance respond in parallel. A shipowner may decide that calling at a particular port is no longer worth the scrutiny. An insurer may decide that renewing cover for a certain trade invites questions it would rather avoid. The visible behaviour is route adjustment or non-renewal. The abstraction of *future risk* appears as a missing line on a policy schedule. The implication is that physical movement declines before any ban is declared.

There is a historical precedent that underscores how long this pattern has existed. In the early 1980s, well before comprehensive international sanctions against apartheid South Africa, many multinational companies withdrew voluntarily. Public campaigns, university divestment movements and shareholder activism created a climate in which continued engagement was seen as unacceptable. By the time the United States enacted the Comprehensive Anti-Apartheid Act in 1986, a significant portion of corporate withdrawal had already occurred. The visible metric was declining foreign direct investment. The implication was that moral and reputational pressure can precede legal compulsion by years.

The quiet motif running through these cases is the empty desk. A relationship manager no longer pursues a client. An underwriter removes a category from her book. A port planner stops marketing a route. Nothing dramatic is announced. The desk simply clears. Trade fades from view.

This self-imposed restraint is reinforced by enforcement uncertainty. Firms know that regulators often apply rules retrospectively, judging past behaviour against evolving standards. The fear is not only of breaking today's law, but of failing tomorrow's test. The visible behaviour is conservative interpretation. Grey areas are treated as red. Licences are viewed with suspicion. The implication is that legality becomes necessary but insufficient.

Critics argue that this dynamic produces overreach and collateral damage. They are not wrong. Humanitarian trade suffers. Smaller firms without compliance infrastructure are excluded. Markets distort. There is a credible counter-example, however, that tempers the critique. In some cases, clear and sustained government reassurance has kept trade alive. Specific licensing regimes, public statements of support, and active engagement with banks and insurers have preserved narrow channels. The visible behaviour is continued financing and cover under defined conditions. The implication is that pre-emptive withdrawal is not inevitable.

Reconciling this exception with the broader pattern reveals the core driver. Self-imposed restrictions flourish in uncertainty. They retreat when uncertainty is replaced with credible comfort. The difficulty is that comfort is costly. It requires political capital and administrative effort. Absent that investment, the market chooses safety.

Metrics again expose the mechanism. After high-profile announcements or scandals, analysts observe immediate changes in pricing and capacity. Insurance premiums adjust within weeks. Credit spreads widen. Shipping volumes dip. These are early signals. They precede law. They often outlast it.

The role of internal governance cannot be overstated. Boards demand foresight. Risk committees reward caution. Performance metrics rarely credit staff for navigating controversial trades successfully; they punish those associated with trouble. The visible behaviour is internal escalation that ends in refusal. The implication is cultural. Saying no feels safer than asking how.

This culture spreads across borders. A decision taken in one financial centre influences behaviour elsewhere through shared professional norms. Compliance officers attend the same conferences. Insurers read the same advisories. Port authorities watch the same headlines. The result is synchronised retreat without instruction.

The unresolved tension is practical and immediate. If markets can impose their own embargoes based on expectation and fear, how much formal authority do governments retain over the timing and scope of economic pressure? When does prudent anticipation become unaccountable power? The diagnostic question for the reader is not whether a ban exists, but whether the actors that make trade possible still believe the future will forgive the present. When that belief evaporates, the law arrives late to a decision already made.

Chapter 2

Sanctions Lists and Risk Filters

A name appears on a list. Nothing else changes. The company's offices remain open, its ships are still registered, and its staff are still paid. There is no press conference, no police tape. Yet within days, payments stall, insurance queries multiply, and long-standing counterparties stop returning calls. The list itself is only a few pages long, publicly available, updated with bureaucratic restraint. The effects ripple far beyond it, touching firms and individuals whose names never appear in print.

This is the peculiar power of sanctions lists: they are small, finite documents that generate infinite consequences. They do not merely prohibit. They contaminate. A single entry can cast a shadow across ownership chains, supply routes, and balance sheets that span continents. What looks like a catalogue is, in practice, a trigger.

At first glance, sanctions lists seem deceptively simple. They name people, companies, sometimes sectors or entire jurisdictions. They carry dates, references and legal authority. To the uninitiated, they resemble the most straightforward form of economic control: a register of who may not do what. Yet anyone who has watched a lawful business grind to a halt because of a partial match, an unresolved ownership query or an ambiguous activity knows that the real action begins after the list is published, not with it.

This chapter explores that afterlife. It examines how lists are constructed, interpreted and transformed into living systems of risk management. It asks why lists that are meant to provide clarity often produce confusion, and why the effort to draw sharp legal lines results, paradoxically, in blurred commercial boundaries. Above all, it shows how the quiet embargo is operationalised not through the list itself, but through the filters built around it.

The modern sanctions list is a compromise between precision and breadth. Governments seek to target specific actors without imposing blanket hardship. They name individuals responsible for particular conduct, entities that facilitate it, and sectors deemed strategically sensitive. Sometimes they go further, designating entire countries or regions. Each approach reflects a different political calculation. Naming individuals signals moral condemnation. Targeting entities disrupts capacity. Sectoral measures aim to reshape behaviour across an industry. Country-wide measures declare isolation.

For firms, these distinctions matter less than might be expected. A listed individual can render an unlisted company toxic if ownership or control thresholds are crossed. A sectoral measure can capture transactions that appear innocuous on their face. A country designation can turn routine counterparties into high-risk exposures overnight. The list is the starting point; interpretation does the rest.

Consider a hypothetical shipping company added to a sanctions list. The designation names the legal entity, cites its role in prohibited trade, and sets out the restrictions. On paper, the impact is contained. In practice, the designation radiates outward. Banks examine loans to subsidiaries. Insurers review cover for vessels managed but not owned by the listed company. Charterers reconsider contracts. Ports reassess access. A minority shareholder in a joint venture suddenly finds itself questioned. The list has not grown. The risk universe has.

This expansion is neither accidental nor informal. It is built into the way lists are translated into screening systems. Raw legal texts are unreadable at scale. Banks and insurers therefore ingest lists into automated tools that match names, addresses, identification numbers and other attributes against client databases and transaction flows. What was once a document becomes code.

This translation is an act of interpretation. Decisions must be made about spelling variants, transliteration, aliases, and fuzzy matches. Ownership rules must be modelled. Thresholds must be set. A system that is too permissive invites regulatory criticism; one that is too strict paralyses business. Most institutions err on the side of caution. The visible result is the false positive: a legitimate client flagged because its name resembles that of a listed person, or because it shares an address with an unrelated entity. The system freezes activity while humans investigate.

These moments reveal the tension at the heart of sanctions compliance. Lists promise certainty. Screening systems produce probability. Compliance teams live in the gap between the two. A payment halted by a false match is not evidence of wrongdoing; it is evidence of a risk filter doing what it was designed to do. Yet for the client, the effect is indistinguishable from a ban.

Ownership and control rules deepen this complexity. Sanctions frameworks rarely limit themselves to named entities. They extend to those owned or controlled by them, often defined by percentage thresholds or tests of influence. These rules reflect a reasonable concern: that designated actors will hide behind corporate veils. They also create a vast grey zone. Minority stakes, family relationships, nominee directors and informal influence can all become relevant. Determining control is as much art as science.

A trader may believe it is dealing with an independent counterparty, only to discover, when a compliance query arises, that a distant shareholder has ties to a listed individual. The stake may be small. The influence may be indirect. The legal position may be arguable. None of this prevents banks or insurers from stepping back. The cost of misjudgement outweighs the benefit of nuance. The trader learns, belatedly, that risk travels along hidden lines.

Sectoral and thematic sanctions introduce another layer of interpretation. Instead of naming actors, they define prohibited activities. Energy, shipping, technology and finance are frequent targets. The intent is to constrain capacity without the diplomatic cost of naming every participant. For firms, this shifts the burden of classification onto them. What counts as energy-related? When does a technology become dual-use? Does financing a piece of equipment implicate a restricted sector if the end use is uncertain?

These questions do not admit easy answers. A bank considering a loan for machinery must assess not only the borrower, but the potential application of the equipment. An insurer underwriting cargo must consider not just what is shipped, but where it may end up. Two institutions may reach different conclusions on the same facts, each defensible in isolation. The list does not resolve the ambiguity; it generates it.

Compounding this is the reality that sanctions lists are never complete. They lag events. They reflect political compromise. They are updated periodically, not continuously. Information about ownership, control and activity is often partial or outdated. Firms operate with fragments. One insurer may view a client as acceptable based on available data; another may decline because it weights uncertainty differently. Both are responding rationally to incomplete information.

This divergence is not a failure of compliance; it is a feature of the system. Sanctions enforcement relies on decentralised judgement. Authorities expect firms to take responsibility for their own risk assessments. The price of that responsibility is inconsistency. The quiet embargo emerges not from uniform prohibition, but from overlapping, sometimes conflicting, interpretations of where the line lies.

What gives this chapter its urgency is the way these mechanisms have scaled. As trade has grown more complex, so too have the lists and filters that govern it. Data volumes have increased. Screening has become faster and more automated. Yet the underlying uncertainties have not diminished. If anything, they have intensified. Ownership structures have grown more opaque. Supply chains have lengthened. Political risk has become more volatile.

The result is a world in which lists exert influence far beyond their formal scope. They shape behaviour even where they do not apply directly. Firms avoid counterparties not because they are listed, but because they resemble those who are. They exit sectors not because they are banned, but because classification is uncertain. They withdraw from regions not because trade is illegal, but because the informational burden is too high.

A recurring image in this chapter is the searchlight. Sanctions lists illuminate specific targets, but the beam is narrow. Everything outside it lies in shadow. Firms, wary of what might be hidden there, keep their distance. The searchlight does not move often. Behaviour does.

This dynamic raises questions that extend beyond compliance. Who bears the cost of uncertainty? How much discretion should private actors exercise in interpreting public policy? At what point does caution become exclusion? These are not abstract concerns. They play out in delayed shipments, frozen accounts and abandoned projects. They affect who can trade, who can grow, and who is quietly pushed to the margins.

The pages that follow will examine these questions in detail. They will unpack the anatomy of sanctions lists, trace their journey into screening systems, and explore the fault lines created by ownership rules and sectoral measures. They will linger in the grey areas, where information is incomplete and judgement is contested. The aim is not to offer technical instruction, but to sharpen perception.

By the end of this chapter, the reader should no longer see sanctions lists as static artefacts. They are better understood as catalysts: small inputs that set large systems in motion. To read them well is to look not only at who is named, but at how those names are used, misused and feared. The list is only the beginning. The filter decides what passes.

What sanctions lists actually contain

On 6 April 2018, the United States Treasury added Oleg Deripaska and several companies linked to him, including United Company RUSAL, to its Specially Designated Nationals list. The place was Washington, the effect was global. Within hours, aluminium prices spiked on the London Metal Exchange, banks froze transactions, insurers reviewed exposure, and shipping contracts were suspended. Nothing in the listing mentioned bauxite mines in Guinea, smelters in Ireland, or traders in Singapore. Yet all were affected. A few names on a list had travelled far.

Lists look finite. Effects are not.

Sanctions lists are often described as blunt instruments. In reality, they are carefully tiered documents designed to operate at multiple levels of economic life. They combine precision and ambiguity by design. Understanding what they actually contain—rather than what they appear to contain—is essential to understanding why their reach extends so far beyond the page.

At their most basic, sanctions lists are catalogues of designation. They identify who or what is subject to restrictions and under which legal authority. Yet even this apparent simplicity hides variation. Some entries name individuals. Others name corporate entities. Still others define categories of activity or entire jurisdictions. Each type carries a different logic and produces different downstream behaviour. The list is not a single tool; it is a bundle.

Named individuals are the most recognisable element. These entries typically include a full name, date of birth, nationality, and sometimes aliases or identification numbers. The intent is personal accountability. The visible behaviour that follows is immediate exclusion. Banks block accounts. Employers terminate relationships. Travel and access narrow. The implication seems contained. Yet individuals rarely operate alone. Their designation raises questions about every enterprise they touch.

Entities form the second layer. Companies, partnerships and vessels can be listed directly. These entries often include registered addresses, incorporation details, and known subsidiaries. The intent is to disrupt organisational capacity. The visible behaviour is broader: contracts are voided, insurance is withdrawn, counterparties disengage. The implication is structural. An entity listing does not merely punish; it isolates.

Sectoral and thematic measures widen the aperture further. Rather than naming every actor, authorities define prohibited activities within sectors such as energy, shipping, defence or finance. The intent is efficiency. The visible behaviour is interpretive. Firms must decide whether a given transaction falls inside or outside the restricted activity. Compliance teams debate definitions. Deals pause. The implication is that responsibility for line-drawing shifts from the state to the market.

Finally, there are broad country measures. These range from comprehensive embargoes to more limited prohibitions tied to specific behaviours. The intent is political signalling and systemic pressure. The visible behaviour is sweeping. Entire regions become difficult to trade with, even where exceptions exist. The implication is that geography itself becomes a risk factor.

These layers are not mutually exclusive. They overlap. A single sanctions programme may include individual designations, entity listings, sectoral prohibitions and country-wide measures. The list is less a ladder than a mesh.

To see how this plays out, consider a hypothetical shipping company added to a sanctions list. The designation names the legal entity, its registered address and the vessels it operates. On paper, the restriction applies to that company. In practice, banks examine loans to its affiliates. Insurers review cover for vessels it manages but does not own. Charterers reassess contracts with joint ventures. Ports scrutinise calls by ships under common management. The listing has triggered a cascade.

Show the mechanism and its name becomes clear. This is associative risk. The explanation lies in ownership and control rules embedded within sanctions frameworks. If a listed entity owns or controls another company beyond a defined threshold—often 50 per cent—that company is treated as listed, even if unnamed. The implication is that designation propagates through corporate structures. A minority shareholder with influence can create uncertainty. A family link can invite scrutiny. The list becomes a map of potential contagion.

Two named, checkable examples underline the point. When RUSAL was listed in April 2018, several downstream firms not themselves designated faced immediate disruption. Norsk Hydro, a Norwegian aluminium producer with exposure to RUSAL through joint ventures, announced market uncertainty and operational challenges. The visible metric was share price volatility. The implication was that entity listings can affect firms several steps removed.

A different illustration came in February 2020, when the United States designated COSCO Shipping Tanker (Dalian). The parent group remained unlisted. Yet charterers and traders reassessed dealings with vessels managed or chartered through related structures. Freight rates for compliant tonnage rose. The visible behaviour was rebooking and rerouting. The implication was again associative. The list did not need to name every vessel to change the market.

There is a credible counter-example worth noting. Some firms successfully ring-fence exposure through clear corporate separation and transparent governance. In such cases, banks and insurers may continue business with unlisted affiliates. The limitation is practical. Ring-fencing must be legible and trusted. Where information is incomplete or contested, caution prevails.

Reconciling this exception with the broader pattern clarifies why lists are structured as they are. Authorities rely on private actors to extend the effect of designations through judgement. Lists provide anchors. Interpretation supplies reach.

The structure of lists also reflects political economy. Naming individuals is symbolically powerful but operationally limited. Entity listings disrupt commerce more directly but risk collateral damage. Sectoral measures avoid the diplomatic cost of naming yet demand interpretation. Country measures are blunt but unmistakable. Policymakers choose combinations based on objectives and tolerance for spillover. The list records the choice. The market executes it.

A quiet motif runs through this architecture: the nameplate. A company name on a list functions like a label affixed to a door. It does not block the hallway. It signals danger. Those who walk past adjust their pace. Some turn away. Others pause to read the fine print. Few proceed without hesitation.

The abstraction of *clarity* is often invoked in discussions of sanctions lists. In practice, clarity is uneven. Lists are precise about what they name and deliberately vague about what they imply. This is not an accident. Vagueness creates flexibility. It allows authorities to adapt enforcement without constant revision. The visible behaviour is private caution filling public silence.

Metrics again expose the effect. After major listings, transaction volumes drop not only with listed parties but with adjacent actors. Insurance capacity tightens. Financing costs rise. These shifts can be measured in weeks. They do not wait for guidance notes.

This dynamic places a heavy burden on compliance functions. They must translate list entries into decisions that balance legal obligation, commercial viability and reputational exposure. The list does not tell them what to do; it tells them what to worry about. The implication is that lists are prompts rather than prescriptions.

The unresolved tension at the end of this section is deceptively simple. If sanctions lists are designed to be precise but operate through diffusion, how much uncertainty is acceptable? At what point does a list cease to be a targeted measure and become a cloud? The answer is not written in the document itself. It is written in the choices made by those who read it and decide, quietly, to step back.

From legal lists to screening systems

On 27 July 2020, in Washington, the US Treasury's Office of Foreign Assets Control announced a settlement with Commerzbank AG for apparent violations of multiple sanctions programmes. The penalty—publicly stated at $2.3 million—was not the largest of its kind. Its details were more instructive. OFAC described breakdowns in screening and processing that allowed prohibited transactions to pass through systems that were meant to stop them. For compliance teams elsewhere, the message landed with familiar weight: your filters must work, and you must be able to show how they work.

Machines decide first.

The transformation from a published sanctions list to a working screening system is where law becomes friction. Lists are legal artefacts: enumerations of names, entities, programmes and authorities. Screening systems are operational machines: they ingest data, match it against other data, and trigger decisions at speed. The two are often spoken of as if they were the same thing. They are not. The list is a text. The filter is a judgement engine built from code, thresholds and assumptions.

The first step in that transformation is ingestion. A bank or insurer receives updates from official sources—such as OFAC's SDN list, the European Union's consolidated list, or the United Nations sanctions lists—and loads them into internal systems, either directly or via commercial vendors. The visible behaviour is mundane: a scheduled update, a file transfer, a system refresh. The name for this step is list management. The explanation is necessity. Lists change. Aliases are added. Dates of birth are corrected. New programmes appear. The implication is that timeliness matters. A late update is an open gate.

Ingestion, however, is not neutral. Data must be normalised. Names appear in different scripts and formats. Addresses are incomplete or inconsistent. Identification numbers vary by jurisdiction. A list may include multiple aliases and transliterations for the same individual. Systems must decide what counts as the "primary" name and how to store alternatives. The visible behaviour is a decision in data mapping: which fields are mandatory, which are optional, how to handle blank entries. The implication is subtle. A mapping choice can change what gets flagged.

The second step is matching, and this is where most of the quiet embargo is manufactured. Matching can be exact—an identical name and date of birth—or fuzzy, using algorithms that capture similar spellings, partial overlaps, and phonetic resemblance. Banks and insurers choose sensitivity settings based on risk tolerance. A high sensitivity system flags more potential matches. A low sensitivity system misses more. This trade-off is not philosophical; it is operational. It can be measured in alert volumes. Some large banks generate thousands of sanctions alerts each day. The implication is workload. Alerts require human review, and human review takes time.

Addresses complicate matching further. Many sanctions lists include addresses that are old, vague, or formatted differently from internal records. A street name may be transliterated inconsistently. A city may have multiple spellings. Postcodes may be absent. Systems therefore rely on partial address matching, which increases both coverage and error. The visible behaviour is an alert triggered by a shared city or a similar street name. The implication is that geography becomes a proxy, often imperfect.

Ownership links are the third and most complex element. Lists themselves do not always enumerate corporate families. They often name one entity and assume that ownership and control rules will extend restrictions to subsidiaries. Screening systems must therefore incorporate ownership data from corporate registries, commercial databases, and internal client information. This is where insurers and banks become, reluctantly, corporate investigators. The visible behaviour is the construction of relationship graphs: who owns whom, at what percentage, through which layers. The name for this is beneficial ownership screening. The explanation is regulatory expectation. Authorities expect firms to identify whether an unlisted entity is owned or controlled by a listed party. The implication is uncertainty. Ownership data is often incomplete, delayed, or deliberately obscured.

Two named, checkable examples illustrate how these systems have become central to enforcement. In February 2019, Standard Chartered reached settlements with US and UK authorities over sanctions and anti-money laundering controls, including weaknesses in screening and monitoring. The case spanned multiple jurisdictions and years. The visible behavioural response across the sector was immediate: institutions increased investment in screening technology and expanded model validation functions. The implication was that regulators were judging not only outcomes but systems.

A second example comes from the European context. In April 2020, the UK's Office of Financial Sanctions Implementation published guidance emphasising the importance of effective screening and reporting, reflecting an expectation that firms maintain adequate controls and demonstrate them. The document did not prescribe specific algorithms. It set a standard of defensibility. The implication was predictable: firms tuned systems to avoid criticism, even at the cost of higher false positives.

False positives are not an inconvenience; they are a structural feature of automated screening. Consider a legitimate client—say, a mid-sized exporter in Manchester—whose director shares a common surname with a listed individual. A payment is initiated to a customer overseas. The screening tool flags the name as a potential match. The bank's policy requires an automatic stop until review. Funds are held. The exporter is asked for identification documents, corporate records, and confirmation of beneficial ownership. The compliance team checks dates of birth, addresses, and nationality. The match is ruled out. The payment is released days later. No law was broken. Yet the exporter's contract may have been jeopardised, and the bank has expended scarce compliance time.

Show the outcome and the system's logic becomes visible. The name for this is conservative tuning. The explanation is asymmetry: a missed true match can bring regulatory penalty and reputational damage; an extra false positive brings customer frustration and operational cost. The implication is that banks and insurers tolerate friction as the price of safety.

Insurers experience the same dynamic, with additional constraints. An insurer must screen not only insureds but vessels, cargoes, beneficiaries, intermediaries and sometimes even ports. Claims handling adds another layer. A claim payment that touches a sanctioned party can create legal exposure. As a result, insurers often build sanctions checks into underwriting and claims workflows. The visible behaviour is delay at renewal, conditional cover, or requests for extensive documentation. The implication is that risk filters shape market access.

The operational burden created by screening systems is significant. It can be measured in staffing and turnaround times. Large institutions maintain dedicated sanctions teams, escalation committees, and model risk functions that test and validate screening tools. Model validation is a discipline in itself. It asks whether the system is calibrated appropriately, whether data feeds are reliable, and whether tuning decisions are documented. The name for this is governance. The explanation is that regulators now expect not just compliance, but demonstrable control. The implication is that compliance becomes a form of institutional infrastructure.

There is, however, a credible limitation to automated screening. Algorithms cannot resolve ambiguity when the underlying data is poor. A system can match a name, but it cannot always determine identity. It can flag an ownership link, but it cannot always verify control. It can detect patterns, but it cannot infer intent. Over-reliance on automation can therefore create false comfort. A "no match" result is not proof of safety; it is proof that a particular dataset and algorithm did not detect a match.

Reconciling this limitation with the need for scale explains why human judgement remains central. Screening systems triage. They do not decide in the full sense. They generate alerts that must be interpreted by analysts who weigh context: the customer relationship, transaction history, geography, and documentation. The visible behaviour is escalation: from analyst to manager to committee. The implication is delay and variability. Two institutions may treat the same alert differently because their risk appetites differ.

This variability is amplified by the incentives set by enforcement. Authorities rarely punish a firm for being overly cautious, but they do punish for missing prohibited activity. That encourages higher sensitivity settings, broader watchlists, and stricter internal policies. The effect can be measured in alert volumes and customer attrition. Some firms accept the operational cost. Others choose to exit higher-risk business entirely. The quiet embargo is often the output.

A quiet motif threads through this process: the red flag on a screen. It appears, it halts motion, it demands attention. Most flags are resolved as false positives. The work is repetitive, sometimes tedious. Yet the existence of the flag changes behaviour. Relationship managers avoid clients likely to generate flags. Underwriters decline business that will cause operational friction. The screen becomes a gate.

The ethical tension is unavoidable. Automated screening protects financial systems from abuse and supports the enforcement of public policy. It also imposes costs on legitimate actors, particularly those with common names, complex corporate structures, or connections to regions under scrutiny. The cost is visible in delayed payments, lost contracts, and increased documentation burdens. These are not abstractions. They are lived experience.

The forward test is not whether screening systems will become more pervasive—they will—but whether institutions can measure and manage the trade-off between sensitivity and harm. A system tuned to catch everything may freeze the innocent. A system tuned to avoid disruption may miss the guilty. The diagnostic question is simple and uncomfortable: when the red flag appears, what, exactly, is your institution optimising for?

Ownership, control and hidden links

On 6 April 2018, when the United States Treasury designated Oleg Deripaska under its Russia sanctions programme in Washington, the legal action named a man and a finite list of companies. Within days, banks in London and Frankfurt began asking questions of firms that had never dealt with Deripaska directly. Minority shareholdings were scrutinised. Board appointments were re-examined. Joint ventures stalled. The designation of one individual had exposed a web of ownership links that few counterparties had previously mapped in full.

Control does not announce itself.

This is the central difficulty of ownership-based sanctions. Unlike lists that prohibit dealings with a named person or entity, ownership and control rules operate by implication. They extend restrictions beyond what is written, pulling in companies and transactions that sit at one or two removes from the designation. The intent is clear enough: sanctioned actors should not be able to evade measures by hiding behind corporate structures. The execution is anything but simple.

At the heart of the problem lies a deceptively modest question. Who really owns this business? In ordinary commerce, the answer is often taken at face value. A register shows shareholders. A board is listed. Audited accounts are filed. For sanctions purposes, this surface clarity is rarely sufficient. Authorities expect firms to look beyond formal titles and percentages, to consider who exercises influence, who benefits, and who might pull the strings informally. Ownership becomes a hypothesis rather than a fact.

Show the issue in practice and its contours sharpen. A trader agrees to supply equipment to an unlisted manufacturing firm. The contract is lawful. Initial screening raises no alarms. Then a bank, conducting enhanced due diligence, discovers that a sanctioned individual holds a 30 per cent stake through an offshore vehicle. The stake falls below formal thresholds in many jurisdictions. Yet the individual is known to have close ties to management. The bank escalates. The insurer hesitates. The trader is asked to provide assurances it cannot fully give. The deal pauses.

The name for this uncertainty is *control risk*. The explanation lies in how sanctions frameworks define ownership and control. Many regimes treat entities owned, directly or indirectly, beyond a certain percentage by a listed person as themselves sanctioned. Others go further, capturing entities controlled "in fact" even where formal ownership is lower. Control may be inferred from voting rights, board representation, contractual vetoes, or personal relationships. The implication is that sanctions compliance requires judgement about power, not just arithmetic.

Two named, checkable examples illustrate how far this logic can reach. When RUSAL was designated in April 2018, the company was majority owned by Deripaska at the time. Yet the disruption extended to firms where his influence was indirect. Glencore, which had commercial relationships with RUSAL, publicly disclosed its exposure and began reassessing arrangements. The visible metric was market volatility and renegotiated contracts. The implication was that even arm's-length relationships became suspect when ownership questions arose.

A different case emerged in December 2020, when the United States designated several Chinese companies for alleged links to the military. While the designations named specific entities, global investors and banks began reassessing holdings in affiliated firms, unsure where influence ended. Index providers announced removals. Funds divested. The visible behaviour was rapid portfolio adjustment. The implication was that uncertainty around control can radiate through capital markets.

Minority stakes are particularly destabilising. In many corporate contexts, a 10 or 20 per cent holding conveys little day-to-day power. In sanctions analysis, it can be decisive. A minority shareholder may enjoy special rights, informal influence, or family ties that amplify their role. Compliance teams must therefore ask questions that are uncomfortable and sometimes unanswerable. Who sits on the board? Who appoints management? Who provides financing? Who is related to whom? Each answer opens another door.

Family ties complicate matters further. Sanctions regimes often designate individuals precisely because of their proximity to political power. Their relatives may appear nowhere on a list, yet exercise significant influence through shared interests and trust. A company owned by a spouse, sibling or adult child may be formally independent and practically aligned. The visible behaviour this produces is cautious association. Firms avoid not just listed individuals, but their extended networks. The implication is that personal relationships become risk factors.

Nominee structures add another layer of opacity. Shares held on behalf of another, trusts established in distant jurisdictions, and management companies acting as fronts are familiar features of global commerce. They are also fertile ground for sanctions evasion. Compliance systems attempt to pierce these veils using corporate registries, leaked datasets and commercial intelligence. The results are uneven. A nominee arrangement may be perfectly lawful and still unacceptable to a risk committee. The implication is that legality does not resolve suspicion.

A brief illustrative example shows how easily unsuspecting counterparties are drawn in. A European commodities trader sources material from a mid-sized supplier incorporated in Southeast Asia. The supplier is not listed. Its shareholders appear to be local entrepreneurs. During a routine review triggered by a bank query, the trader learns that one shareholder holds a 15 per cent stake via a holding company in another jurisdiction. Further inquiry reveals that this holding company is linked to a sanctioned individual through a family trust. The stake is small. The influence is unclear. The trader's bank decides the risk is too high. Payments are halted. The trader is left explaining a problem it did not know existed.

Trust is often invoked in discussions of ownership. In this context, trust manifests as a decision to proceed or to step back. It is visible in approvals granted or withheld. Efficiency, another abstraction, appears as turnaround time for due diligence or the length of a questionnaire. Risk takes the shape of a declined transaction or a terminated relationship. These are not metaphors; they are operational facts.

There is a credible counter-example that tempers the picture. Some jurisdictions and institutions have developed clearer guidance on ownership thresholds, providing firms with greater certainty. Where ownership is demonstrably below defined limits and governance structures are transparent, banks and insurers may accept the risk. The visible behaviour is continued service provision. The limitation is that such clarity is rare and often jurisdiction-specific. In cross-border trade, the most restrictive interpretation usually prevails.

Reconciling this exception with the broader pattern reveals why ownership and control remain such powerful tools. They introduce ambiguity that forces private actors to exercise caution. Authorities need not list every affiliate or associate. They rely on firms to infer where influence might lie and to act accordingly. This decentralised extension of sanctions is efficient, but it transfers responsibility and cost to the market.

The quiet motif threading through this section is the shadow share. It does not appear in annual reports or marketing materials. It surfaces only when someone looks closely enough, often too late. Once seen, it is difficult to ignore. Deals unravel not because ownership is proven, but because it cannot be disproven.

The burden of this uncertainty falls unevenly. Large multinationals can invest in forensic due diligence and bespoke analysis. Smaller traders cannot. Charities and humanitarian actors, already stretched, struggle to meet escalating documentation demands. The result is exclusion by complexity. Transactions that might be permissible in principle become impractical in execution.

This dynamic also shapes behaviour upstream. Firms redesign corporate structures to avoid concentrated ownership. They dilute stakes. They rotate directors. They avoid joint ventures in sensitive regions. These changes are visible in governance charts and shareholder registers. The implication is that sanctions policy influences corporate architecture itself.

The unresolved tension at the end of this discussion is stark. If ownership and control are defined broadly enough to capture hidden influence, how much uncertainty can commerce bear? At what point does the effort to prevent evasion suffocate legitimate exchange? The forward test is constant and uncomfortable. When a name does not appear on a list, but its shadow does, who decides how far that shadow falls?

Sectoral and thematic sanctions

On 16 July 2014, in Washington, the United States Treasury announced a new wave of Russia-related measures that did not rely on an ever-expanding roll-call of banned counterparties. Instead, through OFAC's sectoral sanctions directives, the US targeted *activities*: certain kinds of financing and dealings with specified firms in energy, defence and finance. The legal architecture was spare. The operational effect was immediate. Banks re-cut credit lines, shortened maturities, and turned away trades that had been commercially routine a month earlier, not because the borrower's name was newly infamous, but because the *type* of transaction had become suspect.

Definitions do the damage.

That is the essential character of sectoral and thematic sanctions. They do not merely ask, "Who is prohibited?" They ask, "What counts?" The question sounds technical, but it is existential for the institutions that must act on it. A person or company can be screened against a list. An *activity* must be interpreted. Once interpretation becomes necessary, private risk appetite becomes policy.

Sectoral measures emerged from a practical dilemma. Governments wanted to apply pressure without reaching for comprehensive embargoes that can be politically costly and economically indiscriminate. They also wanted to avoid the whack-a-mole logic of listing every subsidiary, proxy and affiliate in a sprawling corporate universe. The solution was to constrain capability by targeting categories of conduct: specific types of financing, investment, services, technology transfer, or operational support, often tied to sectors that matter strategically. Energy, shipping, advanced technology, and financial services recur because they are both central and controllable.

Show how this works and the shape becomes clearer. A bank does not need to be told never to deal with a named firm; it is told it may not extend credit beyond a certain term, or may not participate in certain instruments, or may not finance certain projects. The bank's compliance system can flag the counterparty and the jurisdiction, but it must also classify the product and measure the transaction's features. The abstraction of *risk* appears as a concrete internal decision: reduce tenor from 90 days to 30, refuse to roll over an existing facility, require cash collateral, or demand enhanced documentation on end use. The implication is that legal nuance translates into commercial contraction.

Thematic sanctions widen the frame further. Here the logic is less about traditional sectors and more about a theme—cyber activity, corruption, human rights abuses, illicit finance, proliferation—implemented through tools that can include targeted designations, service restrictions, export controls and procurement bans. The theme may be morally compelling and politically resonant, but for firms it poses a familiar problem: mapping a broad normative category onto a transaction file. How does one measure a "human rights risk" in a shipping contract? What does "material support" look like in a software licensing arrangement? The answer, in practice, is that firms create proxies: country risk scores, sector exclusions, and lists of red-flag goods or services.

This is where dual-use technology becomes the recurring stress test. Dual-use is not an exotic corner case; it is the daily reality of industrial modernity. The same high-performance bearings that keep a wind turbine turning can also support a missile system. The same advanced chips that power medical imaging can also enable surveillance or weapons guidance. Export control regimes have long recognised this, and the European Union's dual-use framework—now consolidated in Regulation (EU) 2021/821—codifies how certain goods, software and technology require controls depending on destination and end use. Sanctions measures often intersect with these rules, creating layered obligations and interpretive friction.

Consider an example that compliance officers will recognise instantly, even when details vary. A mid-sized European bank is asked to finance a shipment of precision machine tools to a customer in a third country. The customer is unlisted. The route is ordinary. The goods are not obviously military. Yet the bank's trade finance team notices that the machine tools match technical parameters associated with controlled dual-use items under EU rules. The exporter supplies an end-user statement describing civilian production. The bank is still unsure whether the product's specifications trigger additional scrutiny under thematic restrictions aimed at preventing military capability enhancement in a sanctioned jurisdiction. The file reaches a committee. The committee asks for more comfort. Time passes. The exporter loses the deal, not because a law forbade it in plain terms, but because the classification could not be settled quickly enough to satisfy a cautious institution.

Five words matter here: *What counts as restricted?* The question reappears in different guises. It is asked in underwriting rooms when insurers decide whether a service is "support" for a sanctioned sector. It is asked in shipping companies when they decide whether a cargo is "related to" a prohibited activity. It is asked in ports when they decide whether accepting a vessel could be construed as facilitating restricted trade. The motif is the boundary line drawn in pencil: it can be sharpened, smudged, or erased, and everyone acts as if they might be judged for how they drew it.

A second named, checkable example shows how sectoral definitions can reshape markets even when firms remain otherwise tradable. On 2 August 2017, in Washington, the United States enacted the Countering America's Adversaries Through Sanctions Act (CAATSA). Among its many provisions, CAATSA created new bases for sanctions related to Russia, Iran and North Korea, including measures that could reach certain investment and support activities in energy export pipelines. The legislative text did not have to list every relevant engineering firm or shipping intermediary. It threatened penalties for categories of involvement. Firms responded with visible behaviour: legal reviews, project delays, restructuring of participation, and in some cases withdrawal. The implication was classic sectoral logic. Constraint travelled through activity risk.

Sectoral and thematic measures also work because they exploit how modern institutions already organise decision-making. Banks, insurers and large corporates manage their businesses by product lines, industry groupings and risk categories. A sectoral prohibition plugs straight into existing systems. It can be turned into a rule: "No debt beyond X days for Y category," or "No cover for projects involving Z." The abstraction of *efficiency* becomes measurable: fewer bespoke decisions, faster automated rejection, lower compliance variance. The implication, however, is that sectoral rules encourage broad-brush avoidance. When classification is difficult, a firm can protect itself by stepping back from the entire category.

Shipping illustrates this with particular clarity because the sector itself is both a target and a conduit. A measure may restrict services to certain vessels, restrict transport of certain commodities, or restrict insurance for certain trade patterns. Firms must interpret whether an activity is "shipping support" or "energy support," whether a cargo is "originating from" a prohibited area, whether a route implies sanctions exposure. The visible behaviour is operational: vessels are re-routed, flagged differently, charter terms rewritten, ports substituted. The metric is cost. Freight rates and insurance premiums diverge between "clean" and "questionable" corridors, reflecting the market's internal classification of risk.

For all their potency, sectoral and thematic sanctions have a built-in limitation: they demand interpretive capacity that many institutions do not possess evenly. Large banks can maintain specialist teams. Global insurers can consult counsel and data vendors. Smaller firms cannot. The result can be uneven application—some institutions treat a category as manageable with controls; others treat it as untouchable. That inconsistency is not a bug from the regulator's perspective; it is often the mechanism by which pressure spreads. But it can lead to unintended consequences: lawful trade blocked, humanitarian supply chains delayed, and competitive advantage shifting to actors willing to operate nearer the line.

There is another limitation that is less discussed and more strategic. Broad activity-based measures can sometimes incentivise clever compliance rather than genuine behavioural change. If the rule prohibits financing beyond a certain tenor, financing structures may be chopped into shorter pieces. If the rule targets certain project types, activity may be repackaged. If the rule focuses on direct involvement, involvement becomes indirect. This does not make sanctions ineffective; it shows that their effectiveness depends on how well definitions anticipate adaptation. The implication is that sectoral sanctions are a contest of classification, not merely of enforcement.

Reconciling these limitations with the continued appeal of sectoral and thematic measures requires acknowledging their core advantage: they allow pressure without total rupture. They can degrade capability while leaving room for negotiation, exemptions, and selective continuity. They also scale. A government need not chase every shell company if it can deter the enabling services—finance, insurance, specialist engineering—from supporting the prohibited activity. The price is ambiguity. The system runs on grey.

In practice, institutions manage this grey by building internal taxonomies. They create "restricted sectors" lists, "sensitive goods" inventories, and "elevated geography" matrices. They set triggers: a certain HS code, a certain end-use statement, a certain counterparty jurisdiction. They measure outcomes through key indicators: alert volumes, escalations, turnaround times, rejection rates. Each abstraction becomes a number or a decision. Trust appears as a cleared transaction. Doubt appears as a hold. Risk appetite appears as a policy line.

This has human consequences, and not only for sanctioned actors. The exporter whose machine tools are delayed because of dual-use uncertainty learns that compliance is not a question of innocence but of legibility. The bank's committee does not need to believe the goods are destined for harm; it needs to believe it can defend its decision under scrutiny. That defensibility, rather than truth, often becomes the operational criterion. It is a subtle but profound shift.

The boundary line in pencil returns at the end because it captures the enduring challenge. Sectoral and thematic sanctions promise precision: target the activity, not the population. Yet precision depends on classification, and classification depends on information, and information is rarely complete. The forward test, then, is not simply whether a transaction is permitted, but whether the institution can *name* what it is doing with confidence. When the file lands on a desk and the question arises—does this product, this service, this financing arrangement belong on the wrong side of the line?—who has the authority, the evidence, and the appetite to answer without reaching for the safest refusal?

Grey areas and incomplete information

On 6 April 2018, in Washington, the United States Treasury added Oleg Deripaska and several companies linked to him, including United Company RUSAL, to its Specially Designated Nationals list. The designation was unambiguous in form: names, identifiers, legal authority. The market reaction exposed a different truth. Within hours, banks and insurers began asking questions that the list could not answer: which subsidiaries were caught; which joint ventures were safe; which contracts could still be performed; which payments might be trapped mid-flight. The law spoke in clean lines. The data did not.

The map is outdated.

Sanctions regimes depend on lists, but lists are snapshots of a moving target. They are updated in bursts, shaped by diplomacy, and constrained by what authorities can prove and publish. Between updates, the world changes. Ownership structures mutate. Companies rename and re-register. Addresses shift. Individuals acquire new passports, new roles, new proxies. A list can be perfectly accurate at the moment it is issued and still fail to capture the reality a week later. This gap—between the list as a legal artefact and the world as a living system—is where grey areas breed.

The first grey area is incompleteness. Lists are not meant to enumerate every risk. They are meant to name what a government has chosen, and is able, to designate. That choice is strategic. A regime may target a handful of prominent actors to send a message, expecting markets to widen the effect through caution. Or it may target a narrow slice of a sector, hoping to constrain capability without triggering broad collateral damage. Either way, the list is not a census. It is a signal.

Show how incompleteness behaves in a compliance setting and it becomes something measurable. A bank screens a customer base and finds no direct matches to a new designation. Yet it sees transactions involving counterparties in the same corporate family, or cargoes moving on the same vessels, or payments routed through the same intermediaries. The name for this is adjacency risk. The explanation is that sanctions frequently aim at networks, not isolated entities. The implication is that firms must act on patterns that are not explicitly named.

The second grey area is delay. Official lists update on official schedules, but commercial realities move at market speed. A compliance team may receive a list update hours after it is published, depending on data vendors, internal change controls, and system refresh cycles. Even when updates are timely, the supporting information—corporate registries, shipping databases, beneficial ownership records—may lag far behind. The visible behaviour is a file stuck in review while staff wait for documents, confirmations, translations, or third-party intelligence. Time becomes the instrument. The implication is that lawful trade can be slowed to a halt by the pace of information, not the content of the law.

The third grey area is conflict. Different sources can disagree about the same fact. One database may show a shareholder at 49 per cent; another at 51. One registry may list an address that has been superseded; another may still carry the old one. One intelligence report may suggest control by a designated individual; another may call it unproven. Firms do not receive a single authoritative narrative. They receive a stack of partial stories. The visible behaviour is divergence: one institution proceeds, another declines, both convinced they are acting responsibly. The implication is that compliance outcomes are shaped as much by epistemology—what you believe you know—as by law.

A second named, checkable example illustrates how lists can be clear while the surrounding facts remain contested. On 8 August 2022, in Washington, OFAC added Tornado Cash, a crypto mixing service, to the SDN list. Whatever one thinks of the policy, the operational problem was immediate and novel: how does a bank, exchange, or insurer treat an entry that is not a conventional person or corporation, but a set of blockchain addresses associated with software? Market participants had to translate a legal designation into technical controls, and they did so unevenly. Some froze broad categories of activity to be safe. Others tried to implement narrow address-based blocks. The list was definitive. The implementation lived in uncertainty.

This is a useful reminder that grey areas are not always caused by bad actors. They can arise from novelty. When sanctions regimes expand into new domains—digital infrastructure, cyber activity, novel financial products—the boundary between "listed party" and "listed pattern" blurs. Firms must build controls faster than they can build understanding. The visible metric is policy lag: internal rules updated in weeks, staff training updated in months, systems tuned over quarters. The implication is predictable: in the meantime, the safest refusal often wins.

The burden of incomplete information does not fall evenly across sectors. Marine insurance offers a particularly sharp lens because it depends on identifiers that are both precise and, at times, inadequate. A vessel has an IMO number. That helps. A port call can be tracked. That helps too. But the entity that owns, manages, charters, or benefits from the voyage may be hidden behind layers of companies incorporated in jurisdictions that disclose little. The insurer can see the ship. It may not see the hands steering the business.

Here the grey area often crystallises around ownership and control. Lists name an entity. Rules extend to entities owned or controlled by that entity. Determining whether a subsidiary falls under that extension requires corporate data that is frequently opaque. When the data is incomplete, firms substitute proxies: the presence of a politically exposed person, links to a sanctioned geography, unusual corporate changes, a mismatch between declared business and observed trade patterns. Each proxy can be defended. None is conclusive. The implication is that compliance becomes a craft of inference.

A brief illustrative example shows how two insurers can reach different conclusions on the same client without either behaving irrationally. A shipping company seeks renewal of hull and machinery cover. It operates mainly in the Mediterranean, with occasional voyages to ports near jurisdictions under intense sanctions scrutiny. Its beneficial ownership appears clean in commercial databases, but one data feed shows a minority shareholder linked to a family trust with historic ties to a designated individual. The link is indirect and the percentage appears below formal thresholds. Insurer A, with a large US reinsurance programme and a strict internal policy, treats the uncertainty itself as unacceptable. It declines renewal or offers cover with broad sanctions exclusions that render the policy commercially unattractive. Insurer B, with less US exposure and a more permissive risk appetite, requests additional documentation, obtains written assurances, and proceeds with pricing that reflects heightened monitoring rather than outright refusal. The same facts. Two outcomes. The divergence is not legal disagreement so much as differing weights assigned to uncertainty.

This is the quiet embargo's most persistent feature: discretion hidden inside process. Firms rarely say, "We believe you are sanctioned." They say, "We cannot get comfortable." Comfort becomes a measurable operational state: an approval granted, a premium quoted, a payment released. Discomfort becomes delay and withdrawal. In grey areas, comfort is scarce.

A credible counter-example should be faced squarely. There are domains where identifiers and documentation can reduce ambiguity significantly. In shipping, the combination of IMO numbers, classification records, and AIS histories can provide a relatively robust picture of a vessel's identity over time. In banking, strong "know your customer" documentation and audited corporate records can resolve many questions, particularly in jurisdictions with transparent registries and reliable enforcement. When data quality is high and governance is clear, firms can and do proceed. The visible behaviour is straightforward: faster approvals, fewer escalations, lower premiums relative to comparable risk corridors. The limitation is that these conditions are not universal. Many of the transactions that matter most in sanctions policy occur precisely where transparency is weakest.

Reconciling the counter-example with the broader reality clarifies the structural nature of grey areas. Uncertainty is not an aberration. It is concentrated where sanctions regimes aim their pressure: at complex networks, cross-border intermediaries, and politically sensitive industries. Firms operating there cannot wait for perfect information. They must decide under partial knowledge. The result is unevenness that is both rational and destabilising.

This unevenness is reinforced by institutional incentives. Regulators and prosecutors judge outcomes retrospectively. They ask whether a firm *should* have known, whether warning signs were missed, whether controls were adequate. Firms therefore build systems that prioritise defensibility. The visible behaviour is documentation inflation: questionnaires, certifications, end-user statements, beneficial ownership declarations, shipping route confirmations. Each document reduces one uncertainty and reveals another. The implication is that transaction costs rise until some trades, though lawful, no longer clear.

Media and political scrutiny intensify the grey. A firm may accept a transaction legally but fear that a headline will frame it differently. Where facts are contested, perception fills the gap. Reputation becomes an additional filter. The visible decision is self-imposed restriction: declining a category of clients, excluding a geography, or exiting a line of business pre-emptively. The implication is that grey areas expand beyond what law requires because uncertainty attracts attention, and attention attracts risk.

The quiet motif that threads through this section is the stale file: a dossier with missing pages, outdated addresses, contradictory charts of ownership. It sits on a desk while someone tries to make a binary decision from non-binary information. The stale file creates friction by its mere existence. It also creates divergence, because different desks will tolerate different degrees of staleness.

These grey areas also affect the broader economy of compliance. They encourage a market for data vendors, investigators, and screening tools that promise clarity. They produce escalating expenditure on compliance staff and systems. They alter who can compete: firms with resources can chase information; those without step back. The implication is a quiet redistribution of trade capacity away from smaller actors and towards institutions able to absorb uncertainty.

The unresolved tension is not whether sanctions lists can be made perfect. They cannot. It is whether markets can develop a mature way to live with imperfection without turning every unknown into a veto. The forward test arrives whenever a file contains just enough to worry but not enough to prove. Do you treat uncertainty as a reason to stop, or as a reason to measure, monitor, and proceed with limits? In the grey, the decision is the policy, and the policy is made one stalled transaction at a time.

Chapter 3

Reinsurance, P&I Clubs and Lloyd's

In October 2018, a tanker sat idle in a Mediterranean anchorage, its paperwork in order and its destination unchanged. There was no interdiction, no legal notice taped to a gangway. What had changed was quieter. The ship's insurer had informed the owner that renewal terms would not be offered on the same basis. Behind that decision lay another, taken further upstream, by a reinsurer that had reassessed its exposure to a particular route. The cargo was lawful. The voyage was routine. Yet without affordable cover, the ship did not sail.

Insurance, it turns out, can stop a ship as effectively as a blockade.

For centuries, maritime trade has depended on the promise that loss can be absorbed and shared. Ships sink. Cargoes spoil. Accidents happen. Insurance exists to make risk survivable. What has changed is not the need for insurance, but its role as an instrument of policy and pressure. In the contemporary world of sanctions and compliance, insurance no longer merely responds to risk; it shapes what risks may be taken at all. The quiet embargo often begins not with a ban, but with a clause.

This chapter examines the strata beneath the visible surface of insurance markets: the reinsurers who provide capacity, the mutual clubs that govern shipping liabilities, and the peculiar marketplace of Lloyd's, where hundreds of syndicates converge under shared rules. These institutions rarely appear in headlines, yet their decisions determine which trades are possible, which routes are viable, and which regions become commercially unreachable long before any law declares them so.

Reinsurance is the least visible and most powerful of these layers. Primary insurers, the firms that issue policies to shipowners, traders and operators, do not carry all that risk themselves. They pass portions of it upward, spreading exposure across global markets. This structure allows insurers to write policies that would otherwise be too large or volatile. It also creates a choke point. When reinsurers tighten terms or withdraw from a category of risk, the effect cascades downward. Primary insurers may still wish to insure a voyage, but without reinsurance support their balance sheets will not permit it. Capacity evaporates without announcement.

The logic is straightforward. Reinsurers sit furthest from the individual client and closest to systemic exposure. They view risk in aggregates: regions, sectors, correlations. A cautious shift at this level is rarely about a single ship or contract. It is about portfolio coherence, regulatory expectations, and reputational posture. When that shift occurs, it is transmitted through pricing, exclusions and non-renewals. Entire routes can become uninsurable because the top of the chain has blinked.

Protection and indemnity clubs operate differently, yet with comparable influence. These mutual associations exist to cover shipowners against liabilities that conventional insurance does not readily absorb: pollution, crew injury, collision, wreck removal. P&I clubs are not merely insurers; they are communities with rules, traditions and collective discipline. Members share losses. They also share norms. When a club issues a circular warning about a particular trade, port, or counterparty, it is not issuing law. It is signalling collective discomfort. Members who ignore that signal may find themselves isolated or unsupported when trouble arises.

This soft governance is one of the most effective forms of control in shipping. A P&I club does not need to prohibit a cargo explicitly. It can remind members of their obligations, highlight emerging risks, and suggest prudence. The result is often behavioural change that goes beyond legal necessity. Ships avoid certain trades not because they are forbidden, but because the mutual safety net feels less secure.

Lloyd's of London adds another dimension. It is neither a single insurer nor a regulator, but a marketplace where syndicates underwrite risk under a common banner. Lloyd's sets standards, issues guidance, and enforces compliance expectations across its market. When Lloyd's speaks, it speaks to hundreds of underwriting desks simultaneously. A shift in tone or interpretation can ripple quickly, harmonising caution across otherwise independent actors.

This collective sensitivity makes Lloyd's a powerful amplifier of sanctions risk. A single high-profile claim dispute, or a regulatory warning addressed to the market, can recalibrate attitudes overnight. Underwriters adjust appetites. Wordings tighten. Questions once answered routinely become escalations. The market moves together, not because it is ordered to do so, but because shared infrastructure and shared scrutiny encourage convergence.

Threaded through all of this is language: the clauses, exclusions and carve-outs that translate political risk into contractual reality. Sanctions exclusions are often short, dense and overlooked until they matter. A phrase such as "to the extent prohibited" or "where performance would expose the insurer to sanction" can decide whether a claim is paid or denied. These words embed policy into private agreement. They are negotiated quietly, renewed annually, and invoked decisively when loss occurs.

For the insured, the effect can be jarring. A claim that would have been paid a decade earlier is now declined, not because the loss itself is excluded, but because paying it would create sanctions exposure for the insurer or its reinsurers. The knock-on effects are immediate. Financiers reassess collateral. Charterers reconsider contracts. Ports question access. One denied claim can echo through a commercial network.

The most subtle form of pressure, however, is disappearance. Cover is not always cancelled. More often, it is not renewed, or it returns with higher premiums, narrower terms and more exclusions. Clients are not told that a route is impossible; they are shown that it is unaffordable. This gradual constriction is a hallmark of the quiet embargo. It avoids confrontation. It leaves no single decision to contest. It simply changes the economics until behaviour adjusts.

A shipping company that once traded freely across several regions may find its options shrinking year by year. Each renewal brings new questions, new endorsements, new conditions. Eventually, certain voyages drop out of the business plan. Ships are redeployed. Routes are redrawn. The embargo has taken hold without a proclamation.

What makes this chapter urgent is not novelty, but accumulation. Sanctions regimes have grown more complex. Compliance expectations have intensified. Public scrutiny of insurers has sharpened. Reinsurance markets have become more concentrated. Each of these trends reinforces the others. Together, they place extraordinary influence in the hands of actors whose primary mandate is not geopolitics, but solvency and reputation.

Yet this is not a story of villains. Reinsurers, P&I clubs and Lloyd's respond to incentives and constraints that are real. They face regulators who expect vigilance, shareholders who demand caution, and public opinion that punishes perceived complicity. Their decisions are rational within that environment. The consequence is a system in which private risk management becomes a form of global governance.

A recurring image in this chapter is the tightening valve. No single turn stops the flow. Each adjustment seems minor, defensible, technical. Together, they reduce pressure until movement slows and then ceases. By the time observers notice, the system has already rebalanced.

The pages that follow will descend into these mechanisms with care. They will examine how reinsurance shapes capacity, how P&I clubs guide behaviour, how Lloyd's disseminates caution, how policy wordings decide outcomes, and how cover vanishes without noise. The aim is not to demystify insurance in the abstract, but to show how its architecture has become one of the most consequential arenas in modern trade conflict.

If earlier chapters revealed how banks and compliance systems apply the brakes, this chapter reveals who controls the brake fluid. The question that hangs over it is simple and unsettling: when the ability to insure determines the ability to trade, who is really setting the limits, and how visible are they to those who must live with the consequences?

Why reinsurance controls capacity

In March 2022, in Zurich, Swiss Re informed a number of cedants that it would significantly restrict reinsurance support for risks connected to Russia and Ukraine. The announcement was not framed as a political statement. It arrived through technical notices, revised appetites, and altered treaty terms. Within weeks, smaller marine and energy insurers across Europe and Asia adjusted their own offerings. Routes remained legally open. Capacity did not. Ships that could once secure cover found premiums doubled or offers withdrawn altogether.

The tap closed upstream.

Reinsurance is the quiet architecture that allows insurance markets to exist at scale. Primary insurers—those that issue policies to shipowners, traders, energy companies and logistics firms—rarely retain all the risk they underwrite. They pass portions of it to reinsurers, distributing exposure across global balance sheets. This arrangement permits insurers to write policies that would otherwise exceed their capital limits. It also concentrates power. When reinsurers become cautious, the ability of primary insurers to operate contracts with it.

The mechanics are simple and decisive. A reinsurer sets terms for how much risk it will accept, at what price, and under what conditions. Those terms are embedded in treaties that govern vast swathes of an insurer's portfolio. If a reinsurer excludes a geography, tightens a sanctions clause, or reduces line sizes for a class of business, the effect is not incremental. It is systemic. Primary insurers must either mirror the restriction or retain more risk on their own books than regulators and rating agencies will tolerate. Most choose to mirror.

Capacity follows capital.

Show this in a concrete transaction and the leverage becomes visible. A regional insurer may wish to underwrite hull and machinery cover for voyages through a contested corridor. The premium looks adequate. The claims history is acceptable. Yet the insurer's reinsurance treaty includes an exclusion or sub-limit for that corridor following a reinsurer's review. The insurer can technically write the policy, but only by retaining a disproportionate share of the risk. That decision affects solvency ratios and capital charges. The visible behaviour is refusal or repricing. The implication is that reinsurer appetite becomes the market's appetite.

Reinsurers justify this stance in the language of aggregation. They see portfolios, not individual risks. A single insured voyage may look manageable; hundreds of correlated exposures in a volatile region do not. Sanctions risk compounds this concern because it is binary. A claim denied under a sanctions exclusion may still generate litigation, regulatory inquiry and reputational damage. From a reinsurer's perspective, the safest loss is the one never assumed. The visible metric is reduced aggregate exposure by region or sector. The implication is that entire routes become commercially marginal.

A second named, checkable example underscores the point. In January 2019, in Munich, Munich Re announced tighter underwriting and reinsurance support for coal-related risks, citing long-term transition risk and policy uncertainty. While the announcement focused on primary underwriting, its reinsurance implications were immediate. Insurers with coal exposure found reinsurance terms narrowing. Smaller insurers withdrew from coal-linked business altogether. The visible behaviour was market exit. The implication was that a decision taken at the reinsurance level reshaped the downstream insurance landscape.

Reinsurance controls capacity not only through explicit exclusions but through pricing. When reinsurers perceive heightened risk, they raise rates, impose higher deductibles, or reduce commissions. These changes cascade. Primary insurers pass costs to clients or decide that certain business no longer meets return thresholds. Premium increases can be measured in percentages; withdrawal is measured in absence. Both alter behaviour.

Trust is often invoked in discussions of reinsurance relationships. Here, trust manifests as willingness to share risk. A reinsurer that trusts an insurer's controls, underwriting discipline and compliance framework may maintain support in challenging environments. One that doubts those controls will retreat. The abstraction of *trust* becomes a tangible decision: renew the treaty unchanged, or rewrite it with carve-outs. The implication is competitive differentiation. Insurers with stronger governance retain capacity longer.

Efficiency, another abstraction, appears in treaty structures. Quota share arrangements distribute risk proportionally and make reinsurer sentiment immediately consequential. Excess-of-loss treaties introduce thresholds, but once those thresholds are breached, reinsurer participation becomes decisive. In both cases, the architecture ensures that upstream caution transmits rapidly. The system is designed to propagate signals.

Sanctions intensify this transmission because they introduce uncertainty that reinsurers are structurally ill-suited to absorb. Unlike natural catastrophes, sanctions risk does not lend itself to probabilistic modelling. It depends on politics, enforcement discretion and public perception. Reinsurers respond by simplifying. They exclude. They cap. They withdraw. The visible behaviour is treaty revision following major sanctions announcements. The implication is that capacity contracts pre-emptively.

A recurring motif in this process is the narrowing funnel. At the wide end sit thousands of insured risks. As they pass upward through layers of reinsurance, the funnel tightens. By the time exposure reaches the top, only what fits the reinsurer's appetite emerges. Everything else spills away. No one announces the spillage. It is inferred from what no longer flows.

The concentration of reinsurance capital magnifies this effect. A relatively small number of global reinsurers dominate certain lines. Their views carry disproportionate weight. When several move in the same direction—often informed by shared regulatory expectations and market intelligence—the impact is swift. Primary insurers find that alternative capacity is scarce or equally cautious. The visible metric is alignment: similar exclusions appearing across competing policies within a single renewal season.

There is a credible counter-example that deserves attention. In some niche markets, specialist reinsurers or alternative capital providers step in when traditional capacity retreats. Parametric covers, captives, and bespoke structures can preserve limited capacity for specific risks. The visible behaviour is innovation. The limitation is scale. These solutions rarely support mainstream trade at volume. They mitigate at the margins while the core market contracts.

Reconciling this exception with the dominant pattern clarifies why reinsurance remains the fulcrum. Alternative capacity thrives where risks are well-defined and contained. Sanctions-related risks are neither. They sprawl across legal systems and public opinion. Reinsurers, tasked with protecting capital over decades, respond accordingly.

The human consequences are often indirect but material. A shipping company renewing its fleet insurance may learn that certain routes now attract punitive premiums or are excluded entirely. It adjusts schedules. Cargo owners seek alternative carriers. Ports see fewer calls. None of these actors receive a letter from a government agency. They read the signal in the market.

Regulators reinforce this dynamic through capital requirements and supervisory scrutiny. Insurers are expected to demonstrate prudent risk management, including sensitivity to sanctions exposure. Reinsurers, subject to the same expectations, act conservatively. The visible behaviour is alignment with the strictest plausible interpretation. The implication is that the system rewards caution and penalises creativity.

This creates a feedback loop. As primary insurers withdraw, data on claims and losses in certain regions becomes thinner. Reinsurers, lacking fresh information, perceive higher uncertainty. They tighten further. The funnel narrows again. Capacity reduction becomes self-reinforcing.

The unresolved tension at the end of this chain is practical. If reinsurance controls capacity, and capacity determines which trades can occur, who bears responsibility for the economic consequences of upstream caution? Is it acceptable that decisions taken in Zurich, Munich or Bermuda reshape trade patterns in ports thousands of miles away without public debate? The forward test confronts every insurer at renewal: retain exposure and risk capital and scrutiny, or step back and let the market recalibrate without you. The answer is written not in policy papers, but in the routes ships quietly stop sailing.

How P&I clubs manage shipping risk

On 2 March 2022, in London, the International Group of P&I Clubs issued a series of circulars following the expansion of sanctions related to Russia's invasion of Ukraine. The language was measured. No club announced a prohibition. Yet within days, shipowners quietly declined to fix fixtures for certain cargoes and ports. Chartering desks adjusted instructions. Brokers warned clients off trades that had been routine weeks earlier. Nothing in statute had changed overnight. The clubs had spoken, and members listened.

Mutuals govern by consent.

Protection and indemnity clubs occupy a distinctive place in maritime commerce. They are not insurers in the conventional sense, nor are they regulators. They are mutual associations through which shipowners pool liability risk that is too large, too uncertain, or too legally complex for standard insurance markets to bear alone. Pollution, wreck removal, cargo damage, crew injury, collision—these exposures can run into the hundreds of millions. P&I clubs exist to make them survivable. Their power lies not only in what they cover, but in how they set expectations for those who depend on them.

The mutual structure matters. Members are both insureds and contributors. Losses are shared. Governance is collective. When a club issues guidance, it is not an external imposition; it is a conversation within a community that has a shared interest in staying solvent, reputable, and insurable. This creates a form of discipline that is subtle but effective. Rules are followed not because they are policed aggressively, but because the cost of ignoring them is borne by peers.

Show this dynamic in action and its reach becomes clear. A P&I club circulates a notice highlighting increased sanctions risk associated with a particular trade. The notice reminds members that liabilities arising from sanctions breaches may fall outside cover, or that reimbursement could be delayed pending legal review. The name for this instrument is a circular. The explanation is risk signalling. The implication is behavioural change. Members reassess voyages that sit near the line, not because the club has forbidden them, but because the safety net now looks thinner.

Club rules provide the formal backbone for this influence. These rules set out conditions of entry, scope of cover, exclusions, and obligations of disclosure. Sanctions clauses are embedded here, often granting clubs wide discretion to withhold cover where compliance risk arises. The language is deliberate. It protects the collective from being dragged into liability by the actions of a few. The visible behaviour is caution in claims handling and underwriting advice. The implication is that members internalise the club's risk posture.

Guidance extends beyond the rulebook. Clubs issue advisories on emerging risks, legal developments, and enforcement trends. They interpret sanctions measures, highlight areas of uncertainty, and suggest prudent approaches. This guidance does not carry the force of law, yet it often carries more practical weight. A shipowner who disregards a club's advice may find itself unsupported when a claim arises. Trust, here, is reciprocal and conditional.

A second named, checkable example illustrates how this operates. In April 2019, following heightened scrutiny of ship-to-ship transfers involving Iranian oil, several P&I clubs issued guidance warning members of the risks associated with such operations. The guidance referenced enforcement actions and emphasised the difficulty of maintaining cover where sanctions exposure could not be ruled out. The visible outcome was a reduction in members' willingness to engage in those transfers. The implication was not a ban, but a chilling effect driven by collective caution.

P&I clubs also influence behaviour through claims practice. When a claim touches on sanctions risk, clubs may reserve rights, seek external legal opinions, or delay payment pending clarity. These steps are defensible and often necessary. They also send a signal. Members observe which claims are straightforward and which become protracted. Over time, this experience shapes operational decisions. Trades associated with slow, uncertain claims resolution become less attractive.

Efficiency is an abstraction that becomes tangible in this context. A voyage that triggers extensive pre-voyage consultation with the club, enhanced documentation, and post-incident scrutiny consumes time and management attention. A voyage that does not is simpler. The visible metric is administrative burden. The implication is route selection. Shipowners gravitate towards trades that minimise friction.

The International Group of P&I Clubs amplifies this effect. Comprising thirteen clubs that collectively cover the majority of the world's ocean-going tonnage, the Group coordinates reinsurance and shares information. When one club identifies a risk, others take note. Guidance issued by one often finds echoes in the circulars of others. This is not collusion; it is information sharing within a tightly knit professional network. The implication is convergence. Behaviour changes across the fleet, not just within a single membership.

Sanctions sharpen this convergence because they threaten the Group's collective reinsurance arrangements. If sanctions exposure jeopardises the Group's reinsurance programme, the risk is existential. Clubs therefore err on the side of caution. The visible behaviour is aligned messaging and conservative interpretation. The implication is that even permissive readings of the law may be overtaken by the Group's risk appetite.

A credible counter-example exists and deserves attention. There are instances where P&I clubs have supported members in navigating sanctioned environments through careful structuring, licensing, and documentation, particularly for humanitarian or essential trades. In these cases, clubs work closely with members to manage risk rather than simply signalling withdrawal. The visible behaviour is engagement rather than avoidance. The limitation is that such support requires clarity, resources, and a defensible legal position. It cannot be offered universally.

Reconciling this exception with the broader pattern highlights the clubs' central calculus. They balance member service against collective exposure. Where risk can be bounded and justified, they assist. Where it cannot, they caution. This balance is recalibrated continuously, informed by enforcement trends, political developments, and claims experience. Members learn to read the signals.

The quiet motif threading through this section is the circular itself: a document that lands in an inbox, often read quickly, sometimes skimmed, but rarely ignored. Its tone, footnotes, and references matter. A sentence noting "increased scrutiny" can carry more weight than a page of prohibition. The circular does not shout. It nudges.

This nudging has macro consequences. When P&I clubs collectively signal discomfort with a trade, chartering patterns shift. Ports see fewer calls. Cargoes seek alternative routes or remain unsold. The effect resembles an embargo, but it arises from mutual governance rather than decree. The clubs do not intend to set foreign policy. They intend to protect their members and themselves. The outcome, however, is political in effect.

There is an ethical dimension to this power. P&I clubs occupy a space between private association and public impact. Their decisions influence who can move goods, where, and under what conditions. Yet their deliberations are internal, their guidance cautious, their accountability diffuse. This opacity is part of their strength and their vulnerability.

For shipowners, the lesson is not simply to follow guidance, but to understand its provenance. A club's warning reflects not only law, but collective sentiment and upstream pressure from reinsurers and regulators. Ignoring it is a gamble. Following it may foreclose opportunities. The choice is rarely framed starkly. It emerges through habit and risk culture.

The unresolved tension at the end of this discussion is practical and persistent. If P&I clubs manage shipping risk through shared norms rather than commands, how transparent should those norms be to those affected downstream—charterers, traders, ports, and communities that depend on shipping? When a cargo disappears from the market because clubs have signalled discomfort, who explains why? The forward test confronts every member: when the circular arrives, do you read it as information, or as instruction? In that distinction lies the quiet power of the mutual.

The Lloyd's marketplace and sanctions

On 10 September 2018, in London, a dispute over a marine insurance claim connected to Iranian cargo reached the underwriting floors of Lloyd's. The claim itself was modest by market standards. Its implications were not. Questions arose about whether paying the claim would expose participating syndicates to United States secondary sanctions. The debate did not stay confined to the slip. Within weeks, underwriters across multiple syndicates were revisiting sanctions wordings, declining similar risks, and escalating marginal cases that would previously have been written with little comment. One contested loss had shifted the market's mood.

Lloyd's listens to itself.

The Lloyd's marketplace is often described as an insurance market, but this is only half true. It is a governance system layered over competition. Hundreds of syndicates, each with its own capital, management and risk appetite, underwrite business under a shared brand and a shared rulebook. They compete fiercely for premium. They also submit to central oversight. This duality is what gives Lloyd's its peculiar influence in sanctions compliance. When caution spreads here, it spreads quickly and with authority.

At the centre of this system sits Lloyd's Corporation. It does not underwrite risk, but it sets standards, issues guidance, and enforces compliance across the market. Sanctions controls are part of this remit. When Lloyd's publishes guidance on sanctions interpretation, reporting expectations, or risk management, syndicates are expected to align. The guidance is not law. It is governance. The implication is that deviation carries consequences: scrutiny, remediation plans, reputational cost.

Show how this works in practice and the mechanism becomes clear. A syndicate considers underwriting a risk linked to a jurisdiction subject to complex sanctions. The legal analysis suggests the risk may be permissible. However, Lloyd's has recently issued a market bulletin emphasising conservative interpretation and escalation of ambiguous cases. The syndicate's compliance team advises caution. The visible behaviour is referral to senior management or outright declinature. The implication is that central tone shapes decentralised decisions.

Sanctions amplify this effect because they threaten the market's collective standing. Lloyd's trades on trust: with regulators, with cedants, with governments. A perception that the market is lax on sanctions could invite regulatory intervention or reputational damage that affects all syndicates, not just the offender. This shared vulnerability encourages alignment with the strictest plausible reading of risk. Efficiency gives way to defensibility.

A second named, checkable example illustrates how precedent operates. In 2019, following enforcement actions against insurers accused of breaching Iran-related sanctions, Lloyd's issued guidance reminding managing agents of their obligations and the potential consequences of non-compliance. The guidance referenced public enforcement outcomes and emphasised the need for robust controls. The visible metric was increased referral rates to compliance committees. The implication was market-wide tightening, even in lines not directly implicated.

This process relies less on command than on signalling. Lloyd's rarely instructs syndicates to stop underwriting a class of business. Instead, it highlights risks, expectations, and consequences. Managing agents, conscious of oversight and peer comparison, adjust behaviour. The abstraction of *reputation* becomes a concrete decision: write the risk and explain later, or decline now and avoid scrutiny. Most choose the latter.

The structure of Lloyd's accelerates convergence. Syndicates often co-insure risks, sharing slips and following leaders. When a leading syndicate declines a risk on sanctions grounds, followers take note. Brokers relay market sentiment. What begins as one syndicate's decision becomes the market's position. The visible behaviour is uniform pricing or blanket refusal. The implication is that caution compounds through imitation.

Sanctions clauses are a focal point for this dynamic. Lloyd's standard wordings and market clauses are widely used. When these are updated to reflect heightened sanctions risk, the change propagates instantly. A revised exclusion inserted into a model clause appears across multiple policies within a renewal cycle. Clients experience this as a sudden narrowing of cover. The cause lies in central standard-setting rather than coordinated action.

Trust, in the Lloyd's context, is institutional. Regulators trust the market to police itself. The market trusts managing agents to enforce standards internally. When that trust is tested by a high-profile dispute or enforcement action, corrective action follows. The visible behaviour is increased audit activity and conservative underwriting. The implication is resilience at the cost of flexibility.

Efficiency is sacrificed deliberately. Lloyd's governance framework prioritises stability over speed. Sanctions-related referrals slow underwriting processes. Deals that once closed in hours now take days. This friction is tolerated because it reduces the risk of missteps. The metric is turnaround time. The implication is that some business migrates elsewhere, while Lloyd's retains a reputation for caution.

A credible counter-example tempers this picture. Lloyd's syndicates do not always move in lockstep. Specialist teams with deep expertise in certain regions or sectors sometimes continue to underwrite risks others avoid, supported by detailed analysis and bespoke wordings. The visible behaviour is selective engagement. The limitation is exposure. These syndicates operate under close scrutiny and often cap line sizes. Their actions do not reverse the broader trend.

Reconciling this exception with the dominant pattern reveals Lloyd's core function. It allows diversity of judgement within a common framework. That framework tightens when sanctions risk rises. Diversity narrows, not because dissent is forbidden, but because the cost of being wrong increases. The market self-corrects towards caution.

The quiet motif threading through this section is the underwriting room itself: desks aligned under a single roof, screens flickering with the same news alerts, conversations overlapping. Information travels fast. So does anxiety. A dispute discussed at one desk becomes a reference point at another. Culture spreads as much as policy.

This cultural transmission has tangible consequences beyond Lloyd's walls. Brokers advise clients that "the market" is uncomfortable. Clients adjust expectations. Trades are redesigned or abandoned. The market's discomfort becomes a fact of life, even for those who never place business at Lloyd's. The brand's influence extends outward.

There is an inherent tension here. Lloyd's prides itself on innovation and risk-taking. It was built on underwriting the unusual and the uncertain. Sanctions pressure pulls in the opposite direction, encouraging uniformity and restraint. The marketplace adapts by shifting innovation to safer domains and applying conservatism where politics intrudes.

For intelligent observers, the lesson is not that Lloyd's dictates sanctions policy, but that it translates policy into practice. It does so through governance, precedent and shared standards rather than edict. The result is a market that can pivot quickly when the risk environment changes, without waiting for legislation to catch up.

The unresolved question that closes this discussion is structural. When a marketplace with global reach internalises sanctions risk and responds collectively, how transparent should that response be to those affected downstream? When a claim dispute in London reshapes underwriting decisions across continents, who explains the chain of cause and effect? The forward test confronts Lloyd's continuously: maintain its reputation as a disciplined market without becoming an invisible regulator of trade. Where that balance settles will shape not just insurance outcomes, but the contours of global commerce itself.

Carve-outs, exclusions and small print

On 25 October 2017, in London, the High Court handed down judgment in *Mamancochet Mining Ltd v Aegis Managing Agency Ltd* [2017] EWHC 2643 (Comm), a dispute involving a political risk policy underwritten in the Lloyd's market. The insured sought cover for losses connected to mining rights in Venezuela. The underwriters resisted payment, arguing that the policy's terms did not respond in the way the claimant asserted. The case did not turn on sanctions. It turned on the language. Yet it became a quiet warning across insurance desks: in high-risk jurisdictions, the policy is only as strong as its wording, and courts will read what is written, not what was hoped.

Words decide outcomes.

Sanctions risk enters insurance not chiefly through headlines but through clauses. Most disputes in this domain are not about whether a country is sanctioned in the abstract; they are about whether a particular payment, service, or claim is prohibited or exposes the insurer to penalty. Those questions are resolved, in practice, by small print that many buyers never negotiate and few read carefully until something goes wrong. The quiet embargo often begins here: not in a refusal to insure, but in an insurance contract that will not pay when it matters.

The contemporary sanctions clause is a response to a structural problem. Insurers promise indemnity. Sanctions can make indemnity illegal, punishable, or reputationally toxic. The insurer therefore inserts an escape hatch: a clause that permits it to deny, delay, or limit performance if doing so would expose it—or its reinsurers, banks, or intermediaries—to sanctions. These clauses are drafted to be broad, because the consequences of a narrow clause can be severe. For the insured, the broadness is unsettling. It turns a clear promise of payment into a conditional one.

Show how the clause operates and its logic is plain. A policy is issued. Premium is paid. Risk attaches. Then, after a loss, the insurer assesses whether paying the claim would breach sanctions or trigger secondary sanctions risk. If the answer is yes—or even if it cannot be ruled out—the insurer invokes the clause. Payment is withheld. The name for this mechanism is a sanctions exclusion or sanctions limitation of liability clause, often framed in terms such as "to the extent that… payment would expose the insurer to any sanction, prohibition or restriction". The explanation is self-protection. The implication is that the insured's risk has not been transferred fully; it has been transferred conditionally.

The small phrases matter because they determine who bears uncertainty. Consider the difference between "payment is prohibited" and "payment would expose the insurer to sanction risk". The first is a legal threshold. The second is a judgement threshold. Under the first, the insurer must show a prohibition. Under the second, the insurer may rely on a reasoned apprehension of exposure. That is not a technical nuance; it is a shift of power from contract certainty to insurer discretion.

Carve-outs complicate matters further. Many policies contain exceptions designed to preserve cover for certain activities—humanitarian goods, lawful trades under licence, or transactions with specified safeguards. Carve-outs signal an intention to keep legitimate trade flowing. Yet a carve-out is only as effective as its integration into the policy's wider architecture.

If the sanctions clause is drafted to override all other terms, the carve-out may be illusory. If the carve-out requires documentation that is hard to obtain, it becomes a barrier. The visible behaviour is delayed claim processing or refusal pending "satisfactory evidence". The implication is that carve-outs can exist on paper and fail in practice.

A second named, checkable reference point helps ground the broader phenomenon. The International Group of P&I Clubs has, for years, published sanctions-related guidance and model wordings warning members that cover may not respond where sanctions restrict payment or where involvement in sanctioned trade creates exposure. The language is typically cautious, emphasising that clubs cannot provide cover or pay claims where doing so would breach sanctions. The visible outcome is behavioural. Members adjust trades to avoid falling into the grey zone where a claim might be disputed. The implication is that wordings shape routing decisions long before any loss occurs.

The most instructive way to understand the power of small print is to walk through a plausible claim scenario in detail. A shipping company carries a cargo of industrial equipment to a port near a heavily sanctioned jurisdiction. The trade is structured to comply with relevant rules, and the buyer is not listed. During discharge, a mechanical failure causes damage to the cargo and part of the vessel. The shipowner presents a claim under its policy. The insurer acknowledges the loss event is covered in principle. Then the sanctions clause enters. The insurer asks for confirmation of the ultimate consignee and end use. It asks whether any parties in the transaction chain are owned or controlled by designated persons. It asks whether the cargo might be re-exported into a restricted area. The shipowner provides documentation, but some elements are incomplete: a consignee address differs from one in a database; a shareholder link cannot be ruled out; a local agent is used whose ownership is opaque. The insurer's compliance team flags residual exposure. Payment is withheld.

At this point the claim dispute becomes an economic event. The shipowner's bank, expecting the insurance proceeds, reassesses credit. The charterer withholds payment under the charter party pending resolution. The port authority, seeing uncertainty around cover, imposes additional requirements on the shipowner's next call. The shipowner diverts vessels away from the corridor, not because the corridor is prohibited, but because the insurance promise has become unreliable. This is the knock-on effect that matters. A clause in a policy has altered trade patterns.

The abstraction of *trust* becomes a measurable behaviour here: whether counterparties accept a certificate of insurance as evidence that losses will be paid promptly. When trust declines, they demand additional guarantees or decline the trade. The abstraction of *efficiency* becomes claim-cycle time: days versus months. The abstraction of *risk* becomes premium pricing for renewals and the willingness of the market to offer terms. Small print becomes market structure.

Exclusions do not operate only at the claims stage. They shape underwriting from the outset. Underwriters know that broad sanctions clauses allow them to write business in uncertain regions without taking unbounded exposure. Buyers accept those clauses because they need cover, and because the clause may never be invoked—until it is. The visible behaviour is an expansion of cover in form paired with contraction in substance. The implication is that the market can appear liquid while being brittle.

This brittleness is not accidental. It reflects upstream pressures from reinsurers and regulators. Reinsurers demand that primary insurers avoid exposures that could entangle them in sanctions disputes. Regulators expect insurers to maintain controls and avoid facilitating prohibited activity. Claims teams know that a single mistaken payment can trigger consequences beyond the value of the claim. Underwriters respond by drafting clauses that grant discretion. The clause is a compromise between writing business and protecting the institution.

There is a credible counter-example that prevents this picture from becoming fatalistic. In some situations, carefully drafted clauses and clear licensing pathways have preserved meaningful cover. Where the trade is clearly within humanitarian or licensed parameters, where documentation is strong, and where insurers have established protocols for sanctions review, claims can be paid without protracted dispute. The visible behaviour is prompt settlement and stable renewal terms. The limitation is that such conditions are not guaranteed, and they often require sophisticated counterparties with resources to provide documentation and engage counsel.

Reconciling the exception with the broader pattern clarifies the role of small print as a sorting mechanism. Clauses do not merely exclude; they discriminate between transactions that can be made legible and those that cannot. Legibility becomes a prerequisite for coverage. That requirement favours large firms with compliance infrastructure and penalises smaller actors. The quiet embargo, again, is not a single barrier but a shift in who can pass.

The motif that threads through this section is the footnote. Sanctions clauses are often introduced as standard endorsements or boilerplate wordings, accompanied by brief explanatory notes. They sit at the back of the slip, rarely negotiated. Yet in a crisis, the footnote becomes the main text. It determines the fate of the claim, and by extension the viability of the trade.

This is why seemingly minor phrases attract intense attention in underwriting rooms. Does the clause refer to sanctions "applicable to the insurer" or to sanctions "in any jurisdiction"? Does it require that payment be "prohibited" or merely that it would "expose" the insurer? Does it permit delay pending review, and if so, for how long? Each variation allocates power between insured and insurer. Each variation shapes the market's appetite.

The unresolved tension is therefore contractual and political at once. If insurers must protect themselves against sanctions exposure, and do so through broad exclusions, how can insureds assess what they are truly buying? At what point does a policy become a certificate rather than a guarantee? The forward test is practical and immediate: when a loss occurs in a contested corridor, do the words on the page transfer risk, or do they return it—quietly, and at the worst possible moment—to the party who thought it had been insured?

When cover quietly disappears

In August 2018, from Copenhagen, A.P. Moller–Maersk announced that it would cease taking new business involving Iran as United States sanctions were reimposed. The statement was framed as compliance with "applicable sanctions". For many firms down the chain, the more immediate experience was not a dramatic prohibition but a narrowing of options: fewer carriers willing to call, fewer insurers prepared to quote, more questions from banks, longer delays. Iran did not vanish from the map. Cover did.

Renewal is the real moment.

Insurance seldom ends with a bang. It ends with an email. A policy reaches its expiry date and, instead of the familiar renewal terms, the insured receives a polite message: the insurer will not renew, or will renew only with revised conditions, or will quote at a price that makes the business irrational. No law is cited. No accusation is made. The language is managerial: a change in appetite, a portfolio rebalancing, a requirement to align with reinsurance terms. This is the quiet embargo's most reliable instrument. Cancellation makes enemies. Non-renewal creates drift.

The mechanics of disappearing cover begin upstream. Reinsurers restrict capacity for a geography, a cargo type, or a set of counterparties. Primary insurers respond by tightening terms. Underwriters insert broader sanctions clauses, reduce line sizes, increase deductibles, and ask for more documentation. Clients feel this as friction before they feel it as denial. The visible behaviour is the renewal process elongating: more questions, more referrals, more "subject to" language. The implication is that what used to be a commodity becomes a negotiation.

The non-renewal itself is often defensible. Insurers are not public utilities. They choose their risks. Yet in sensitive corridors, the decision is rarely about actuarial loss alone. It is about compliance exposure and reputation. A voyage that looks profitable can still be unattractive if it triggers sanctions screening, media scrutiny, or regulatory enquiry. The abstraction of *reputational risk* becomes a concrete underwriting decision: "We will not offer terms for this route." The implication is that lawful trade can be priced out of existence.

A second factor is internal governance. Most insurers have sanctions committees and escalation thresholds. When the geopolitical environment shifts, these committees tighten the thresholds. A trade that once required routine checks now demands senior sign-off. Senior sign-off is scarce. The visible metric is referral rates: more files pushed up the chain, fewer cleared quickly. The implication is an unspoken rationing of appetite.

Small changes in wording accelerate the disappearance of usable cover. A sanctions clause that permits the insurer to withhold payment if performance would "expose" it to sanctions risk may be enough to make a bank reject the policy as collateral support. A port may refuse entry without unequivocal evidence of cover. A charterer may decline a ship whose insurance contains broad exclusions. The insured technically has a policy. Practically, it cannot trade. The implication is that cover can disappear without ever being withdrawn.

Price is the most socially acceptable form of refusal. When underwriters wish to reduce exposure but avoid explicit declinature, they reprice. Premiums rise. Deductibles increase. Coverage limits shrink. The effect is predictable. Some clients pay and stay; others leave. Most cannot absorb repeated increases. The visible behaviour is route change. The implication is economic sorting: those with greater margins continue, those without are excluded.

The quiet motif that threads through this section is the renewal notice. It arrives on schedule, unremarkable in form, decisive in effect. Each year, it forces the same question: can this business still be insured? The answer, increasingly, determines which trades exist at all.

To grasp the consequences, consider a shipping company that has historically operated a mixed fleet of product tankers and bulk carriers. Its niche is the movement of agricultural products and refined fuels between the Eastern Mediterranean and ports near a sanctioned jurisdiction. The trade is structured to comply with relevant laws. The company has no appetite for evasion. It relies on reputable insurers and on P&I cover through an International Group club. For years, the route has been viable: higher premiums than the safest corridors, but manageable.

Then the renewal season changes character. The hull insurer requests more information about counterparties, ports, and cargo documentation. The company provides it. The insurer responds with a quote that is 60 per cent higher than the previous year and includes a broad sanctions limitation clause. The company's bank, reviewing the policy as part of a financing package, warns that the clause may undermine collateral comfort. The P&I club issues a circular emphasising heightened scrutiny for the region and reminding members of sanctions-related limitations on cover. The company's broker canvasses the market and discovers that several underwriters have quietly exited the class of business. Alternative quotes arrive with even higher pricing and narrower terms. No one has said the route is prohibited. The market has said it is no longer worth supporting.

The company adapts. It redeploys vessels to routes that attract lower premiums and faster clearance. It declines fixtures it would once have pursued. It reduces calls to certain ports. Cargo owners find fewer ships available. Freight rates rise. Some goods move via longer routes, adding time and cost. Others do not move at all. The embargo appears not as a ban but as a reconfiguration of logistics driven by the disappearance of affordable cover.

This is not a hypothetical fantasy. The underlying pattern can be observed in multiple episodes. After major sanctions expansions, insurers and reinsurers have publicly signalled withdrawal from certain exposures, and markets have adjusted accordingly. Following Russia's invasion of Ukraine in February 2022, for example, the rapid reassessment of war risk and sanctions exposure led to sharply higher premiums for vessels transiting the Black Sea and to tightened underwriting conditions. The London insurance market's war risk ratings and pricing became a practical indicator of where trade could proceed. The implication was immediate: some voyages were delayed or cancelled not because they were illegal, but because the cost and uncertainty of cover changed overnight.

A second checkable example comes from environmental and transition risk rather than geopolitical sanctions, yet it demonstrates the same mechanism of silent withdrawal. In the late 2010s, major European insurers such as AXA and Zurich Insurance announced progressive restrictions on underwriting coal-related risks. Many projects remained lawful. Yet financing and insurance capacity tightened as cover disappeared or became prohibitively expensive. The visible behaviour was the cancellation or delay of coal projects. The implication is that markets can impose de facto embargoes through withdrawal of services even without legal prohibition. The same dynamic operates in sanctions-sensitive trade, with compliance and reputation replacing climate policy as the trigger.

There is a credible counter-example that prevents the argument from becoming deterministic. In some cases, specialist insurers or state-backed mechanisms maintain capacity where mainstream markets retreat. Certain trades continue under licences, supported by dedicated insurance arrangements and enhanced documentation. The visible behaviour is continued underwriting at a price. The limitation is fragility. These arrangements are often narrow, contingent and politically sensitive. They do not restore normality; they create exceptions.

Reconciling this exception with the broader pattern shows why quiet disappearance is so effective. It does not require coordination. It does not require public explanation. It flows naturally from incentives: reinsurers reduce exposure, primary insurers follow, banks become cautious, ports demand certainty. Each actor can claim prudence. The aggregate outcome is restriction.

The disappearance of cover is also self-reinforcing. As fewer insurers write a class of risk, competition declines. Prices rise further. Remaining underwriters become more selective. Clients with the best documentation and the lowest exposure survive. Others exit. The market's memory hardens: "That corridor is difficult." Difficulty becomes a reason for avoidance, even if conditions improve.

For those outside the insurance world, the most counterintuitive aspect is that nothing needs to be declared. No official must say "stop". The system stops by itself. Renewal notices do the work that embargo orders once did, and they do it with less drama and less accountability.

The unresolved tension lies in the gap between public intent and private withdrawal. Sanctions regimes often contain exceptions, licences, and policy aims that assume some trade will continue—humanitarian goods, lawful essentials, carefully structured transactions. If insurance cover disappears through non-renewal and silent repricing, those policy aims can fail without any change in law. The forward test is therefore not legal but operational: when the next renewal notice arrives, will the market still provide usable cover for lawful trade, or will it continue to withdraw until legality becomes irrelevant?

Chapter 4

Over-Compliance and De-Risking

In late 2016, a small humanitarian organisation working out of Amman received a brief letter from its bank in London. The account would be closed within thirty days. No breach was alleged. No suspicious transaction cited. The charity's work involved food distribution near the Syrian border, fully licensed and audited. The bank's explanation was spare: a strategic decision to reduce exposure to certain regions. The funds were returned. The projects stalled. Aid workers learned, belatedly, that compliance can exceed the law with devastating efficiency.

This is not caution taken too far by accident. It is design responding to fear.

Over-compliance is the point at which risk management stops asking what is permitted and begins asking what is survivable. It is the practice of going beyond legal requirements in order to eliminate even the faintest possibility of regulatory trouble, reputational harm, or future scrutiny. In the world of sanctions, finance, and trade, over-compliance is rarely announced as such. It appears instead as policy simplification: whole countries deemed "off-limits", entire sectors labelled "high risk", client types quietly declined. The quiet embargo reaches maturity here, not through rules imposed, but through rules abandoned.

The paradox at the heart of this chapter is unsettling. The more complex and conditional sanctions regimes become, the more likely firms are to ignore that nuance altogether. Faced with ambiguous guidance, finite resources, and asymmetrical penalties, institutions retreat to blunt instruments. It is safer to say no to everything than to say yes once too often. Compliance teams understand this intuitively. So do boards.

Historically, trade restrictions were explicit and bounded. An embargo named a country, a commodity, a port. Merchants adapted within those lines. Over-compliance dissolves the boundary. It creates shadow zones where lawful trade becomes impractical because intermediaries will not touch it. These zones expand and contract with enforcement moods, media cycles, and internal risk metrics. They are rarely mapped, never legislated, and deeply consequential.

This chapter sits at the point where the book's earlier mechanisms converge. Banks that act as choke points. Insurers that withdraw capacity. Sanctions lists that are incomplete by design. Add to these the institutional memory of punishment and the result is de-risking: the deliberate exit from clients, regions, or activities deemed more trouble than they are worth. De-risking is often defended as prudence. Its effects, however, are distributive and political.

The logic that drives over-compliance begins with asymmetry. A firm that complies strictly with the letter of the law but misjudges a grey area can face penalties measured in the hundreds of millions, along with public censure and years of remediation. A firm that declines lawful business rarely faces sanction for doing so. The visible metric is enforcement history. The implication is clear. Rational institutions respond by avoiding exposure altogether.

Past enforcement actions loom large in this calculus. High-profile penalties are studied not for their precise legal reasoning, but for their scale and reputational fallout. Lessons are generalised aggressively. A settlement involving one jurisdiction becomes a cautionary tale applied globally. Internal policies are rewritten. Thresholds are lowered. What began as a response to a specific failure hardens into a universal rule. This is how a single case can reshape global behaviour.

Internal risk models accelerate the process. These models promise objectivity. They translate diffuse concerns into scores, colours, and categories. Geography becomes a risk input. So does cargo type, payment chain complexity, corporate structure. A transaction that crosses too many "red" variables is flagged, escalated, or rejected automatically. The human judgement that once weighed context is replaced by thresholds embedded in systems. The visible behaviour is denial by algorithm. The implication is that contesting a decision becomes difficult, sometimes impossible.

The attraction of these models is not only consistency but defensibility. When challenged—by a client, a regulator, or a court—firms can point to established processes rather than individual discretion. Responsibility diffuses. "The model flagged it" becomes an explanation that closes conversation. Over time, the model's assumptions become policy. Policy becomes reality.

Resource constraints reinforce this drift. Compliance teams are under pressure to do more with less. Deep, transaction-specific analysis is expensive. Blanket rules are cheap. It is easier to exit an entire region than to evaluate dozens of marginal cases. This is particularly true for smaller institutions and for business lines with thin margins. The visible behaviour is portfolio pruning. The implication is that risk is managed by withdrawal rather than engagement.

Reputational concern adds another layer. Firms operate under constant observation by media, activists, and investors. Even lawful involvement in controversial regions can attract criticism. The cost of defending nuance in public is high. Silence is safer. By exiting early and broadly, firms minimise the chance of being drawn into a narrative they do not control. The quiet embargo is thus also a communications strategy.

The human cost of this strategy is often treated as collateral. When banks close accounts for charities, the justification is rarely hostility to aid. It is exposure management. When insurers price cover so high that no one buys it, the rationale is actuarial prudence. Yet the outcomes are tangible. Shipments delay. Projects collapse. Communities lose access to goods and services that sanctions regimes often claim to protect. Over-compliance does not distinguish well between bad actors and inconvenient ones.

This chapter will follow that damage without resorting to melodrama. It will look at how lawful trade is stranded not by prohibition but by process. It will examine the way small exporters, niche traders, and humanitarian organisations are disproportionately affected because they lack the scale to absorb friction. It will show how de-risking shifts economic activity towards larger players with greater compliance infrastructure, reinforcing concentration.

A recurring image throughout the chapter is the empty corridor. Not closed by a gate, but abandoned because too many doors along the way are locked. The corridor once carried goods, money, and trust. Now it carries silence. Each actor along the chain has a defensible reason for stepping back. No single decision is decisive. Together, they change the map.

The intellectual challenge here is to resist caricature. Over-compliance is not simply cowardice or ignorance. It is an emergent property of a system that punishes error far more severely than omission. Understanding it requires empathy for institutional incentives alongside clear-eyed analysis of consequences. This chapter aims to provide both.

What follows will move from definition to mechanism to impact. It will show what over-compliance looks like in practice, why firms de-risk entire regions, how past enforcement shapes present fear, how internal models harden judgement, and where the damage lands. The reader is not asked to choose sides, but to see the system whole.

The question that closes the introduction, and animates the pages ahead, is deliberately uncomfortable. If lawful trade can be choked off by institutions acting rationally within existing rules, where does accountability sit? When everyone complies beyond what is required, who decides what is lost—and who bears the cost?

What over-compliance looks like

If a transaction is lawful, licensed, and documented, why does it still fail? Consider a simple datum: in a 2017 survey by the Charity Finance Group in the United Kingdom, over 40 per cent of charities reported difficulties accessing banking services because of perceived sanctions or counter-terrorism risk. How can legality coexist with exclusion at that scale?

Because risk is being managed elsewhere.

Over-compliance begins where the question changes. Institutions stop asking *is this permitted?* and start asking *what could go wrong for us?* The shift is subtle, but decisive. It moves decision-making away from statutory interpretation and towards institutional self-preservation. Over-compliance is not the breach of law. It is the abandonment of nuance. It is the replacement of conditional judgement with categorical refusal.

Five words capture it: *we cannot take this.*

In practical terms, over-compliance appears as blanket rules. Entire countries are coded as “no-go”, even when sanctions regimes are partial. Whole sectors—shipping, remittances, charities—are designated high risk irrespective of individual counterparties. Client types are excluded not because of conduct, but because of proximity. Proximity to a sanctioned jurisdiction. Proximity to a controversial activity. Proximity to scrutiny.

Show this at ground level and it becomes tangible. A bank updates its internal policy following a sanctions review. The policy states that accounts connected to certain regions require enhanced due diligence and senior approval. That approval pipeline is slow and resource-intensive. Relationship managers learn, quickly, which cases stall. Over time, they stop proposing them. The name for this phenomenon is policy chilling. The explanation is organisational learning. The implication is silent refusal.

One of the most visible manifestations is the closure of accounts held by charities and non-governmental organisations operating near sanctioned zones. These organisations often deal in small amounts, operate transparently, and carry licences where required. Yet they sit at the intersection of multiple sensitivities: cross-border payments, high-risk geographies, and public scrutiny. For banks, the revenue is modest and the potential downside unbounded. The visible behaviour is account termination with minimal explanation. The implication is that lawful humanitarian activity is squeezed out of the formal financial system.

Efficiency, here, is measured not in transaction speed but in staff time. Enhanced due diligence consumes analysts, compliance officers, and managers. When resources are finite, institutions triage. They prioritise clients whose risk profile is simple and whose commercial value justifies scrutiny. Others are exited. This is not ideological. It is arithmetic.

Risk, another abstraction, is operationalised through internal thresholds. A jurisdiction may be rated "high risk" because of sanctions, corruption indices, or enforcement history. Once that label is applied, every client connected to it inherits the rating. A local exporter selling agricultural goods becomes indistinguishable, in system terms, from a complex trading house. The visible metric is a risk score. The implication is loss of differentiation.

Trust becomes procedural rather than relational. Where once a long-standing client relationship might have mitigated concern, now the system demands documentation and verification at every turn. If that documentation is unavailable—or simply slow—the relationship cannot compensate. The abstraction of *trust* collapses into checklists. The implication is that human judgement recedes.

A second named, checkable example illustrates the pattern without relying on anecdote. In 2014, following substantial penalties imposed by United States authorities on several global banks for sanctions breaches, numerous European banks reviewed their exposure to money service businesses and charities operating in high-risk regions. Public reporting by organisations such as the Overseas Development Institute documented widespread account closures and service refusals affecting aid agencies, despite the absence of legal prohibitions on their work. The visible outcome was disruption to aid delivery. The implication was that enforcement history, not current legality, drove behaviour.

Over-compliance also manifests as the refusal to engage with complexity. A transaction involving multiple jurisdictions, layered ownership, or unconventional payment routes may be lawful but demanding. Compliance teams, under pressure to process volume, learn to prefer simplicity. Complex trades are escalated, delayed, or declined. The visible behaviour is delay followed by attrition. The implication is that lawful complexity is penalised.

This pattern is reinforced by the internal language of risk committees. Minutes record decisions in terms of "exposure", "appetite", and "tolerance". Rarely do they record opportunity cost or downstream impact. When a committee decides that a region is "outside appetite", that phrase carries enormous weight. It does not mean illegal. It means unwelcome. Appetite becomes destiny.

A quiet motif runs through these decisions: the map with areas shaded. Not red for prohibited, but grey for avoided. The grey expands. Each expansion is defensible. Each removes another set of transactions from consideration. No one announces the map's revision. Clients discover it when doors close.

There is a credible counter-example that prevents caricature. Some institutions invest heavily in specialist compliance teams capable of nuanced analysis. They continue to service complex clients and regions by applying granular controls rather than blanket bans. The visible behaviour is selective engagement. The limitation is scalability. Such approaches require investment and carry residual risk. They are easier for large institutions with diversified revenue than for smaller firms.

Reconciling this exception with the dominant trend clarifies why over-compliance persists. The system rewards avoidance more reliably than engagement. Regulators punish failures, not refusals. Markets remember scandals, not missed opportunities. Internal incentives align accordingly.

The cost of this alignment is borne unevenly. Large multinational firms with dedicated compliance resources adapt. Small exporters, charities, and niche traders do not. They lose access to banking, insurance, and logistics despite operating within the law. The visible behaviour is market exit. The implication is concentration of trade and finance among those who can afford friction.

Over-compliance thus becomes a form of private regulation. It redraws the boundaries of permissible commerce without legislative debate. It privileges certainty over proportionality. It treats risk as something to be eliminated rather than managed. The quiet embargo is most complete at this stage because it requires no coordination and provokes little resistance.

The unresolved tension at the end of this section is diagnostic. If institutions systematically go beyond what the law requires to protect themselves, how can policymakers ensure that the law's intended balance—between pressure and permission—survives? When a bank closes an account not because it must, but because it prefers not to explain itself later, who decides whether that caution is prudent or excessive? The next section follows that question into the logic of regional de-risking, where over-compliance hardens into geography.

Why firms de-risk entire regions

On 2 March 2012, in Brussels, SWIFT announced that it would disconnect certain Iranian banks following European Union sanctions. The decision did not outlaw all trade with Iran. It did not inspect a single container. Yet it removed a region from the ordinary financial bloodstream. Banks elsewhere took note. Correspondent relationships were reviewed. Payment routes were closed. What looked like a targeted measure became, in practice, a broad signal: this geography is trouble.

Geography becomes a proxy.

De-risking entire regions is not a failure of intelligence. It is a response to incentives that make nuance expensive and error catastrophic. When institutions label a country, port, or industry "not worth it", they are not always saying it is illegal. They are saying that the cost of *proving* it is legal, the cost of *staying* legal as rules shift, and the cost of *defending* legality under scrutiny exceed the revenue or strategic value of the business. De-risking is the market's way of buying certainty.

Show the chain of reasoning and it becomes almost banal. A compliance team faces a rising volume of alerts connected to a region under sanctions pressure. Each alert demands investigation: ownership checks, end-use statements, vessel histories, bank routing analysis. These investigations consume staff time. Staff time is finite. The institution therefore either expands resources—expensive and slow—or reduces exposure—cheap and immediate. The name for this choice is portfolio triage. The explanation is capacity constraint. The implication is withdrawal.

Resource constraints are not merely about headcount. They are about expertise. Many institutions do not have enough staff who can read corporate registries in multiple languages, interpret shifting sanctions guidance, or assess maritime risk patterns. Outsourcing due diligence to vendors helps, but vendors themselves rely on incomplete data. The visible behaviour is the use of simplified rules: "no clients with operations in X", "no payments routed through Y", "no cover for voyages calling at Z." The implication is that complexity is treated as guilt by association.

Unclear guidance makes this worse. Sanctions regimes often include phrases that are legally meaningful yet operationally slippery: "owned or controlled", "material support", "significant transaction", "related to". Institutions must translate these into internal rules. Where guidance is ambiguous, internal policies become conservative. Committees do not want debates that end in "it depends". They want thresholds. The visible behaviour is the creation of blanket exclusions to eliminate judgement calls. The implication is that ambiguity produces overreach.

Reputational concern supplies the final push. An institution may be able to manage legal risk with careful controls, yet still fear that any involvement with a contested region will attract criticism. This fear is not theoretical. Media scrutiny and activist reporting often focus on the optics of involvement, not the technical legality. Shareholders ask whether the institution is "exposed". Boards ask whether it is "worth it". The visible behaviour is pre-emptive exit announced as "strategic focus". The implication is that public perception becomes a veto.

This logic is especially visible in insurance, because insurance can refuse without breaking a contract. Underwriters are not obliged to quote. They can price. They can exclude. They can delay. When a region becomes politically sensitive, insurers often respond with pricing that functions as a polite refusal. Premiums rise sharply. Deductibles increase. Sanctions clauses widen. Capacity shrinks. The offer may still exist, but it is no longer usable.

Consider an example that captures how de-risking works without formal prohibition. A mid-sized insurer is approached to provide marine cargo cover for shipments of agricultural equipment to a port near a sanctioned jurisdiction. The cargo is lawful. The buyer is unlisted. The exporter can provide licences and end-user assurances. The insurer's compliance team flags residual uncertainty: the route involves transhipment through a high-risk hub; the consignee's ownership cannot be fully resolved; the insurer's reinsurer has recently imposed tighter aggregate limits for the region. The underwriter quotes at a premium several times higher than comparable routes and includes a sanctions limitation clause that permits non-payment if exposure arises. The exporter declines. The trade does not move. No one has said "no". The market has said "not at this price".

Price is policy.

A second named, checkable example shows the same pattern in financial services. The Financial Action Task Force has, over many years, warned about "de-risking" as a response to anti-money laundering and counter-terrorist financing expectations, noting that wholesale withdrawal from correspondent banking can harm financial inclusion and legitimate trade. The FATF's 2016 report on correspondent banking services and de-risking documented how banks curtailed relationships in certain regions, not always because of proven wrongdoing, but because of compliance cost and perceived risk. The visible metric was declining correspondent relationships. The implication is that entire economies can be pushed towards informal channels.

This phenomenon is often defended as rational. In narrow terms, it is. A bank that earns modest fees from a high-risk corridor and faces substantial compliance burdens and potential regulatory scrutiny is acting logically when it exits. An insurer that can earn similar premiums in safer lines is acting logically when it withdraws. Yet rationality at the firm level can produce distortion at the system level. When many institutions make the same calculation, regions become under-served. The quiet embargo takes shape as an aggregate outcome of private optimisation.

The motives are not identical across institutions, but the behaviours converge. Banks close correspondent accounts. Insurers reduce capacity or reprice. Shipping firms avoid ports that trigger scrutiny. Inspection companies decline to certify in difficult jurisdictions. Each decision is defensible in isolation. Together, they constrict lawful trade.

A credible counter-example deserves attention. Some institutions choose selective engagement rather than blanket exit. They concentrate on a narrow set of clients with strong documentation, they ring-fence exposure, and they invest in specialist teams. They may even develop regional expertise that becomes a competitive advantage. The visible behaviour is continued service provision with stricter controls. The limitation is scale and appetite. Selective engagement works when the institution can absorb cost and when regulators accept the approach. It fails when uncertainty is too high or when reputational risk becomes unmanageable.

Reconciling this exception with the dominant pattern clarifies the role of uncertainty as the real driver. Where rules are clear, data is strong, and enforcement expectations are stable, institutions can price risk and proceed. Where rules are ambiguous, data is poor, and enforcement signals are volatile, institutions step back. De-risking is a response not to risk alone, but to risk that cannot be bounded.

The quiet motif threading through this section is the shrinking map: a set of regions slowly shaded out of acceptable business, not by law but by policy. Each shading decision is made in a committee room, translated into a system rule, and experienced by clients as silence. The map shrinks until trade corridors harden around a few "safe" nodes.

These dynamics have distributional consequences. Firms in de-risked regions face higher costs and fewer options, even for lawful business. They turn to smaller, less regulated intermediaries or to informal networks. This can increase the very risks regulators seek to reduce. The system becomes less transparent. Enforcement becomes harder. De-risking, intended as protection, can generate fragility.

The forward test at the end of this section is therefore pointed. If institutions retreat from regions because they cannot price or defend uncertainty, what would make them return? Clearer guidance? Better data? Safe harbours for good-faith compliance? Or will the map continue to shrink until only the lowest-friction trades remain, leaving lawful but complex commerce to wither in the grey?

The role of past enforcement actions

On 30 June 2014, in New York, BNP Paribas pleaded guilty to charges relating to sanctions violations and agreed to pay $8.9 billion in penalties and forfeiture, as announced by the US Department of Justice that day. Within weeks, compliance teams across banks that had never processed a BNP transaction began rewriting policies as if the judgment had been handed down against them personally. Credit committees demanded tighter controls. Correspondent banks asked more questions. Entire corridors of trade became harder to finance, not because the law had changed, but because the memory of punishment had sharpened.

Fear has a long tail.

Enforcement actions are not merely retrospective. They are predictive signals, read by markets as clues about what regulators will tolerate next. A single settlement can do what dozens of guidance notes cannot: it can change behaviour at scale. This is partly because enforcement is vivid. Numbers are published. Executives resign. Monitors are appointed. The story travels. Compliance, often an invisible function, is suddenly placed under a harsh light. The market responds by tightening its own internal boundaries, frequently far beyond the facts of the case.

Show the mechanism and its name becomes clearer. An enforcement action arrives with a narrative: what went wrong, how it was detected, what a firm failed to do, and what it must now build. The narrative is absorbed by three audiences at once. Regulators read it as precedent. Boards read it as threat. Front-line staff read it as warning. The implication is straightforward. Risk appetite contracts.

The most consequential feature of enforcement is asymmetry. A firm can be punished spectacularly for missing prohibited activity. It is rarely punished for refusing lawful business. That imbalance creates an institutional bias: it is safer to over-correct than to calibrate. In practical terms, over-correction looks like universal rules derived from particular cases. A settlement involving US-dollar clearing becomes, in internal policy, a reason to treat any connection to a sanctioned geography as unacceptable, regardless of currency. A case involving concealment of Iranian nexus data becomes, in internal training, a reason to reject any transaction with imperfect documentation, even where concealment is not alleged. The abstraction of *prudence* becomes a concrete decision: decline now; explain later.

BNP Paribas is useful precisely because it was so large and so public. The size of the penalty, cited by the Department of Justice in 2014, communicated something more important than the details of any individual transaction. It communicated will. It told the industry that sanctions enforcement could carry the same gravity as major criminal conduct. The visible behavioural response was not confined to French banks or to Iran-related business. Global banks tightened controls on multiple programmes, expanded sanctions screening, and increased compliance headcount. The implication was not that all those banks were guilty of similar wrongdoing, but that they had learned a lesson about the cost of error.

This lesson is generalised through institutional psychology. Compliance departments are not merely rule interpreters; they are custodians of organisational memory. They keep files of past cases, circulate summaries, and turn enforcement actions into training modules. The story is told and retold until it becomes doctrine. A case involving deliberate evasion is quietly converted into a lesson about ordinary ambiguity. The phrase "we cannot afford this" migrates from the exceptional to the routine.

Visible metrics follow. Transaction monitoring thresholds are lowered. Alert volumes rise. Escalation rates increase. Turnaround times lengthen. Client attrition climbs in categories associated—sometimes loosely—with previous enforcement. These are measurable behaviours, and they explain why enforcement has an impact beyond the boundaries of law. When a bank changes its sanction screening sensitivity after a major case, it is not changing the statute. It is changing the lived economy of trade.

A second named, checkable example shows how one enforcement action can drive global policy change at speed. On 19 February 2019, Standard Chartered reached settlements with US and UK authorities relating to sanctions and anti-money laundering controls, as publicly announced by relevant regulators. The precise legal findings mattered, but the operational message mattered more: deficiencies in controls, governance, and escalation will be treated as serious failures even where intent is disputed. In response, many institutions reviewed not only their sanctions policies but their governance structures: committee mandates, model validation, audit trails, escalation protocols. The visible behaviour was structural investment. The implication was that enforcement reshapes institutions, not only transactions.

This is where over-compliance draws nourishment. Enforcement cases are often complex, involving specific patterns: stripping information from payment messages, using cover payments, routing around controls, or maintaining business with clearly prohibited counterparties. These are not subtle mistakes. Yet the fear they induce spreads to unrelated situations: lawful trade with difficult documentation, humanitarian shipments, small charities operating near sanctioned zones, exporters selling dual-use-adjacent goods under licence. The market's internal logic is blunt: if the worst-case scenario is ruinous, treat anything that resembles the worst case as unacceptable.

The resemblance need not be strong. It can be aesthetic. A country name in a payment narrative. A port call near a disputed coastline. An intermediary with a confusing ownership chart. A client who cannot provide immediate documentation in the preferred format. These are not proof of wrongdoing.

They are friction points. After enforcement actions, friction points acquire new gravity.

This gravity is amplified by the role of monitors and remediation programmes. When an enforcement settlement imposes multi-year obligations—independent monitors, reporting requirements, mandated system upgrades—it changes the internal politics of decision-making. Managers learn that regulators may ask, years later, why a particular decision was taken. Documentation becomes defensive. Committees prefer decisions that are easy to justify. The abstraction of *accountability* becomes a practice of paper: memos, minutes, evidentiary bundles. The implication is that anything hard to justify is hard to approve.

There is also a reputational multiplier. Enforcement actions are not private scoldings; they are public events. Media coverage often compresses nuance into a headline: "Bank fined for sanctions violations." The public rarely distinguishes between deliberate evasion and control failures. Executives do not want to answer those headlines. Investors do not want to explain them. The visible behaviour is reputational de-risking: exiting certain clients, sectors, and geographies that could generate uncomfortable questions, even where the legal position is defensible.

A quiet motif runs through these decisions: the scar. Enforcement leaves scars—on balance sheets, on executive careers, on institutional culture. Scars are not remembered as detailed narratives; they are remembered as sensation. Pain. Vulnerability. Aversion. An institution that has lived through an enforcement action becomes hypersensitive to anything that might reopen the wound. Even institutions that have not suffered directly behave as if they might, because they see the scar tissue on their peers.

Yet it would be misleading to treat enforcement as mere fear-making. There is a credible counter-example: enforcement can improve precision rather than bluntness when it clarifies expectations and when firms invest in genuine capability rather than blanket refusal. Some institutions respond to enforcement by building stronger analytic functions—better data integration, more sophisticated ownership analysis, clearer escalation protocols—allowing them to distinguish lawful from unlawful more accurately. The visible behaviour is nuanced decision-making supported by evidence, not avoidance. The limitation is that this requires resources, executive commitment, and the confidence to tolerate residual uncertainty. Many firms choose the cheaper path of withdrawal.

Reconciling these divergent responses reveals a deeper truth. Enforcement actions do not dictate a single market outcome. They provide an incentive structure, and institutions choose how to respond within it. When guidance is unclear and internal capacity is weak, firms generalise aggressively and de-risk broadly. When capacity is strong and governance is mature, firms can respond with precision. In both cases, enforcement is the catalyst.

The policy consequences are profound. Enforcement is often intended to deter prohibited behaviour, but it also shapes what lawful behaviour is possible. If banks and insurers respond by withdrawing from entire regions or client types, sanctioned actors may indeed be constrained. So may humanitarian actors and legitimate traders. The resulting system can be perversely selective: well-resourced firms with sophisticated compliance functions continue operating, while smaller actors are excluded. The quiet embargo becomes, in part, a transfer of market share.

There is also a temporal consequence. Because enforcement cases are backward-looking, markets can end up fighting the last war. Institutions design controls to prevent the precise failures of the last major settlement, even as sanctions practice evolves. A case about message stripping leads to investments in payment transparency. Necessary. But the next challenge may lie in ownership obfuscation, shadow fleets, or novel payment methods. Over-focusing on precedent can create blind spots. The visible behaviour is compliance spend aligned with yesterday's scandal. The implication is misallocated vigilance.

This is why enforcement actions are read not just for their legal outcomes but for their rhetoric. What did regulators emphasise? Was the failure framed as poor governance, inadequate systems, reckless culture, or wilful evasion? Institutions listen for tone because tone signals future scrutiny. Tone is then converted into internal policy language: "zero tolerance", "no exceptions", "avoid high-risk geographies". The words migrate from enforcement press releases into underwriting guidelines and credit policies. The quiet embargo thickens.

A further complication is jurisdictional layering. A bank headquartered in Europe may fear US enforcement because of dollar clearing. An insurer may fear exposure through reinsurance placed in markets subject to different regimes. Firms respond by harmonising to the most stringent perceived standard. The visible behaviour is global policy alignment: rules written to satisfy the toughest regulator, applied everywhere. The implication is that enforcement in one jurisdiction can reshape trade far beyond that jurisdiction's borders.

The forward test, then, is not whether enforcement is justified. The question is whether markets can learn from enforcement without paralysis. When an institution confronts a lawful but complex transaction, does it treat past penalties as a reason to refuse, or as a reason to measure more carefully and decide more intelligently? The difference is not academic. It determines whether enforcement strengthens compliance while preserving legitimate trade, or whether it quietly expands the embargo beyond anything the law intended.

Internal risk models and scoring

In December 2020, in London, the UK's Office of Financial Sanctions Implementation published guidance on compliance expectations, emphasising that firms should take "appropriate steps" to identify and manage sanctions risk, with governance, controls and record-keeping that can withstand scrutiny. The document did not instruct firms to build scoring models. It did not prescribe an algorithm. Yet across banks and insurers, the operational response was familiar: translate "appropriate steps" into numbers, thresholds, and automated decisions that can be audited.

The score decides first.

Internal risk models are where vague concerns become hard policy. They convert a messy world—fragmented ownership records, ambiguous end uses, shifting political signals—into an apparently orderly set of categories. Red, amber, green. High, medium, low. Approved, escalated, declined. In a high-volume institution, this conversion is not optional. Humans cannot read every trade file with equal depth. Models triage. They prioritise. They also harden.

Show the model's work and it becomes less mystical. A bank receives a request to process a cross-border payment or finance a shipment. The transaction enters a workflow. Data fields populate automatically: origin, destination, currency, counterparty identifiers, beneficial ownership attributes, industry codes, vessel identifiers, ports. The model assigns weights. Geography contributes a score because certain jurisdictions have higher sanctions exposure. Counterparty type contributes a score because certain sectors—shipping, oil trading, dual-use manufacturing—are associated with enforcement history. Payment chain complexity contributes a score because multiple intermediaries increase the chance of a hidden nexus. The name for this is risk scoring. The explanation is triage under constraint. The implication is that the model becomes a gatekeeper.

A crucial feature of these models is that they treat *proxies* as facts. Geography is not wrongdoing; it is a proxy for sanctions exposure. Cargo type is not illegality; it is a proxy for dual-use risk. A layered ownership structure is not guilt; it is a proxy for concealment potential. These proxies are often reasonable. They are also blunt. Once embedded in a scoring system, they acquire authority. The visible behaviour is automatic escalation or refusal based on category. The implication is that nuance is compressed.

Efficiency is the obvious reason models proliferate. A bank processing millions of payments cannot subject each one to bespoke sanctions analysis. A marine insurer underwriting thousands of voyages cannot convene a committee for every renewal. Risk models allow institutions to allocate effort: more scrutiny where risk proxies cluster, less where they do not. Efficiency becomes a measurable metric: average review time per transaction, number of escalations per thousand payments, compliance headcount per business line. The implication is a system that moves quickly—until it stops.

Trust becomes procedural in this environment. The institution does not "trust" a counterparty in the ordinary human sense; it trusts the score. The score is trusted because it can be documented, audited, and defended. When challenged, staff can point to policy: "This transaction scored above threshold." The abstraction of *trust* becomes an audit trail. The implication is that contesting a decision becomes a negotiation with a machine.

The structure of risk scoring also reflects the enforcement tail described in the previous section. After high-profile penalties, weights shift. Certain jurisdictions are reclassified. Thresholds lower. Model sensitivity increases. This is visible in alert volumes and declinature rates. It is also visible in the language of internal memos: "heightened risk", "zero tolerance", "no exceptions". The model becomes the instrument by which a firm operationalises fear without saying so.

Two named, checkable examples help ground this phenomenon. The Financial Action Task Force's 2014 "Guidance for a Risk-Based Approach" for the banking sector emphasised that institutions should identify, assess, and understand their risks and apply measures proportionate to those risks. Though framed in anti-money laundering terms, the logic has been imported into sanctions compliance: risk-based systems, documented assessments, and demonstrable controls. The visible behaviour is model-building. The implication is governance through scoring.

A second reference point comes from the European Banking Authority. Its 2021 guidelines on money laundering and terrorist financing risk factors encouraged institutions to consider risk factors relating to customers, products, transactions, delivery channels and geography. Again, the guidance did not mandate a particular model, but it validated the idea that geography and transaction features should influence risk assessment. The visible behaviour is the incorporation of these factors into automated scoring. The implication is that institutions are encouraged, indirectly, to treat proxies as policy.

The most significant inputs to these models are predictable because they reflect what institutions can measure. Geography is easy: countries, ports, and regions can be coded. Counterparty identity is partly measurable: names, registrations, ownership data, and screening outcomes. Cargo type is measurable through commodity codes and declared descriptions. Payment chains can be measured through the number of intermediaries, the use of correspondent banks, the presence of nested relationships, and the involvement of higher-risk currencies or clearing channels. Each input is imperfect. Together, they create a score that feels objective.

Objectivity is persuasive.

Yet the model's apparent objectivity can hide fragile assumptions. Weights are chosen by humans. Thresholds are set by committees. Data quality varies. A port might be coded as high risk because it is near a sanctioned jurisdiction, even if trade through that port is lawful and well-regulated. A small exporter might be scored as risky because its ownership documentation is sparse, even if its governance is clean. The visible behaviour is systemic bias against the small, the unfamiliar, and the complex. The implication is exclusion by structure.

Consider a legitimate but complex trade that is nonetheless flagged as high risk. A European manufacturer sells water treatment equipment to a municipal authority in a Middle Eastern country that borders a sanctioned jurisdiction. The deal is lawful and humanitarian in effect. The manufacturer's bank is asked to issue a letter of credit. The counterparty is a public body, not listed. The goods are civilian. Yet the transaction trips multiple model inputs. The destination geography is coded high risk due to proximity and historical sanctions issues. The goods are classified under a code associated with dual-use sensitivity because similar equipment can have industrial applications. The payment chain involves a local bank with a limited international footprint, requiring several correspondents. The model assigns a high score and triggers an automatic escalation.

Escalation is not neutral. It is delay.

The file reaches a compliance committee that meets once a week. Committee members ask for end-use statements, tender documents, corporate ownership confirmations, and proof that the goods will not be re-exported. The municipal authority struggles to provide documentation in the preferred format and language. The exporter becomes frustrated. Costs rise. The bank, facing internal pressure to reduce high-risk exposure, eventually declines the transaction, not because it is prohibited, but because it is difficult to defend. The exporter loses the contract. The municipal authority seeks alternative suppliers, possibly in less regulated markets. The model has reshaped trade.

This example captures a central feature of risk scoring: once a transaction is coded as high risk, it becomes expensive to rescue. Staff time increases. Documentation demands multiply. Senior scrutiny intensifies. The outcome is often predictable. High-risk labels are sticky. The implication is that risk scoring does not merely identify risk; it creates it by altering the process.

The difficulty of challenging a model is structural. Front-line staff can rarely see the full logic. Vendors often treat algorithms as proprietary. Even when models are built internally, the details may be buried in technical documentation. The result is an asymmetry of understanding: the institution claims the score is authoritative, but the client cannot interrogate it. The visible behaviour is the client being told "policy" without explanation. The implication is opacity.

A credible counter-example exists. Some institutions build models with transparent override mechanisms and invest in "second-line" review functions that can assess whether a high score reflects real risk or merely proxy clustering. In these cases, complex but lawful trades can be approved with tailored controls: ring-fenced payments, enhanced monitoring, and clear documentation. The visible behaviour is nuanced approval. The limitation is workload. Overrides require confidence, expertise, and accountability. In environments shaped by enforcement fear, staff may avoid overrides because they concentrate responsibility.

Reconciling the counter-example with the dominant pattern reveals the model's political function. Risk scoring systems distribute responsibility. They turn decision-making into process. When a transaction is declined because of a score, no single person owns the refusal. This diffusion is attractive in a punitive regulatory environment. It also encourages rigid application. Flexibility requires someone to be brave enough to sign.

The quiet motif threading through this section is the traffic light on a screen. Green flows. Amber waits. Red stops. Most institutions would insist that the lights are advisory. In practice, the lights are law inside the organisation. They determine what gets attention, what gets time, and what gets refused.

These systems also shape market behaviour beyond the institution. Brokers learn which banks are strict. Traders learn which routes trigger delays. Insurers learn which cargo descriptions provoke questions. Actors adapt by simplifying transactions, choosing "cleaner" routes, and avoiding complexity. The implication is that risk models sculpt trade towards what is easily classifiable, not necessarily what is most efficient or most needed.

The unresolved tension is therefore epistemic and moral at once. Risk scoring promises rationality, but it rests on proxies and imperfect data. It protects institutions, but it can punish legitimate commerce that happens to be complex. The forward test arrives whenever a transaction is lawful yet hard to explain. Does the institution treat the red light as a verdict, or as a prompt to investigate and decide with human judgement? The answer determines whether the model serves compliance—or whether compliance quietly becomes the model.

Collateral damage to legitimate trade

In February 2016, in London, Barclays confirmed that it would close the remaining accounts of several money service businesses linked to remittance corridors serving Somalia, following years of pressure tied to sanctions and financial crime risk. The decision did not declare remittances illegal. It did not allege misconduct by every customer. Yet for many small traders and families, the effect was immediate: payments could not move, contracts stalled, and lawful commerce became impossible through ordinary banking channels. A compliance decision, defensible on paper, translated into economic silence.

The cost was real.

Collateral damage is the unpriced consequence of over-compliance. It appears where legal activity depends on intermediaries that decide the risk is not worth managing. It shows up as delayed shipments that miss planting seasons, cancelled infrastructure projects that cannot secure payment cover, and cargoes stranded in ports because insurers will not confirm a clause. These outcomes are rarely counted as sanctions effects. They sit in the shadow of enforcement statistics, absorbed by firms and communities with little voice in policy debates.

Show the mechanics and the damage becomes visible. A lawful trade requires a chain: buyer, seller, bank, insurer, shipper, sometimes reinsurer and inspector. Over-compliance at any point can halt the chain. The name for this is friction accumulation. The explanation is defensive decision-making layered across institutions. The implication is that legality alone is insufficient to guarantee movement.

Consider a small exporter of agricultural equipment based in southern Europe, selling to customers in North Africa. The goods are civilian. The buyers are established distributors. Licences are not required. Yet payments begin to fail. The exporter's bank flags the destination country as higher risk due to regional sanctions activity elsewhere. Correspondent banks ask questions. The insurer tightens its sanctions clause. Each intermediary requests additional documentation. Weeks pass. The exporter misses delivery windows. Buyers lose patience. Orders are cancelled. Revenue falls. No law has been broken. The trade dies anyway.

Efficiency is often invoked to justify this outcome. Compliance teams argue that they cannot examine every transaction in depth. They prioritise. That prioritisation has a shape. Smaller firms with limited compliance resources, operating in complex regions, are the first to be cut loose. The visible behaviour is account termination or transaction refusal without explanation. The metric is throughput: fewer alerts, fewer escalations. The implication is exclusion by scale.

Trust erodes quietly in this process. The exporter trusted that meeting legal standards would be enough. The bank trusted its model more than its client. The insurer trusted its reinsurer's caution more than its underwriting judgement. Trust, once broken, is hard to rebuild. The visible behaviour is clients seeking alternative channels—smaller banks, informal payment networks, cash-heavy arrangements. The implication is risk migration rather than risk reduction.

A second named, checkable example underscores the breadth of the issue. The Financial Action Task Force has repeatedly warned about the unintended consequences of de-risking. Its 2016 report on correspondent banking services documented how wholesale withdrawal from certain regions harmed legitimate trade and financial inclusion, even as institutions sought to comply with sanctions and financial crime controls. The visible evidence included declining correspondent relationships and increased reliance on informal channels. The implication was explicit: over-compliance can undermine policy goals.

The human cost is often indirect but acute. Delayed shipments mean perishable goods spoil. Cancelled projects mean workers are laid off. Stranded cargoes tie up capital and storage space. For small firms, these shocks can be fatal. Unlike large multinationals, they cannot absorb repeated losses or redesign supply chains at speed. The abstraction of *resilience* becomes a simple fact: some firms do not survive.

Ports offer a particularly stark illustration. A vessel arrives with lawful cargo, documentation in order. Yet the port authority, under pressure from insurers and banks, delays clearance pending "comfort". Storage fees accrue. Charter rates tick on. The buyer's financing expires. Eventually, the cargo is diverted or sold at a loss. The visible behaviour is administrative delay. The implication is economic penalty without adjudication.

These outcomes are not accidents. They are predictable consequences of incentive structures. Intermediaries face asymmetric risk. Approving a lawful transaction that later attracts scrutiny can be career-ending. Refusing a lawful transaction rarely attracts sanction. The rational response is caution. Multiply that response across banks, insurers, and shippers, and lawful trade becomes fragile.

There is also a geographic pattern. Regions adjacent to sanctioned jurisdictions, or associated in the media with conflict, suffer disproportionate effects. Firms learn that operating "near" trouble is itself treated as trouble. The visible behaviour is regional exclusion lists that grow over time. The implication is that proximity becomes guilt by association.

A credible counter-example complicates the picture. Some sectors and firms have developed shared frameworks to keep lawful trade moving despite sanctions pressure. Industry initiatives around humanitarian trade, for example, have produced standardised documentation and communication channels that reduce uncertainty. In these cases, shipments that once stalled now move with fewer delays. The visible behaviour is coordination.

The limitation is scope. Such frameworks are rare outside high-profile humanitarian contexts and often depend on sustained regulatory engagement.

Reconciling this exception with the dominant pattern reveals the role of clarity. Where regulators provide explicit comfort and intermediaries share information, over-compliance eases. Where guidance is vague and responsibility diffuse, caution dominates. Collateral damage thrives in ambiguity.

The quiet motif threading through this section is the stopped clock. Trade runs on timing. Payments clear by deadlines. Ships sail on schedules. Insurance binds before departure. Over-compliance stops the clock without announcing why. Time becomes the hidden weapon. For small firms, time lost is often business lost.

Collateral damage also reshapes competition. Firms with in-house compliance teams and multiple banking relationships can navigate obstacles. Smaller exporters cannot. Markets consolidate around those able to absorb friction. The implication is a subtle redistribution of opportunity, favouring scale and sophistication over legality alone.

This redistribution has policy consequences. Sanctions are meant to target specific behaviours and actors. When lawful trade is choked instead, political support erodes. Affected communities perceive sanctions not as precise tools but as blunt instruments. Informal economies grow. Transparency declines. The system becomes harder to police.

The forward test is therefore practical and uncomfortable. When an intermediary declines a lawful transaction because it is complex, who bears responsibility for the outcome? The bank that refused? The insurer that tightened terms? The regulator whose guidance was unclear? Or the trader who assumed legality was enough? Until that question has a credible answer, collateral damage will remain the quiet companion of every embargo, shaping trade not through law, but through fear and time.

Chapter 5

Shadow Fleets and Evasive Logistics

At dawn on a calm morning in April 2022, a mid-sized oil tanker altered its name, flag, and registered owner in a single administrative sweep. The paperwork was filed through separate jurisdictions, each lawful on its own terms, each incomplete in the eyes of the others. By the time the vessel reappeared in commercial databases, it was, formally speaking, someone else's ship. Nothing about the steel hull had changed. The crew remained largely the same. The cargo was familiar. Yet to insurers, banks, and port officials scanning their screens, the vessel's past had thinned into ambiguity. Trade resumed.

This is the paradox at the heart of modern sanctions enforcement. As lawful trade is increasingly slowed by caution and compliance, unlawful or borderline trade adapts by becoming lighter, faster, and harder to grasp. The more formal systems tighten, the more value accrues to those who can step between them. Shadow fleets do not announce themselves. They emerge gradually, assembled from the spare parts of global shipping: ageing vessels, permissive registries, shell companies formed for a season and dissolved without ceremony. Their power lies not in defiance, but in persistence.

Shadow logistics is not new. Merchants have long found ways around blockades and monopolies. Yet the contemporary form is distinct in one crucial respect. It thrives not by hiding entirely, but by fragmenting visibility. Each actor in the chain sees something partial and plausible. A registry sees a compliant owner. An insurer sees a vessel with clean papers. A port authority sees a ship that meets entry requirements. No single institution sees enough to stop the movement. The result is a system that functions in the gaps between systems.

This chapter sits at a fault line in the book's argument. Earlier chapters traced how compliance, insurance, and risk models can quietly restrict lawful trade. Here, the focus turns outward, to the adaptive response.

When formal channels constrict, alternative channels do not merely appear; they are engineered. Shadow fleets and evasive logistics are not chaotic improvisations. They are structured responses to pressure, shaped by the same forces that drive over-compliance elsewhere: asymmetry of risk, fragmentation of authority, and uneven access to information.

The term "shadow fleet" itself is misleading. It suggests a coherent armada, moving in concert. In reality, these operations are often loose constellations of vessels and companies that share tactics rather than command. What unites them is not loyalty to a single actor, but familiarity with a method. A tanker is purchased at the end of its commercial life, often through intermediaries. Ownership is layered through holding companies registered in jurisdictions with limited disclosure. The vessel is reflagged, sometimes repeatedly. Names change. Managers rotate. Each step is modest. Together, they create a fog.

The fog is deliberate.

At the centre of this fog lies a tension explored throughout this book: the reliance of enforcement on services rather than borders. Insurers, banks, and ports are powerful chokepoints precisely because they depend on information. When information becomes unreliable, their power weakens. Shadow logistics exploits this dependency. It does not seek to overwhelm enforcement; it seeks to exhaust it. Analysts spend hours reconciling vessel histories that do not quite align. Compliance teams escalate files that never quite resolve. Over time, attention shifts to clearer cases. Ambiguity wins by attrition.

The chapter will move through the anatomy of this system, beginning with how shadow fleets are assembled. This is not a tale of cinematic secrecy, but of administrative accumulation. A vessel with a chequered past is sold to a newly formed company. That company appoints nominee directors. The vessel is registered under a flag that offers speed and discretion. Management is outsourced. Each decision has a benign explanation. Each leaves a trace. The traces, however, do not join up easily. Investigators must cross registries, languages, and legal regimes to reconstruct what has been obscured by design.

From there, the focus shifts to ownership. Control, as earlier chapters showed, is already a fraught concept in sanctions compliance. Shadow operators exploit this fragility. Nominee directors sign where beneficial owners remain absent. Holding companies sit atop other holding companies, sometimes across three or four jurisdictions. Temporary joint ventures appear for a single voyage and dissolve before scrutiny catches up. The question "who controls this vessel?" becomes harder to answer not because the answer is unknowable, but because it is inconvenient to discover.

Tracking technology, often presented as a solution, enters the story with its own ambiguities. Automatic Identification Systems were designed for safety, not enforcement. They broadcast position, speed, and destination. They were never meant to be incontrovertible. Shadow fleets understand this well. AIS signals are switched off for stretches of sea where coverage is thin. Destinations are declared and then quietly altered. In some cases, GPS signals are spoofed. A ship appears to be somewhere it is not. The screen shows compliance. The hull moves elsewhere.

The sea itself offers further opportunities. Ship-to-ship transfers, lawful in many contexts, allow cargoes to be blended, re-labelled, and redistributed. Oil from different sources mixes in offshore anchorages that see the same manoeuvres repeated week after week. Documentation follows the last transfer, not the first. By the time cargo reaches port, its origin is a matter of paperwork rather than chemistry. Tracing becomes an exercise in inference, not proof.

These practices persist not because enforcement agencies are naïve, but because capacity is finite. Authorities must choose where to focus. Private firms face the same constraint. High-profile cases attract attention. Others move on quietly. This selective pressure shapes behaviour. Shadow operators accept that some vessels will be caught. Loss is priced in. The rest continue. The system resembles an insurance pool of its own, with risk spread across assets and time.

Throughout the chapter, a recurring image will surface: the palimpsest. Each layer of registration, each transfer, each data point overwrites what came before without fully erasing it. The past remains faintly visible beneath the present. Analysts read these layers the way scholars read scraped manuscripts, searching for continuity beneath revision. Yet unlike texts, ships move. Time matters. A vessel need only pass once.

Why does this matter beyond the mechanics of shipping? Because shadow logistics reveals the limits of the quiet embargo. Where compliance tightens without coordination, it creates incentives for evasion that are unevenly distributed. Those with capital, expertise, and tolerance for opacity adapt. Those without are excluded. The result is not a binary world of sanctioned and unsanctioned trade, but a stratified one, where visibility itself becomes a resource.

This stratification has consequences. It undermines trust in the very systems designed to manage risk. When insurers and banks see that evasive operators continue while lawful traders struggle, frustration grows. When ports detain ships that appear compliant on paper but later attract scrutiny, local authorities bear costs without clear guidance. The legitimacy of enforcement depends not only on effectiveness, but on perceived fairness.

There is also a moral dimension. Shadow fleets often carry commodities that are central to global welfare: energy, fertilisers, food inputs. When these flows move through opaque channels, accountability weakens. Environmental standards slip. Labour conditions deteriorate. Accidents become harder to attribute. The same invisibility that frustrates sanctions enforcement also obscures harm.

This chapter does not promise neat solutions. It is not a catalogue of tricks for evasion, nor a manual for interdiction. Its purpose is diagnostic. By examining how shadow fleets operate, it clarifies why enforcement based on partial visibility struggles, and why over-reliance on formal indicators can mislead. It also complicates the moral map. Not all shadow activity is driven by malice; some is driven by exclusion. The line between evasion and adaptation is thinner than policy language admits.

As the chapter unfolds, the reader will encounter vessels that change names like actors changing costumes, companies that exist just long enough to sign a contract, and data that appears authoritative until it is compared with something else. Each element is familiar on its own. Together, they form a system that tests the assumptions of compliance, insurance, and trade governance explored earlier in the book.

The momentum at the end of this chapter is not towards closure, but towards recognition. If the quiet embargo constrains trade through caution and fear, shadow logistics responds through ambiguity and motion. The question that lingers is uncomfortable and unavoidable. In a world where enforcement depends on services and information, who truly controls trade: those who set the rules, or those who learn fastest how to slip between them?

How shadow fleets are assembled

On 1 May 2022, in Dubai, the oil tanker *Pegas* quietly ceased to exist. Within weeks it re-emerged in maritime databases under a different name and flag, its ownership transferred to a newly incorporated company with no trading history. The hull was the same. The crew list barely changed. What shifted was the vessel's administrative skin. By July, the tanker was loading again. To insurers and port authorities relying on standard screening tools, it looked new enough to pass.

This is how shadow fleets begin: not with secrecy, but with paperwork.

Shadow fleets are not built in shipyards. They are assembled in registries, corporate service offices, and inboxes. Their raw material is the global shipping surplus: ageing vessels nearing the end of their commercial life, sold cheaply and often overlooked by major operators. These ships are attractive precisely because they have already depreciated. A buyer can afford to lose one. The name for this logic is asset expendability. The explanation is risk pricing under constraint. The implication is resilience through disposability.

The process usually starts with acquisition. A vessel changes hands through intermediaries—brokers, holding companies, or special-purpose vehicles. Each intermediary adds distance between the ship and its effective controller. Trust, in this context, is replaced by opacity. The visible behaviour is a sale recorded at market price, executed through a lawful contract. The implication is that the transaction attracts little attention.

Ownership then fragments. The purchasing entity is often a newly formed company registered in a jurisdiction that allows rapid incorporation and minimal disclosure. Nominee directors are appointed. Shareholders may be trusts or other companies. None of this is illegal. Each layer is defensible. Together, they produce uncertainty. When banks or insurers later ask who controls the vessel, the answer is technically available but practically elusive.

Flags follow ownership. The vessel is re-registered under a flag of convenience offering speed and flexibility. Some registries process applications in days. Others accept provisional registration pending documentation. A change of flag resets parts of a vessel's compliance history. The name changes too. Sometimes more than once. Each renaming severs continuity in databases that rely on text matching rather than hull numbers. The visible metric is frequency: vessels in shadow fleets often change names every few months. The implication is deliberate disruption of traceability.

A second, checkable example illustrates the pattern. Investigations by the NGO Global Witness and reporting by *Reuters* in 2022 documented a cohort of tankers carrying Russian oil after the imposition of price caps. Many had been acquired by opaque companies, reflagged, and renamed repeatedly within short periods. The reporting did not allege that every voyage was unlawful. It showed something subtler: a systematic effort to stay just ahead of scrutiny. The visible behaviour was administrative churn. The implication was continuity of trade through reinvention.

Shell companies play a central role. They are not created to trade; they are created to exist. Their purpose is to hold title long enough to move an asset. Once scrutiny increases, they dissolve or sell on. The efficiency of this model lies in its temporariness. Corporate registries are slow to update. Investigators arrive late. The abstraction of *control* dissolves into a sequence of signatures.

Inconsistent ownership records are not a bug. They are the feature. Maritime databases pull from registries, insurers, classification societies, and AIS feeds. These sources update on different cycles. A vessel's flag may change before its owner. Its manager may change before its name. Analysts see mismatches and flag them, but mismatches alone do not prove wrongdoing. The visible behaviour is a cascade of alerts that require human review. The implication is overload.

A quiet motif threads through this assembly process: shedding skin. Like an organism that moults to survive, the vessel periodically discards identifiers that have grown risky. The steel remains. The identifiers change. Enforcement systems chase the skin, not the body.

Critically, assembly does not require coordination across a single network. Shadow fleets are often decentralised. One operator sells to another. One ship joins another's pattern by imitation rather than instruction. Tactics spread because they work. This diffusion makes enforcement harder. There is no headquarters to raid. No single owner to sanction. The system persists through replication.

Efficiency is measured differently here. For mainstream shipping, efficiency means fuel use, turnaround time, and utilisation rates. For shadow fleets, efficiency means survival time: how long a vessel can operate before becoming too visible. Renamings, reflagging, and ownership transfers are investments in time. Each buys another few voyages. The implication is that administrative agility substitutes for scale.

A credible counter-example tempers the picture. Not every vessel with frequent changes is part of a shadow fleet. Ships are sold, reflagged, and renamed for benign commercial reasons: mergers, fleet rationalisation, or changes in management strategy. The limitation of pattern-based analysis is false positives. Reconciling this requires context. Shadow fleet assembly is identified not by a single change, but by density: the clustering of changes in time, combined with risky routes and cargoes. The visible metric is convergence. The implication is probabilistic judgement, not certainty.

The example of a tanker that has changed identity multiple times captures this dynamic. A vessel originally built in the early 2000s trades under a major flag. After sanctions tighten around a particular commodity, it is sold to a newly formed company. Within six months, it has a new name, a new flag, and a new manager. Six months later, the cycle repeats. Each iteration coincides with heightened scrutiny. The vessel continues to operate. Observers note the pattern. Action lags. Trade moves on.

This lag is structural. Registries prioritise speed and revenue. Classification societies focus on safety. Banks and insurers focus on compliance with their own obligations. No single actor is responsible for continuity of identity. Shadow fleets exploit this fragmentation. The implication is that assembly thrives in institutional seams.

The unresolved tension at the end of this section is deceptively simple. When a vessel's identity is repeatedly reassembled without violating formal rules, who bears responsibility for recognising intent? If each step is lawful, at what point does the pattern itself demand intervention? Until that question has an operational answer, shadow fleets will continue to assemble themselves from the ordinary components of global trade, not in defiance of the system, but by mastering its limits.

Tactics for obscuring true ownership

In April 2016, investigators at the International Consortium of Investigative Journalists opened a tranche of files from Mossack Fonseca, the Panamanian law firm at the centre of what became known as the Panama Papers. Among the millions of documents were shipping companies registered in the British Virgin Islands, directors resident in Cyprus, bank accounts in Latvia, and vessels trading thousands of miles away. The outcome was not a single revelation but a pattern: control without visibility. Even with names, dates, and addresses in hand, tracing who actually *decided* where a ship sailed proved slow and uncertain.

This uncertainty was not accidental. It was engineered.

Obscuring true ownership in shipping relies less on secrecy than on dispersion. Control is stretched across jurisdictions, registries, and legal forms until it becomes difficult to assemble into a single, authoritative picture. The abstraction is *beneficial ownership*. The visible behaviour is the multiplication of entities. The implication is plausible deniability at every step.

Nominee directors are the first layer. These are individuals who lend their names to company boards without exercising real control. In jurisdictions that permit professional directorships, a single nominee may appear on hundreds of company registers. The name is real. The signature is valid. The decision-making power is absent. Investigators see a person; they do not see authority. The risk is misattribution. The metric is frequency: the same director appearing across dozens of unrelated firms.

Layered holding companies deepen the effect. A vessel-owning company is held by another company, which is in turn held by a trust or partnership. Each layer may sit in a different jurisdiction, governed by different disclosure rules. The explanation offered is tax efficiency or corporate structuring. The implication is delay. Each additional layer adds days or weeks to any inquiry, long enough for assets to move.

A second, checkable example illustrates the scale. In 2018, the United States Treasury's Office of Foreign Assets Control identified a network of companies linked to Iranian shipping interests operating through Hong Kong and Singapore. Public statements named dozens of entities, many incorporated within months of each other, sharing nominee directors and registered addresses. The outcome was designation. The deeper lesson was structural: without coordinated disclosures, the network had operated for years. The visible behaviour was corporate replication. The implication was endurance through complexity.

Temporary joint ventures add another tactic. Two companies form a project-specific partnership to move a particular cargo or operate a route. Once the transaction is complete, the venture dissolves. Each partner can claim limited knowledge of the other's activities. Control is shared just long enough to be effective, then dispersed again. The abstraction of *shared risk* masks the reality of shared intent. The visible behaviour is a short-lived entity with a narrow mandate. The implication is that responsibility evaporates when the entity does.

Gaps between registries make these tactics viable. Company registries record incorporation details. Ship registries record flag and ownership.

Banks record account holders. Insurers record policyholders. These datasets are not synchronised. Updates propagate unevenly. A change recorded in one system may not appear in another for months. Investigators confront contradictions rather than answers. The motif here is misalignment: systems designed for their own purposes, not for coherence.

An example from practice shows the friction. Investigators examining a shipping group operating out of the eastern Mediterranean encounter a web of companies registered in Malta, the Marshall Islands, and the United Arab Emirates. Each company appears compliant in its own registry. Directors are named. Addresses exist. Yet attempts to identify the principal decision-maker stall. Requests for information bounce between jurisdictions. Each authority points to another. The outcome is not failure, but exhaustion. The implication is that time becomes the ally of opacity.

Efficiency, in this context, is measured by how little any single document reveals. A nominee appointment form reveals nothing about financing. A share certificate reveals nothing about control agreements. A joint venture contract reveals nothing about side letters. Each document is accurate. Together, they mislead. The visible metric is fragmentation. The implication is that truth emerges only through synthesis, which is resource-intensive.

There are limits to these tactics. A credible counter-example comes from jurisdictions that have strengthened beneficial ownership registries. The United Kingdom's Persons with Significant Control register, introduced in 2016, requires disclosure of individuals exercising control over companies. While imperfect, it has reduced anonymity in domestic structures. The reconciliation lies in scope. Where registries are robust and accessible, obscuring ownership becomes harder. Where they are fragmented or closed, the old tactics persist.

Family ties add another dimension. Control may sit with relatives who do not appear on paper. Shares are held by spouses or adult children. Decision-making occurs informally. Investigators encounter legal owners with no operational role. The abstraction is *influence*. The visible behaviour is aligned decision-making across formally independent entities. The implication is that control can exist without documentation.

Metrics help, but only partially. Analysts look for shared addresses, overlapping directors, synchronised incorporations. These signals suggest coordination. They do not prove it. The risk is false correlation. The implication is cautious inference rather than decisive attribution.

The quiet motif of this section is the vanishing point. As in a perspective drawing, lines converge somewhere beyond the frame. Investigators see the lines—companies, directors, vessels—but the point where they meet remains out of view. Each tactic nudges that point further away.

The unresolved tension is practical and persistent. How much certainty is enough to act when ownership is deliberately diffused? At what point does the accumulation of signals outweigh the absence of a single controlling name? Until institutions agree on answers, obscured ownership will remain less a loophole than a method: lawful in form, evasive in effect, and finely tuned to the spaces between systems.

AIS manipulation and dark activity

On 14 May 2020, in Washington, the US Department of the Treasury issued its "Advisory to the Maritime Industry, Energy and Metals Sectors, and Related Communities" on sanctions evasion and shipping practices. Buried among the cautions about documentation and ownership sat a practical warning: vessels were disabling or manipulating AIS to obscure voyages. The advisory did not invent the practice. It acknowledged it, and in doing so confirmed what many compliance teams had already begun to treat as a hard signal. A ship that goes dark is no longer merely a ship. It is a question.

Screens can lie.

Automatic Identification Systems were created for safety: collision avoidance, traffic management, basic transparency. AIS transponders broadcast a vessel's identity, position, speed, course, destination, and other voyage data. That data is received by coastal stations and satellites, then aggregated into commercial platforms that banks, insurers, charterers, and analysts now consult as routinely as weather. AIS has become a proxy for legitimacy. When a ship's track looks ordinary, intermediaries relax. When it is erratic or absent, they tighten.

That is why AIS manipulation matters so much in the quiet embargo. It strikes at the informational substrate on which cautious markets depend. If sanctions enforcement relies on services and screening, then screening relies on signals. AIS is one of the loudest signals in shipping. When it is silenced or distorted, uncertainty expands, and uncertainty is precisely what triggers refusals, exclusions, and delays.

The simplest form of manipulation is the absence of signal: the vessel stops transmitting. In maritime jargon this is "going dark". There are benign reasons for AIS gaps. Coverage can be patchy. Equipment fails. Some naval or security situations encourage discretion. Yet in sanctions-sensitive trade, prolonged darkness is read differently. It looks like intent. The visible behaviour is a long gap in track history, often coinciding with proximity to high-risk waters or known transfer zones. The implication is escalated scrutiny, sometimes automatic refusal, because the ship has removed a key source of corroboration.

Another tactic is misdirection rather than silence. AIS includes a destination field that can be entered manually. A vessel may broadcast a plausible destination while heading elsewhere. The result is a track that appears consistent at a glance, particularly to systems that prioritise declared fields over route geometry. This is not sophisticated. It is administrative. The visible behaviour is inconsistency between declared destination and observed movement over time. The implication is that some of the most trusted data is also the easiest to manipulate.

Then there is spoofing. In broad terms, spoofing refers to the creation of false location signals, making a ship appear to be somewhere it is not. It is the most alarming tactic because it attacks the premise that position data is a stable truth. Most professionals encounter spoofing as an allegation or suspicion rather than a confirmed event, precisely because proof is hard without independent data. That difficulty is part of its power. The visible behaviour is an implausible jump in position, a track that suddenly relocates inland, or a cluster of vessels whose signals show improbable patterns. The implication is epistemic breakdown: the observer cannot know whether to trust the screen.

The quiet motif in this section is the blackout. Not the dramatic blackout of a city, but the controlled dimming of a single vessel's visibility. The blackout is not total; traces remain. But it is enough to force a choice: treat absence as evidence, or treat it as noise. That choice determines whether trade proceeds.

To see how AIS manipulation integrates into evasive logistics, follow a plausible sequence that mirrors patterns described in enforcement advisories and industry reporting. A product tanker departs a port in a region under heightened sanctions scrutiny. Its AIS track is normal as it passes through monitored sea lanes. Approaching a coastal area with limited shore reception and heavy traffic, the vessel's signal disappears. For several days, it remains dark. It then reappears hundreds of miles away, broadcasting a different destination and showing a draft change consistent with loading or discharge. The cargo documentation later presented to a buyer indicates an origin that does not match the most straightforward inference from the track. No single element proves wrongdoing. Together, they create a file that intermediaries struggle to clear.

The consequences are practical. A bank reviewing a payment linked to the voyage sees the AIS gap and demands additional assurances. The insurer asks for confirmation of port calls and cargo origin, then inserts a sanctions limitation clause or declines cover. A terminal operator asks for more documentation before accepting the ship. Time passes. Costs accumulate. The cargo becomes less profitable to move. The blackout has done its work.

Every abstraction in that story can be tied to a metric. *Risk* becomes an internal score triggered by a dark period longer than a set threshold. *Efficiency* becomes turnaround time in compliance review. *Trust* becomes whether a charterer accepts the vessel or rejects it, fearing future scrutiny. These are not philosophical outcomes. They are operational ones.

AIS manipulation also interacts with other evasive tactics described earlier in this chapter. A vessel that has recently changed name and flag becomes harder to match across databases even when AIS is transmitting. If it goes dark, the difficulty compounds. Ownership opacity and AIS opacity reinforce one another: when the corporate identity is thin and the movement record is broken, verification becomes expensive. Expensive verification often becomes refusal.

A second named, checkable example helps anchor the discussion beyond sanctions advisories. Research and reporting by Global Fishing Watch has documented widespread AIS disabling in the context of fishing, demonstrating that "going dark" can be systematic and geographically patterned rather than random noise (Global Fishing Watch, 2019). The domain differs, but the inference problem is the same. When the signal disappears in precisely the waters where oversight is weakest and incentives to conceal are strongest, observers infer intent. The implication for shipping is straightforward: the technique is not exotic, and the detection challenge is not unique to sanctions.

The maritime industry has not ignored this. The International Maritime Organization has issued guidance over the years emphasising that AIS is intended to be operated continuously except where safety or security concerns justify otherwise (IMO guidance, various circulars). The key point is that AIS was designed to be reliable enough for safety purposes, not to serve as an evidentiary backbone for sanctions enforcement. Compliance has repurposed it. Repurposing creates vulnerability. A system built for collision avoidance becomes, unexpectedly, a battlefield of inference.

This repurposing also creates perverse incentives. When markets treat any AIS anomaly as evidence of wrongdoing, some actors may avoid transmitting even when they are legitimate, fearing misinterpretation of ordinary deviations. Conversely, sophisticated evaders may learn how to craft tracks that look "clean" by transmitting most of the time and going dark only in carefully chosen intervals. The visible behaviour is selective compliance with the signal. The implication is that analysts must judge patterns, not single events.

A credible counter-example is essential here. There are benign explanations for AIS gaps that are common enough to matter. Equipment failures do occur. Coastal reception varies. Satellite coverage is not perfectly continuous. In certain piracy-prone areas, operators may reduce broadcast detail as a security measure, though doing so can itself carry safety risks. Reconciling these realities with enforcement concerns requires a disciplined approach to inference: treat darkness as a trigger for questions, not as proof.

The difficulty is that markets often cannot afford that discipline at scale. Compliance teams and underwriters operate under time pressure and asymmetric consequences. They prefer simple rules. One of those rules becomes: avoid the dark ship. The quiet embargo thus feeds on AIS uncertainty. Even lawful operators can be penalised if their track includes gaps that resemble evasive behaviour. That is where the collateral effects of enforcement meet the adaptive tactics of shadow logistics.

Notice, too, how AIS manipulation turns the ocean into a stage for choreography. The vessel does not need to vanish completely. It needs only to create a discontinuity that breaks the evidentiary chain. Once the chain is broken, the burden shifts to counterparties to prove what happened in the missing interval. Proving a negative at sea is notoriously difficult. The implication is that absence itself becomes leverage.

The relationship between AIS and documentation is especially revealing. Bills of lading, certificates of origin, and port logs are human documents. They can be accurate, forged, incomplete, or delayed. AIS is treated as mechanical truth, yet it is also mediated by human inputs and technical limits. When the two disagree, institutions often trust the machine—until they suspect the machine has been manipulated, at which point they trust neither. The result is an evidentiary vacuum filled by caution. Caution is not neutral. It reallocates trade towards those who can provide redundant proof: multiple data sources, reputable counterparties, strong banking relationships, and insurance support.

The motif of the blackout returns here in a more subtle form. Darkness is not only the absence of AIS. It is also the absence of consensus about what counts as evidence. In that darkness, decision-makers retreat to what they can defend: refusal, delay, exclusion, and repricing. The quiet embargo deepens, not because regulators demand it, but because uncertainty makes it the safest institutional choice.

The forward test is therefore diagnostic. When a vessel's track shows a gap, what would it take—concretely—to restore confidence: independent port call data, satellite imagery, third-party inspections, contractual warranties, or simply the passage of time without incident? If the answer is "nothing, we will not touch it", then AIS manipulation has achieved something larger than concealment. It has altered the market's threshold for engagement, pushing legitimate trade and evasive trade into the same shadowed category. The question that follows is unavoidable: if the screen is now a contested space, who decides what degree of visibility is enough for commerce to move?

Ship-to-ship transfers and mixed cargoes

On 14 May 2020, in Washington, the US Department of the Treasury's maritime advisory on sanctions evasion highlighted ship-to-ship transfers as a recurring method for disguising the origin of oil and other commodities. The advisory was not a maritime textbook. It was a warning to banks, insurers, and shipping firms that the sea had become a place where paperwork could be rewritten without ever touching a port.

At sea, provenance blurs.

Ship-to-ship transfers—STS in industry shorthand—are not inherently suspicious. They are a long-established practice in maritime logistics, used for legitimate reasons: to move cargo from large tankers to smaller vessels that can enter shallow ports, to consolidate shipments, to manage congestion, or to transfer fuel and supplies. The same manoeuvre, however, can also serve a different purpose. It can break the evidentiary chain that links a commodity to its origin, especially when combined with darkness in tracking data, rapid changes in vessel identity, and opportunistic re-documentation.

The core mechanism is simple. Two vessels meet offshore. Cargo is transferred. A new set of documents follows the new vessel. The difficulty begins when observers try to determine what the cargo *now is*, legally and commercially. Oil is not a branded product. It is a mixture of molecules. Once blended, it is hard to assign a single origin with confidence. That physical reality creates a legal and compliance challenge. The abstraction of *origin* becomes a question of documentation rather than chemistry. The implication is that the most important fact in sanctions-sensitive trade can be made contestable.

The patterns that raise risk are, by now, familiar to enforcement agencies and commercial analysts. Repeated transfers in the same offshore locations. Transfers conducted at night or in poor weather. Vessels that go dark before and after a rendezvous. Vessels that appear to hover in loitering patterns without a clear commercial explanation. These patterns do not prove misconduct. They indicate the need for scrutiny. The visible behaviour is clustered manoeuvres. The implication is that trade can be reconstructed only probabilistically.

The quiet motif that threads through this section is the seam. STS transfers create seams in the evidentiary fabric. Each seam marks a place where continuity can be severed and re-stitched. The cargo crosses from one vessel to another, and with it the story of the cargo can change.

To understand how this works in practice, follow a sequence that mirrors many documented cases, without pretending to adjudicate any single voyage. A tanker loads crude oil at Port A, a terminal in a jurisdiction associated with sanctions pressure. Its AIS track is normal as it exits the port and enters open sea lanes. Approaching a known offshore transfer zone, it slows and begins loitering. The AIS signal disappears for several hours. During this period, a second tanker approaches, itself having declared a plausible destination unrelated to the rendezvous. The two vessels come alongside. Cargo is transferred. The first tanker departs with reduced draft, consistent with discharge. The second departs with increased draft, consistent with loading.

From a physical standpoint, the transfer has occurred. From a documentary standpoint, the story is now negotiable. The second tanker may present documents indicating cargo loaded "offshore", with a ship-to-ship transfer noted as the loading point, and with a new origin claim that reflects the last lawful port call rather than the first. If the transferred cargo is mixed with other volumes already on board—common in complex trading operations—the original molecules are now part of a blended pool. The cargo becomes harder to attribute. The compliance challenge is immediate:

where does the sanctions analysis anchor? At the original terminal, or at the offshore seam?

A second STS operation may follow. The second tanker meets a third in a different transfer zone, perhaps nearer a major shipping lane where oversight is intermittent. Another portion is transferred. Documents shift again. By the time the cargo reaches a refinery or storage hub, it is associated with a chain of transfers and mixed volumes. Each transfer may be lawful as an act of seamanship. The legal and compliance question is whether the manoeuvres were used to obscure origin or ownership, and whether the documentation reflects substance or convenience.

Banks and insurers do not need to prove intent to feel exposed. They need only to believe that intent cannot be ruled out. Risk, in this setting, becomes operational. The visible metric is the number of STS events and the consistency of documentation across them. Efficiency becomes the time required to gather and validate evidence: port logs, cargo manifests, bills of lading, vessel tracks, and third-party verification. Trust becomes whether a counterparty's narrative holds under scrutiny. The implication is that STS manoeuvres can convert a manageable trade into an unfinanceable one.

This is why repeated transfers in similar locations matter. Offshore zones develop reputations. Some are well regulated and routinely used for legitimate operations. Others become associated with evasive patterns. The same coordinates appear again and again in datasets. Analysts notice. Compliance systems flag. Insurers ask questions. A ship that has no business loitering in that zone suddenly has a lot to explain.

A second named, checkable example grounds the discussion beyond US advisories. In 2022, *Reuters* and other major outlets reported extensively on ship-to-ship transfers used in the movement of sanctioned or price-capped oil, noting recurring offshore areas near Greece and in other parts of the Mediterranean where tankers were observed conducting transfers. The reporting often relied on AIS data combined with satellite imagery and maritime analytics. The outcome was not always enforcement action. It was a public demonstration that STS transfers had become central to the contemporary evasive playbook. The implication is that the tactic is both widespread and visible in aggregate even if it is contestable in individual cases.

There is, however, a credible counter-example that matters for fairness. STS transfers are integral to legitimate global supply chains. LNG bunkering, fuel transfers, and cargo consolidation often require them. Some regions rely on offshore transfers because ports cannot accommodate large vessels. Treating every STS event as suspicious would be both inaccurate and disruptive. Reconciling this requires context. The difference lies in pattern density, documentation quality, and the presence of other risk signals: identity churn, ownership opacity, anomalous routing, and long AIS gaps. The implication is that STS is a weak signal alone and a strong signal in combination.

Documentation is the pivot. When a cargo changes hands offshore, what documents exist to preserve continuity? Bills of lading can record transfers. Cargo manifests can note volumes. Surveyors can verify quantities. Yet surveyors may not be present. Logs may be incomplete. Offshore operations can occur beyond easy jurisdictional reach. The abstraction of *evidence* becomes a question of who witnessed the transfer and what records were created at the seam. The implication is that the evidentiary burden shifts downstream, onto the party trying to finance or insure the cargo.

The physical reality of mixing compounds this burden. Once oil is blended, forensic certainty declines. Laboratories can analyse chemical fingerprints, but many crude oils are chemically similar, and blending erases distinct markers. Even where fingerprinting is possible, it is not routinely available for commercial deals, and it rarely aligns neatly with legal definitions of origin. The visible behaviour is reliance on documentation as the primary proof. The implication is that the trade can be made legible or illegible depending on paperwork discipline.

This is precisely why STS operations are attractive to evasive logistics networks. They offer a way to create ambiguity without forging documents outright. The documents can be real. They can record a real transfer. They simply do not resolve the deeper question of where the cargo came from originally, or who controlled it along the way. Ambiguity is sufficient. It forces intermediaries to decide how much uncertainty they can bear.

Ports and terminal operators sit in a difficult position. They may have no direct authority over offshore transfers, yet they are asked to accept cargoes whose histories include them. Some respond by demanding stronger assurances: chain-of-custody documentation, vetting of vessels involved, and confirmations from reputable surveyors. Others rely on standard documentation and accept the residual risk. The visible behaviour is divergence in port practices. The implication is that trade routes adjust to the most permissive nodes.

Insurers and P&I clubs also respond through contract language. Policies may exclude claims arising from sanctioned trade or from voyages that involve certain high-risk transfers. Clubs may issue circulars warning members about STS operations in particular zones. These are not proclamations. They are pressure points. The implication is that even lawful STS activity can become commercially unattractive if it is too close to a reputationally tainted pattern.

The seam appears again here, as a metaphor and a practice. Each STS transfer is a seam where responsibility can shift. When a cargo later becomes disputed, parties point to different parts of the chain. The shipowner says it followed orders. The charterer says the shipowner controlled operations. The trader points to documentation. The bank points to compliance policy. Responsibility diffuses. Diffusion is convenient for those seeking to avoid scrutiny. It is corrosive for those seeking accountability.

The forward test at the end of this section is deliberately operational. When confronted with an STS-heavy cargo chain, what would convince a cautious intermediary that the cargo is legitimate: verified survey reports at each seam, continuous AIS with no dark gaps, transparent beneficial ownership for each vessel, or an independent chain-of-custody protocol accepted across the industry? If the answer is "nothing short of certainty", then lawful trade involving offshore transfers will increasingly stall, and evasive operators will continue to exploit the seams. The sea will remain not only a route, but a drafting table where origin can be rewritten.

Limits of enforcement against shadow fleets

In March 2023, in London, the UK Office of Financial Sanctions Implementation published updated guidance acknowledging what many practitioners already understood: enforcement capacity is finite. The document followed months of public debate about vessels moving sanctioned oil despite heightened scrutiny. A handful of ships were named. Several companies were penalised. Most activity continued.

Enforcement selects.

That selection is not random, nor is it evidence of indifference. It reflects structural limits that shape how far states and private actors can realistically pursue complex maritime networks operating across jurisdictions, registries, and oceans. Shadow fleets persist not because no one is watching, but because watching everything is impossible.

The paradox is straightforward. Sanctions regimes have expanded in ambition and scope, while the resources available to enforce them have not grown at the same pace. Each new measure adds reporting requirements, analytical demands, and investigative leads. Each lead competes with others for attention. The result is prioritisation. The visible behaviour is selective action. The implication is that some actors are deterred while others calculate that they can operate beneath the threshold of focus.

The first constraint is information. Even with modern data tools, maritime activity generates more signals than any single authority can exhaustively analyse. Automatic Identification System feeds produce millions of data points daily. Satellite imagery adds layers of confirmation and confusion. Corporate registries differ in quality, accessibility, and reliability. Ownership structures change faster than records update. The abstraction of *visibility* becomes a measurable problem: how many analysts can review how many vessels, how often, and with what confidence?

Consider the public reporting by *Reuters* in 2022 and 2023 on oil shipments moved through complex networks of tankers after the introduction of price caps. Journalists, using open-source AIS data and commercial analytics, identified dozens of vessels engaging in suspicious patterns. Authorities responded by designating or investigating a subset. The remainder were not necessarily lawful; they were simply not the priority. The implication is that exposure does not guarantee enforcement.

Capacity constraints are not limited to governments. Banks, insurers, and shipping firms face their own limits. Compliance teams operate under budgets. Investigators juggle multiple risk domains. A single complex maritime case can consume weeks of effort. The visible metric is case load per analyst. When that number rises, thresholds harden. Trades that require deep investigation are avoided. Shadow operations benefit from this triage. They design transactions to be just complex enough to deter engagement without being so blatant as to force action.

Jurisdiction compounds the problem. Maritime trade crosses legal systems by design. A vessel may be flagged in one state, owned through entities in several others, insured in a third, and financed in a fourth, while operating in international waters. No single authority has complete reach. Mutual legal assistance takes time. Requests queue. By the time information arrives, the vessel may have changed name, flag, and owner. The visible behaviour is delay. The implication is that enforcement often trails the activity it seeks to constrain.

A named example illustrates this dynamic without overstating it. In 2019, the US Department of Justice pursued sanctions-related cases involving shipping companies linked to Iranian oil exports. Several vessels were seized or designated. The cases were public and emphatic. They were also limited. Reporting at the time noted that many other vessels continued operating using similar tactics. Authorities focused on emblematic cases that could demonstrate resolve and clarify expectations. The implication was deterrence by example rather than comprehensive interdiction.

This strategy has logic. High-profile cases shape behaviour across markets. A single enforcement action against a bank can trigger global policy changes, as discussed earlier in this book. The same applies at sea. Designating a vessel or prosecuting a shipping firm sends a signal. Yet signals attenuate with distance. Operators with fewer ties to mainstream finance, insurance, or ports may feel insulated. They weigh the probability of being chosen against the profits of continuing. Risk becomes calculable.

The quiet motif running through this section is the spotlight. Enforcement operates like a moving beam. Where it lands, activity freezes or retreats. Outside its cone, movement continues. Shadow fleets are adept at staying just beyond the brightest light.

There is also a political dimension. Sanctions enforcement is not a purely technical exercise. It reflects diplomatic priorities, alliance management, and economic trade-offs. Authorities may tolerate certain levels of leakage to avoid broader disruption. Energy markets are sensitive. Shipping capacity is finite. Aggressive enforcement can produce unintended consequences: price spikes, shortages, or retaliation. The abstraction of *prudence* translates into decisions about where not to act.

A second named, checkable example highlights this tension. Following Russia's invasion of Ukraine in February 2022, European and US authorities announced sweeping measures targeting Russian oil exports. Enforcement agencies signalled intent. Over time, reporting showed that while some routes were constrained, others adapted. Ship-to-ship transfers increased. New buyers emerged. Authorities pursued selected cases, often where Western intermediaries were involved, while activity routed through less connected channels persisted. The implication is not failure, but calibration.

Private enforcement mirrors this selectivity. Insurers withdraw from certain routes. P&I clubs issue warnings. Banks tighten screening. Yet none can police the entire sea. They rely on risk indicators. When those indicators are ambiguous, decisions diverge. One firm exits. Another stays. Shadow fleets exploit this fragmentation. They seek the weakest link: a permissive registry, a lightly regulated insurer, a port with limited oversight. The visible behaviour is forum shopping. The implication is that uneven standards create corridors of continued operation.

A credible counter-example deserves attention. Enforcement does succeed, sometimes decisively. The near-elimination of certain maritime practices following coordinated action—such as piracy off the Horn of Africa after 2010—shows that sustained, well-resourced efforts can change behaviour. Reconciling this with the persistence of shadow fleets requires recognising differences in objectives and tools. Piracy involved identifiable acts of violence. Shadow trade involves paperwork, ownership, and interpretation. The implication is that the latter resists the same kind of closure.

Another limit is evidentiary. To act decisively, authorities need proof that meets legal standards. Suspicion is not enough. Patterns suggest risk but do not always establish violation. A vessel may engage in ship-to-ship transfers for legitimate reasons. Ownership structures may be opaque without being illicit. Courts require attribution. The abstraction of *proof* becomes a practical hurdle. The implication is that many cases stall at the threshold of action.

This evidentiary burden feeds back into prioritisation. Cases with clear facts, cooperative jurisdictions, and identifiable defendants rise to the top. Complex, transnational cases sink. Shadow fleets design operations to maximise complexity. Complexity is not accidental. It is defensive architecture.

Time also matters. Enforcement operates on institutional timelines. Investigations take months or years. Markets move faster. By the time a case concludes, the operational network may have dissolved and reformed elsewhere. The visible behaviour is organisational churn. The implication is that enforcement often addresses yesterday's configuration.

The role of private data providers complicates the picture. They surface risks. They do not enforce. Their alerts feed into decision-making across firms. When many alerts accumulate without corresponding enforcement, fatigue sets in. Users begin to discount signals. The abstraction of *alert fatigue* becomes observable in higher thresholds for escalation. Shadow operations thrive in that fatigue.

None of this implies futility. It implies trade-offs. Enforcement agencies and firms choose where to concentrate effort. They aim to raise costs, reduce scale, and deter mainstream participation. Complete eradication is not the metric of success. Containment is.

The unresolved tension at the end of this section is strategic rather than moral. Should enforcement continue to rely on exemplary cases and broad signalling, accepting persistent shadow activity as a residual, or should resources be concentrated on closing specific corridors even if that risks wider disruption? For readers navigating this landscape, the diagnostic question is simpler and more personal: when you assess a trade touched by shadow networks, are you comfortable relying on the fact that others are being pursued, or do you assume that the spotlight could move at any time and land on you?

Chapter 6

Tracking Vessels and Trade Data

At 02:17 one morning, a small compliance team noticed that a tanker's position had jumped several nautical miles inland. The ship had not run aground. No accident had occurred. The anomaly sat quietly on a screen: a data point where sea should have been land. By sunrise the point had been dismissed as a technical glitch, one of thousands generated daily by global tracking systems. Weeks later, the same vessel appeared again—this time off a coast it had never declared, carrying cargo it had no obvious way to load. The earlier glitch no longer looked innocent. It looked rehearsed.

Trade now leaves footprints everywhere, yet certainty remains elusive.

This chapter opens where many modern sanctions decisions begin: not with law, not with policy, but with data. Numbers, coordinates, timestamps, registries, feeds. An endless stream of signals that promise transparency while quietly introducing new forms of ambiguity. We live with the assumption that if something moves, it can be tracked; if it can be tracked, it can be understood; and if it can be understood, it can be controlled. Each step in that chain is less secure than it appears.

Maritime trade has always produced records. Logbooks, manifests, port clearances, insurance slips. What has changed is scale and speed. Automatic Identification Systems broadcast positions every few seconds. Satellite constellations watch from above. Commercial databases compile histories that once took months to assemble. The sea, once opaque, now seems illuminated. Yet illumination is not comprehension. The light reveals patterns; it also casts shadows.

The purpose of this chapter is not to teach readers how to operate tracking tools. It is to examine how those tools shape judgement. Data does not merely describe trade; it frames how risk is perceived, how suspicion arises, and how decisions are justified. A vessel's past movements become a proxy for intent. A routing anomaly becomes a question mark over an entire transaction. A clean data profile becomes a source of comfort—sometimes misplaced.

The story of AIS, vessel databases, and trade analytics is therefore not a technical tale but a human one. It is about interpretation under uncertainty. About the limits of observation. About the quiet power of dashboards and alerts to determine whether a shipment proceeds or stalls.

The chapter begins with the basics, because misunderstanding often starts there. AIS was designed as a safety tool, a way for ships to avoid collisions and for coastal authorities to manage traffic. It was never meant to be a compliance instrument. The fact that it has become one explains many of its weaknesses. Broadcast data can be incomplete, manipulated, or absent altogether. Reception depends on geography, infrastructure, and weather. Storage depends on who is listening and how long they keep records. Analysts piece together journeys from fragments, stitching narratives from what is available rather than from what is complete.

From those fragments, patterns emerge. Some are genuinely concerning. Sudden flag changes, repeated calls to the same obscure anchorages, unusual detours near sensitive waters. Others are artefacts: quirks of shipping schedules, weather diversions, clerical errors. The distinction matters. Treating every anomaly as evidence produces paralysis. Ignoring anomalies invites exposure. This tension runs through every data-driven decision in trade compliance.

Commercial data providers sit at the centre of this ecosystem. They aggregate, clean, and enrich information drawn from dozens of sources, presenting it as a coherent picture. Their value is real. Without them, most firms would be blind. Yet their products are not neutral mirrors of reality. They reflect choices about what to include, how to weight sources, how to fill gaps. Two firms using different vendors can look at the same voyage and see different stories. One clears a payment. The other escalates it. Data abundance does not eliminate judgement; it multiplies it.

Inside institutions, these feeds flow into systems designed to manage risk at scale. Dashboards summarise voyages. Watchlists flag vessels. Escalation paths turn anomalies into meetings, memos, and decisions. The analyst at the centre of this process rarely has the luxury of perfect information. Time pressures are real. Commercial relationships hang in the balance. Data becomes a shield as much as a guide: *the system flagged it*, or *the system cleared it*. Responsibility diffuses into process.

Yet data can mislead in both directions. False positives consume resources and damage relationships. False comfort allows carefully engineered trades to pass unchallenged. Some of the most sophisticated evasive strategies are designed not to hide from data, but to perform well within it—to create patterns that look normal, to borrow legitimacy from clean histories, to exploit the assumptions built into screening models. When analysts later discover the truth, the data that once reassured them becomes part of the problem.

This chapter sits at a critical point in the book's arc. Earlier chapters examined how quiet embargoes operate through services, contracts, and behaviour. Later chapters will explore humanitarian carve-outs, governance, and strategy. Here, the focus is the lens through which all of that is seen. Data is the intermediary between policy and action. It is where abstract rules meet concrete movements.

A recurring image will guide the discussion: the chart table. In traditional navigation, charts do not move the ship. They inform the navigator. They require interpretation, experience, and judgement. Modern trade data systems play the same role. They are indispensable. They are also fallible. Confusing the chart with the sea has consequences.

As the chapter unfolds, readers will see how analysts reconstruct journeys from open sources, how risk patterns are identified and misidentified, how commercial data products both illuminate and obscure, and how internal teams wrestle with signals that refuse to resolve neatly into yes or no. They will also see why data-driven compliance can never be a purely technical exercise. It is, at its core, a practice of decision-making under uncertainty.

The questions that close this chapter are not about better algorithms or more feeds, though those matter. They are about posture. When data conflicts, which signals do you trust? When systems disagree, who decides? When the numbers look clean, what do you still ask? And when the data is noisy, incomplete, or contradictory—as it often is—what level of doubt is acceptable?

The sea may be more visible than ever. That does not mean it is easier to read.

Basics of AIS and vessel databases

In December 2002, in London, the International Maritime Organization adopted amendments to the SOLAS Convention requiring most large commercial vessels to carry Automatic Identification Systems. By July 2004 the requirement was in force. The intent was simple: reduce collisions at sea. The outcome was more complex. A safety tool became a global sensor network, quietly recording the movements of tens of thousands of ships, minute by minute, across every ocean. Trade acquired a memory.

Ships now speak.

They speak in bursts of data: identity numbers, positions, courses, speeds, declared destinations. The messages are routine, repetitive, and, at first glance, unremarkable. Yet those fragments form the backbone of modern maritime visibility. For analysts, insurers, banks, and regulators, AIS is no longer background noise. It is evidence, context, and sometimes accusation.

AIS works by broadcasting information over VHF radio frequencies. Each transmission contains a vessel's Maritime Mobile Service Identity, its GPS-derived position, heading, speed, and a handful of static fields such as name and call sign. Some fields are set by crew and change rarely. Others update every few seconds. The abstraction of *transparency* becomes a measurable behaviour: a ship announcing where it is, continuously, to anyone listening.

Who listens matters. Coastal authorities receive AIS signals directly when vessels pass within range of shore-based receivers. Satellite operators capture signals far offshore, albeit with gaps and delays. Commercial aggregators buy, combine, and normalise these feeds, storing years of historical positions in searchable databases. What begins as a local safety broadcast becomes a global archive.

The implication is profound. A ship's past movements are no longer ephemeral. They persist. They can be replayed, analysed, and compared. A tanker's call at a port three years ago may resurface during a sanctions review today. Memory changes behaviour. It also changes risk.

AIS data does not stand alone. It sits alongside vessel registries, classification society records, port call logs, insurance certificates, and corporate ownership filings. Vessel databases weave these strands together, creating profiles that feel authoritative. Name, flag, owner, operator, insurer, class, history. Each field suggests certainty. Each rests on assumptions.

Consider how analysts reconstruct a journey. A payment linked to a crude oil cargo triggers review. The vessel's IMO number is entered into an open-source database. AIS tracks show departure from a Black Sea port in March, a long period of silence mid-voyage, and reappearance weeks later near the eastern Mediterranean. Port call records suggest a ship-to-ship transfer off Cyprus. Satellite imagery confirms two hulls alongside. None of this proves a violation. Together, it raises questions. The visible behaviour is pattern recognition. The implication is scrutiny.

The power of AIS lies in continuity. It provides a time series rather than a snapshot. Risk is inferred not from a single point but from a narrative: where a ship has been, how often, and in what sequence. Analysts do not ask only *where is it now?* They ask *where has it been willing to go?*

Yet the system's limits are as important as its strengths. AIS relies on self-reported data. Crews enter destinations manually. Errors are common. "For orders" appears where a port name should be. Spelling varies. A vessel bound for Rotterdam may declare "RTM", "ROT", or something else entirely. The abstraction of *accuracy* becomes a question of data hygiene rather than intent.

Coverage is uneven. Satellite reception suffers from message collisions in busy sea lanes. Coastal receivers do not reach far offshore. Weather and terrain interfere. A vessel disappearing from AIS does not necessarily signal misconduct. It may signal geography. Treating absence as guilt produces false alarms.

A named limitation illustrates this clearly. During the COVID-19 pandemic in 2020, global shipping patterns shifted abruptly. Port congestion, crew changes, and quarantine rules forced vessels into unusual anchorages. AIS histories from that period are riddled with anomalies that had nothing to do with sanctions or evasion. Analysts who ignored context misread risk. Reconciling this requires humility: data reflects reality filtered through circumstance.

Vessel databases attempt to add stability by anchoring movements to identity. The IMO number, introduced in the late twentieth century, is designed to remain with a hull for life. Names and flags change; numbers persist. This continuity allows histories to be stitched across decades. The implication is trust in identifiers.

Trust can be misplaced. Data quality varies by source. Some registries update ownership promptly; others lag. Some commercial databases correct errors quickly; others propagate them. Two analysts using different platforms may see different owners listed for the same date. One clears a transaction. The other escalates. The abstraction of *consistency* turns into a practical divergence.

A second named example underscores this point. In 2018, investigative journalists working with *Lloyd's List* traced a series of tankers involved in sanctioned trades by correlating AIS tracks with registry data that had not yet been updated to reflect recent sales. Ownership appeared benign in one database and risky in another. The difference lay not in the vessels but in update cycles. Data timing mattered.

This raises a critical implication for compliance. AIS and vessel databases do not deliver truth. They deliver signals. Those signals require interpretation, corroboration, and restraint. The temptation to treat a clean track record as proof of innocence is strong. So is the urge to treat irregularity as proof of wrongdoing. Both are errors.

A quiet motif threads through this discussion: the logbook. Traditional logbooks were written by hand, subject to omission, correction, and judgement. AIS is a digital logbook. It is more complete, more accessible, and still imperfect. Like its predecessor, it tells a story shaped by who writes and who reads.

The relationship between AIS and behaviour is reflexive. Once operators understand how data is used, they adapt. Some broadcast diligently, cultivating a record of regularity. Others manipulate fields, within technical limits, to create plausible narratives. This does not negate AIS's value. It reframes it. Transparency invites performance.

A credible counter-example deserves mention. There are trades where AIS scrutiny adds little. Short-sea shipping within well-regulated regions produces dense, repetitive data that offers minimal insight beyond confirming normal operations. In such contexts, other risk indicators matter more. Reconciling this reinforces a broader point: AIS is most useful at the margins, where behaviour deviates from established baselines.

For institutions, the visible metric is not how much data they possess but how they use it. Storing years of AIS history is easy. Interpreting it responsibly is not. Decisions must balance sensitivity and scepticism. Over-reliance leads to paralysis. Under-reliance invites surprise.

As this chapter unfolds, later sections will examine how patterns are flagged, how commercial providers shape perception, and how internal teams integrate data into decisions. The foundation matters. Misunderstanding the basics produces compounded errors downstream.

The unresolved question that closes this section is deceptively simple. When you look at a vessel's track and feel either reassurance or concern, are you reacting to the ship's behaviour, or to the limits of the system that recorded it?

Patterns that suggest higher risk

On 14 May 2020, in Washington, the US Department of the Treasury warned the maritime industry that certain observable behaviours—unexplained AIS gaps, loitering, and ship-to-ship transfers—were being used to evade sanctions. The advisory did not claim that every anomaly was illicit. It did something more operational: it gave institutions permission to treat patterns as prompts for scrutiny. From that moment, a new kind of evidence began to matter in trade. Not proof. Pattern.

Patterns guide attention.

They are the currency of modern compliance because most institutions cannot investigate everything. They must choose where to look. Patterns provide a way to allocate scarce judgement. That is their value. That is also their danger. Patterns can be over-read. They can be engineered. They can be innocent. The discipline required is to treat them as *questions*, not verdicts.

A five-word sentence belongs here: Patterns are not proof.

Start with irregular port calls. A vessel that normally trades between predictable hubs suddenly calls at an obscure anchorage, or makes a detour to a port that does not fit its usual commercial logic. That irregularity is a data signal. The name for the signal is route deviation. The explanation can be benign—weather, congestion, mechanical issues, charter changes—or it can be strategic, designed to obscure cargo origin or counterparties. The implication is not guilt, but uncertainty worth examining.

Irregularity becomes more salient when it clusters with other signals. A detour followed by an AIS gap. A port call near a known ship-to-ship zone followed by a draft change. A vessel that declares "for orders" repeatedly, then appears to loiter offshore. Each element alone is weak. Together, they form a story that demands corroboration.

Sudden flag changes are another classic pattern. Flags change for many reasons: commercial strategy, tax, regulatory preferences, or changes in ownership. Yet frequent reflagging, especially in short time windows and combined with name changes, can suggest an attempt to disrupt continuity in screening systems. The visible behaviour is administrative churn. The implication is that the vessel may be trying to become harder to track and harder to classify.

This is where databases matter. A compliance analyst will not merely note that a flag changed; they will ask how often, and whether ownership records changed in parallel. They will compare the vessel's IMO number history against name and flag histories. They will check whether the new flag is associated with rapid registration and limited disclosure. They will measure density: how much change, how quickly. Density is the difference between routine commerce and deliberate disguise.

Another pattern sits in the rhythm of movement. Vessels engaged in evasive trade often display loitering behaviour—slow circles, repeated course changes, long stops in open water—near places where transfers are feasible and oversight is weaker. Loitering can be legitimate; ships wait for berths, pilots, weather windows. Yet loitering in the same offshore box repeatedly, especially when matched with AIS anomalies or repeated rendezvous with the same counterparties, becomes a signal. The name is suspicious loitering. The explanation is the search for transfer opportunities or coordination. The implication is an increased likelihood of concealed operations.

A cluster example illustrates how patterns become persuasive without becoming decisive. In 2022, analysts tracking tanker movements in the eastern Mediterranean observed multiple vessels taking unusual routes near waters associated with heightened scrutiny, including prolonged loitering and repeated proximity events consistent with transfers. Some vessels showed AIS gaps timed around these loitering periods. Others broadcast implausible destinations. The cluster, taken together, suggested a transfer corridor: a set of ships behaving in ways that were statistically unusual relative to normal traffic. The visible behaviour was convergence in time and space. The implication was a pattern of coordinated activity, even if any single vessel could claim innocent explanations.

Clusters matter because they change the burden of interpretation. A single odd track may be noise. Ten similar odd tracks in the same patch of sea look like a method. Compliance teams often formalise this intuition by building "hot zones" or "watch areas" into dashboards. When a vessel enters such a zone, its risk score increases. This is not legal analysis. It is triage.

Risk, here, is operationalised as friction. A flagged pattern triggers additional checks. Those checks take time. Time delays trades. Delays raise costs. Costs can kill deals. The implication is that pattern detection does not simply identify risk; it reshapes trade by changing how easily transactions clear.

Draft anomalies are another pattern, particularly for tankers. AIS data includes draft information, though it is not always reliable and can be manually entered. A sudden change in draft can suggest loading or discharge. When such changes occur without corresponding port calls, analysts infer offshore transfers. The visible behaviour is a draft shift in open water. The implication is a transfer seam where origin may be obscured.

Payment and document patterns can align with vessel patterns. A bank may see invoices that do not match the vessel's likely route or timing. A bill of lading may declare a loading point inconsistent with AIS tracks. An insurance certificate may be issued by an unfamiliar provider shortly after a vessel's ownership change. These are not maritime patterns alone; they are trade patterns. When they align with vessel anomalies, suspicion hardens. The implication is not certainty, but enough doubt to justify refusal or escalation.

A second named, checkable example helps anchor the discussion beyond advisories. The International Maritime Organization has repeatedly stressed that AIS is intended to be operated continuously except where safety or security concerns justify otherwise. This guidance matters because it defines a baseline expectation. Deviations from baseline become meaningful. Yet the same guidance also recognises exceptions. Reconciling these points requires judgement: a gap may be defensible in a piracy-prone area; it may be indefensible if timed around a rendezvous in a known transfer zone. The implication is context-dependent interpretation rather than mechanical scoring.

This is where false positives enter. Not every detour signals evasion. Not every flag change signals concealment. Shipping is complex. Charter parties change. Ports congest. Weather reroutes. Treating every anomaly as illicit will flood compliance systems with noise, degrade decision quality, and push institutions towards blanket avoidance. The visible behaviour is alert fatigue. The implication is that real risk may be missed because everything is flagged.

There is also the opposite risk: false comfort. Sophisticated operators learn which patterns trigger scrutiny and design their behaviour to avoid them. They keep AIS on most of the time. They use plausible destinations. They vary transfer locations. They distribute activity across many vessels rather than concentrating it. They maintain clean-looking tracks while obscuring ownership and documentation. The visible behaviour is conformity to expected patterns. The implication is that a "normal" track can be a performance.

A credible counter-example clarifies the need for restraint. Consider seasonal shipping patterns around grain exports. During harvest periods, ports become congested and anchorages fill. Vessels loiter. Routes change. AIS tracks become messy. A compliance analyst unfamiliar with seasonal rhythms could misread normal congestion as evasive behaviour. Reconciling this requires domain knowledge: compare a vessel's behaviour not against an abstract ideal, but against peer traffic in the same corridor and season. The implication is that context reduces false suspicion.

The quiet motif of this section is the fingerprint. Patterns are treated like fingerprints—unique marks that can identify a method. But unlike fingerprints, shipping patterns are not unique. Many vessels share similar behaviours for legitimate reasons. The fingerprint metaphor is therefore both useful and dangerous. It reminds us that patterns can identify methods. It also tempts us to overstate certainty.

Institutions respond by building layered review. A pattern triggers a question. The question triggers corroboration: port logs, bills of lading, inspection reports, ownership checks, sanctions screening, satellite imagery. This is the "show → name → explain → implication" engine in practice. Show the anomaly. Name it. Explain plausible causes. Consider what follows if the risk is real. Then decide.

The decision itself is often less about truth than about tolerance. If the transaction is small, margins thin, and documentation imperfect, firms may refuse rather than investigate. If the transaction is strategic and counterparties are reputable, firms may invest in verification. The implication is that risk patterns do not operate equally across the market; they interact with power, profit, and capacity.

The forward test that closes this section is diagnostic. When a pattern triggers concern, what would change your mind: an independent verification of port calls, a consistent chain of documentation, a credible explanation supported by third-party data, or simply the absence of future anomalies? If the answer is "nothing", then patterns have become pretexts for withdrawal. If the answer is "evidence can resolve it", then patterns remain what they should be: prompts for scrutiny rather than instruments of quiet embargo.

Commercial data providers and limits

On 1 March 2021, in London and New York, S&P Global announced it would acquire IHS Markit, a deal framed in the language of indices and information advantage. The corporate logic was plain enough: in markets where uncertainty is costly, the firm that sells usable data sells confidence. The shipping world had already learned that lesson. Over the prior decade, vessel tracking and trade intelligence had become a commercial industry in its own right, with platforms that turned radio signals, port notices, corporate registries, and satellite imagery into something that looked like a coherent picture of the sea.

The map is not territory.

Commercial maritime data providers exist because the underlying information is plentiful but messy. AIS messages are abundant, yet inconsistent. Port calls are recorded, but not uniformly. Corporate ownership is discoverable, yet fragmented across jurisdictions. Even the same vessel can appear under different names, managers, and flags depending on which source is consulted. What the vendor sells is not merely data; it sells *integration*. Integration becomes a product, a subscription, and sometimes an institutional dependency.

At their best, these services do three things in sequence. They aggregate raw inputs from many sources; they clean and normalise them; and they enrich them with interpretation. Aggregation means pulling in AIS from coastal receivers and satellites, combining it with vessel registries, classification society details, and port call logs where available. Cleaning means resolving duplicated identifiers, correcting obvious errors, and standardising formats so that a vessel's name, IMO number, and MMSI do not appear as three separate entities. Enrichment is the step that changes the game: adding inferred ownership links, labelling "high-risk" zones, estimating cargo flows, and producing risk scores that can be embedded into compliance systems.

Each step adds value. Each step adds judgement.

Aggregation itself is not neutral. Providers do not all listen in the same places. Coastal receiver networks vary by geography. Satellite coverage depends on commercial arrangements and technical capabilities. Some vendors specialise in particular regions or vessel types. A platform with excellent coverage of European coastal traffic may be weaker in remote offshore zones where evasive transfers often occur. The abstraction of *coverage* becomes a measurable constraint: which waters are seen continuously, which are seen intermittently, and which are seen mostly through inference.

Cleaning introduces another layer of choice. AIS contains fields that are manually entered by crews, including destination and, often, draft. Errors range from innocent misspellings to deliberate misdirection. Vendors decide what to treat as error and what to preserve as signal. If a ship's destination field oscillates between two ports, is that noise, or a sign of obfuscation? A cleaning algorithm can "correct" away the very ambiguity a compliance analyst might want to see. The visible behaviour is a smoother, more readable track. The implication is that readability can conceal uncertainty.

Enrichment is where vendors become most influential. A vessel's track becomes a narrative. A cluster of loitering points becomes an inferred ship-to-ship transfer. A chain of corporate filings becomes an estimated beneficial owner. A history of flag changes becomes a risk tag. These inferences can be excellent. They can also be wrong, and when wrong they can travel far, because many institutions use the same providers and many internal systems consume vendor outputs as if they were facts.

This is why two firms can reach different views on the same case. One bank subscribes to a vendor whose AIS feed has stronger satellite coverage in a particular offshore zone; it sees a vessel's signal persist through what would otherwise look like a "dark" period, and it concludes the voyage is consistent with normal routing. Another bank uses a different vendor with weaker reception in that zone; it sees a long gap, and its system flags the vessel for possible concealment. Both banks believe they are acting on evidence. Both are acting on the limits of their sensors. The first clears the payment. The second escalates it. The cargo does not become more or less lawful in the meantime; it becomes more or less *legible*.

Legibility is an economic force.

A second divergence can arise from how vendors model port calls. Some platforms infer port calls from AIS proximity to port polygons. Others rely on port authority notifications or agent reports where obtainable. A ship that drifts at anchorage can be classified as "in port" by one system and "near port" by another. For a compliance team evaluating whether a vessel called at a restricted terminal, that difference is not pedantic; it is decisive. The visible metric is a port call entry in a timeline. The implication is whether a transaction is treated as routine or suspect.

Named examples help keep this grounded without pretending that any single vendor holds the whole truth. The US Department of the Treasury's 14 May 2020 maritime advisory explicitly encouraged industry participants to use "available maritime data" and to pay attention to indicators of deception, including AIS manipulation and ship-to-ship transfers. It did not endorse a particular provider. It effectively endorsed the practice of treating commercial intelligence as a compliance input. The implication is that private data services have become part of the enforcement environment, even when they remain private products.

Another anchor point comes from the Financial Action Task Force's repeated focus on information sharing and risk-based controls in the financial system, including its 2016 work on correspondent banking and de-risking. While not maritime-specific, FATF's logic has been imported into sanctions compliance: use data to allocate attention, document decision-making, and demonstrate that risk signals were considered. Commercial maritime data vendors thrive in that environment because they help firms show work. The visible behaviour is audit-ready dashboards and alerts. The implication is that compliance increasingly depends on external data infrastructure.

The advantages of commercial providers are substantial and worth stating plainly. They compress time. They lower the cost of initial screening. They allow non-specialist teams to detect patterns that would otherwise require deep maritime expertise. They enable cross-referencing: a vessel's track alongside ownership changes, alongside historic port calls, alongside sanctions screening outcomes. For time-conscious professionals, this is transformative. What once took a week of phone calls and manual searches can be done in minutes.

They also create a common language. When underwriters, banks, and traders consult similar platforms, they can discuss risk in comparable terms: "dark activity", "loitering", "STS zone", "flag change frequency". This shared vocabulary can improve coordination, particularly when decisions must be made quickly. The implication is smoother risk communication across institutions that otherwise operate in separate worlds.

Yet the blind spots are not incidental. They are structural.

One blind spot is provenance of the underlying sources. Many users treat a vendor's interface as if it were the sea itself. In reality, the interface is an editorial product built from inputs of varying reliability. Coastal receivers can fail. Satellites can miss messages in crowded areas. Corporate registries can be outdated. Port call data can be inferred. When a platform shows a clean voyage, the cleanliness may reflect missing data rather than benign behaviour. The abstraction of *certainty* becomes a design choice: how much uncertainty does the platform display to the user?

Another blind spot is the risk of herd thinking. If many institutions rely on the same vendor tags and risk scores, they can converge on the same decisions. That convergence can be efficient when the vendor inference is correct. It can be damaging when the inference is wrong. A vessel misclassified as high risk may find itself unable to obtain insurance or financing across multiple firms at once. Conversely, a vessel that learns how to "score well" against a dominant vendor's indicators may pass through multiple gatekeepers. The implication is that concentration in data services can create systemic vulnerability.

A third blind spot is adversarial adaptation. Vendors publish marketing materials and, sometimes, methodology outlines. Industry advisories describe common evasion indicators. Over time, operators learn what triggers suspicion. They do not need to defeat the system. They need to avoid detection thresholds. A vessel can maintain AIS transmissions most of the time, vary transfer locations, keep port calls within plausible patterns, and still participate in evasive activity through ownership opacity and documentation games. The visible behaviour is compliance with observable indicators. The implication is false comfort.

There is also a human blind spot: the temptation to treat vendor outputs as a substitute for judgement. Compliance teams under time pressure may rely heavily on a platform's risk rating. Underwriters may decline cover because a screen is red. Banks may freeze payments because a vendor flag appears. These actions can be defensible, but they can also become self-reinforcing. If a platform labels a region or vessel as risky, institutions withdraw. Withdrawal reduces legitimate activity. Reduced legitimate activity increases the proportion of suspicious activity observed. The platform's risk label appears validated. The implication is a feedback loop where data products shape reality by shaping participation.

A credible counter-example complicates the scepticism. There are contexts where commercial providers genuinely improve accuracy and reduce over-compliance by supplying missing context. A bank that would otherwise reject a transaction because of an AIS gap can, with a richer dataset, see that the gap coincides with known reception limitations rather than suspicious behaviour. An insurer can distinguish routine anchorage waiting from loitering associated with transfers by comparing the vessel's behaviour against peer traffic patterns. In such cases, better data reduces unnecessary refusals. Reconciling this is crucial: the problem is not data providers as such; it is unexamined dependence and misplaced certainty.

The quiet motif for this section is the "single pane". Firms often speak of wanting a single pane of glass—a dashboard where everything can be seen at once. The desire is understandable. It is also seductive. A single pane can conceal how many pieces were cut, polished, and fitted together to create the appearance of unity. When a decision depends on what is shown in that pane, the craft behind the pane matters as much as the view.

The practical implication for institutions is governance. If a bank or insurer embeds vendor feeds into decision engines, it must understand—not merely purchase—the underlying logic: source coverage, update cycles, error handling, and inference methods. Otherwise, the firm is outsourcing not only data collection but risk judgement. Outsourcing judgement can be efficient. It can also be indefensible when challenged, because responsibility remains with the institution even when the signal originated elsewhere.

The unresolved tension that ends this section is a test of maturity. When two reputable vendors disagree about the same voyage, what do you treat as truth: the higher-risk view, the lower-risk view, or the fact of disagreement itself? In a world where trade increasingly turns on data-driven legibility, the most important signal may not be the track on the screen, but the confidence you can reasonably place in the machinery that produced it.

Using data inside compliance teams

In December 2020, in London, the UK Office of Financial Sanctions Implementation issued guidance that placed a quiet emphasis on systems: firms were expected to have controls proportionate to their exposure, to document decisions, and to demonstrate that they could detect and manage sanctions risk. There was nothing in that guidance about dashboards. Nothing about watchlists. Yet within weeks, many institutions updated theirs. A regulatory expectation had been translated into a user interface.

The screen becomes policy.

Inside banks, insurers, and trading houses, vessel and trade data rarely sits in a standalone "maritime" tool used by specialists. It is pulled into operational workflows—payment processing, underwriting, customer due diligence, claims handling—and made legible to generalist teams under time pressure. The objective is not to know everything about the sea. It is to decide whether to proceed.

Show how this works and the quiet embargo becomes visible in its modern form. A transaction arrives: a payment instruction, a request for cover, a chartering decision, a claim notification. The system extracts identifiers—vessel name, IMO number, port, counterparty, commodity—and pings multiple datasets. Sanctions screening tools check names against lists. Maritime data feeds provide voyage history and risk tags. Ownership tools suggest links. The outputs are assembled on a dashboard. The user sees a simplified verdict: clear, review, escalate.

This translation is unavoidable. A compliance team cannot stare at raw AIS messages. It needs an interface that turns noise into prompts. The name for that translation is operationalisation. The explanation is the need to compress complex information into decisions that can be made at speed. The implication is that design choices in dashboards shape what firms treat as risk.

Dashboards typically prioritise three things: identity, movement, and context. Identity includes the vessel's IMO number, flag, name history, and sometimes inferred beneficial ownership. Movement includes recent tracks, port calls, AIS gaps, and proximity to known high-risk zones. Context includes commodity, counterparties, payment route, and any prior internal alerts or decisions. Each element is partial. Together, they create a narrative that feels complete. The temptation is to treat that narrative as truth.

Watchlists are how institutions hold memory. A vessel triggers an alert today; it is placed on a list for future reference. A port or corridor becomes "high risk" based on repeated anomalies. A counterparty is tagged because it appears repeatedly in transactions linked to certain routes. Watchlists feel like prudence. They can also become self-fulfilling. Once something is on the list, it is more likely to be scrutinised, and scrutiny generates more records, which justifies continued scrutiny.

This is not a moral failing. It is a structural feature of bounded attention. It is also where the quiet embargo takes on a distinctive texture: decisions are shaped not only by law, but by institutional memory encoded in tags.

Escalation paths turn signals into authority. Most firms draw a boundary between front-line staff and specialist reviewers. A junior analyst sees an alert and escalates. A second-line team reviews. Sometimes a committee or senior manager decides. The design of the escalation path matters because it determines what kind of evidence is required at each stage, and how risk is framed as it travels upwards.

In many institutions, escalation is itself a form of risk control. It diffuses responsibility. A front-line analyst does not "decline" a transaction; they "escalate". A manager does not "refuse"; they "follow policy". Policy becomes a shield, and data becomes the justification. The implication is that the system encourages caution, because caution is defensible.

A five-word sentence belongs here: Screens make choices feel objective.

To see the process in motion, follow a plausible case from the desk of a compliance analyst in a mid-size European bank. A corporate client instructs a payment for equipment sold to an overseas buyer. The invoice references a shipment already en route. The payment message includes the name of a vessel as part of the shipping documents. The bank's system pulls the vessel's IMO number and queries a maritime data vendor. The dashboard flashes an amber warning: "recent AIS gap" and "proximity to STS zone". The counterparty names do not match sanctions lists. The goods are not obviously restricted. The payment route involves a correspondent bank that has recently tightened its own policies.

The analyst's first move is to compare. They open the vessel's track. The AIS gap is real, but it falls in a region where satellite reception is known to be patchy. The vessel's declared destination field shows "for orders" for several days, then updates to a port that matches the bill of lading. Draft data suggests loading, but draft fields are manually entered and can be unreliable. The vessel's ownership profile shows a recent change in management to a company registered in a jurisdiction associated with rapid incorporations. The flags have changed twice in the past year. None of this is conclusive. All of it is legible as risk.

Show → name → explain → implication becomes the analyst's internal engine. Show: an AIS gap and administrative churn. Name: potential concealment indicators. Explain: possible reception limitations and routine commercial changes, but also potential evasion. Implication: if the transaction later attracts scrutiny, the bank may face questions about why it ignored the indicators.

The analyst requests additional documents from the business team: the charter party excerpt, the bill of lading, proof of cargo origin, confirmation of the buyer's beneficial ownership, and a statement that no sanctioned parties are involved. The business team complains about delay. The client pushes back. The bank's internal clock starts. Every day the payment is delayed increases the chance the client takes its business elsewhere. Every day the payment is delayed reduces the bank's exposure to a surprise. The analyst feels the asymmetry. They also feel alone.

The case escalates.

At the second-line review, a more experienced officer looks for a decisive factor. Is the vessel on any sanctions-related watchlists? Has it been identified in public advisories? Does the client have a history of similar trades? Is the commodity sensitive? What is the bank's appetite for exposure in this corridor? These questions are not always about law. They are about institutional tolerance. The officer may consult a sanctions counsel, but legal advice often confirms what everyone already knows: the transaction may be permissible, yet still risky.

The decision hinges on interpretive thresholds. Some banks operate with an internal rule that any vessel with multiple recent identity changes triggers a presumptive decline unless exceptional justification exists. Others treat such indicators as reasons for enhanced monitoring rather than refusal. The same data yields different outcomes because appetite differs. The implication is that "data-driven" compliance still rests on human governance.

This governance is shaped by enforcement history. A bank that has paid a major penalty in the past tends to embed stricter thresholds into systems. Alert rules are tuned to be more sensitive. Watchlists are broader. Escalations are more frequent. These settings are not technical optimisations; they are organisational scars. The abstraction of *risk culture* becomes visible in alert volumes and declinature rates.

Insurers use similar structures, though the decision object differs. Underwriting teams integrate vessel data into risk selection and pricing. A vessel with erratic routing or ownership opacity may be offered cover with exclusions, higher premiums, or tighter warranties. Claims teams use data retrospectively: they reconstruct voyages to determine whether a loss occurred within coverage and whether sanctions exclusions apply. Here, data is not a prompt but a forensic tool. The implication is that a vessel's track can decide whether a claim is paid.

Trading houses occupy a different position. They often have stronger incentives to keep deals moving, and in many cases deeper maritime expertise. Their compliance functions still rely on dashboards and watchlists, but the business may push for nuanced solutions: rerouting cargo, changing counterparties, seeking alternative banks, or strengthening documentation. The visible behaviour is adaptation rather than refusal. The limitation is exposure. Trading houses that push too hard can find their financing and insurance lines tightening, which brings the quiet embargo back through the side door.

A credible counter-example is important to avoid fatalism. Data integration can reduce over-compliance as well as increase it. In a firm that previously relied on broad geographic prohibitions, better vessel data can show that a trade corridor is cleaner than assumed, allowing lawful transactions to proceed with confidence. In such cases, dashboards become instruments of precision rather than blunt restraint. Reconciling this depends on how institutions treat uncertainty: as a reason to decline, or as a reason to investigate.

The blind spot, however, remains the same. Data systems can create the illusion of completeness. A clean screen can be a product of missing inputs. A red flag can be a product of noise. Both can mislead. Mature compliance teams therefore develop habits that look almost old-fashioned: they cross-check sources, they ask what is not shown, they document uncertainties, and they treat vendor outputs as evidence to be weighed rather than verdicts to be obeyed.

The quiet motif that threads through this section is the "case file". Every alert becomes a file. Every file becomes a narrative. Over time, firms build an internal archive of suspicion and clearance, woven from data points and decisions. That archive shapes future judgements. It also shapes future trade. Counterparties learn which narratives persuade and which do not. Some improve transparency. Others learn to perform.

The forward test that closes this section is a question of discipline rather than technology. When a dashboard flags a voyage and the law remains permissive, what will govern the decision: the institution's appetite, the analyst's courage, the quality of corroboration, or the fear of being the one case that becomes an example? The answer determines whether data serves as a tool of discernment—or as the quiet machinery of embargo.

False positives, false comfort

On 14 May 2020, in Washington, the US Department of the Treasury issued its maritime advisory on sanctions evasion, urging industry to treat certain behaviours—AIS disabling, ship-to-ship transfers, ownership opacity—as red flags. The document's practical effect was immediate. Firms tuned their systems to catch more. Alerts rose. So did refusals. Yet a second, quieter effect followed. As institutions trained themselves to recognise a set of conspicuous patterns, the most adaptive operators began to design voyages that avoided them.

The screen learnt. So did the ship.

False positives and false comfort are the twin pathologies of data-driven compliance. One punishes the innocent by mistaking noise for intent. The other absolves the risky by mistaking coherence for safety. Both errors are predictable. Both are costly. And in a world of quiet embargoes—where decisions are shaped as much by defensibility as by law—both errors can harden into policy.

False positives begin with a technical truth: maritime data is incomplete. AIS coverage varies. Fields are manually entered. Satellites miss transmissions in congested seas. Port call detection depends on polygon definitions and reception quality. Corporate registries update unevenly. When data is patchy, algorithms fill gaps or flag uncertainty. Humans then interpret those outputs. The abstraction of *risk* becomes a coloured banner on a dashboard. The visible behaviour is escalation or refusal. The implication is commercial harm inflicted without wrongdoing.

A five-word sentence belongs here: Data is never complete.

Consider a vessel transiting near a coastline with poor terrestrial reception. Its AIS track breaks for six hours. A vendor platform displays a "dark period" flag. A bank's system is tuned to treat darkness above a threshold as a sanction-evasion indicator. The payment is held. The client is asked for additional documentation. The deal slows. The gap, however, was a reception artefact. The ship never disabled AIS. It simply moved beyond the sensor network. In that moment, a technical limitation becomes a commercial barrier. That is a false positive.

Show → name → explain → implication clarifies the mechanism. Show: missing signals. Name: AIS gap. Explain: coverage limitation rather than concealment. Implication: if systems treat gaps as intent, lawful trade will be penalised, and institutions will drift into over-compliance.

False positives also arise from the complexity of normal shipping. Weather reroutes vessels. Ports congest. Charter parties change. Seasonal patterns alter anchorages. During the COVID-19 pandemic in 2020, many vessels waited at unfamiliar anchorages because port protocols changed rapidly. Tracks looked strange. Port calls became irregular. Draft changes occurred as ships waited for discharge windows. An analyst who treats deviation from normality as deviance will over-flag. The implication is wasted effort and damaged relationships, followed by a strategic retreat into blanket de-risking.

A second, checkable example broadens the point beyond sanctions. Global Fishing Watch's research and public reporting has documented widespread AIS gaps in fishing, many linked to deliberate disabling but also to reception limitations and equipment issues (Global Fishing Watch, 2019). The pattern is instructive: the same signal can reflect both wrongdoing and noise. The implication for compliance is humility. The signal must be weighed, not worshipped.

False comfort is the opposite error. It arises when data looks clean and institutions relax. A vessel's track shows continuous AIS transmissions. Port calls appear routine. Flags and names are stable. Ownership records seem benign. A bank clears payments, an insurer binds cover, a trader closes a deal. Months later, an enforcement action or investigative report reveals that the cargo originated from a sanctioned source and was laundered through a series of transfers and intermediaries designed precisely to keep the visible patterns normal. The data was not false. It was curated.

The quiet motif that threads through this section is the mask. False positives mistake a shadow for a face. False comfort trusts the mask as a face. Both errors come from the same desire: to turn complexity into certainty quickly.

Sophisticated evasion does not always involve darkness and chaos. It often involves *tidiness*. Operators learn what compliance systems flag—AIS gaps, loitering in known STS zones, rapid name changes—and they avoid those signatures. They keep AIS on. They declare plausible destinations. They route through ports that look ordinary. They use intermediaries with clean profiles. They structure ownership through entities that pass basic screening. The visible behaviour is conformity. The implication is that the absence of red flags is not proof of legitimacy; it may be the result of design.

An example shows how this can unfold. A trading house receives an offer for a cargo of refined product. The vessel is a familiar type, flagged in a mainstream registry. The AIS track shows consistent transmissions. Port calls include a recognised export terminal, a short transit, and arrival at a known import hub. No suspicious loitering. No obvious STS indicators.

The counterparty's company documents appear in order. The bank clears the payment. The insurer binds cover.

What the data does not show is the pre-history. Weeks earlier, the cargo was blended offshore, not at the export terminal. The export terminal served as a convenient documentary anchor, allowing the cargo to be re-described through a lawful chain of paperwork. The vessel's clean track was part of the plan: it did not go dark because darkness would attract attention. Instead, the cargo moved in a way that looked like ordinary commerce. The mask held until an external investigation connected the offshore blending to the sanctioned source. The apparent safety was engineered.

This is not a story about omniscient evaders. It is a story about incentives. Compliance systems are built around indicators. Indicators become targets. Targets can be gamed.

Commercial data providers can unintentionally amplify both pathologies. When vendors smooth tracks, infer port calls, or assign risk scores, they can reduce noise in ways that lower false positives. They can also create false comfort by presenting a more coherent picture than the underlying inputs justify. Conversely, when vendors flag too aggressively, they can inflate false positives and push institutions towards conservative withdrawal. The visible metric is alert volume and declinature rates. The implication is that data products shape market behaviour, not merely perception.

Internal governance then decides how these pathologies manifest. A bank under intense regulatory pressure may treat any unresolved anomaly as unacceptable, producing many false positives. Another bank may rely heavily on clean vendor outputs, producing false comfort. Both are defensible in their own internal logic. Both can be wrong.

A credible counter-example helps reconcile the tension. There are situations where good data genuinely correlates with lower risk. A vessel operating within tightly regulated coastal corridors, with consistent ownership, clear port calls, and a long history with reputable counterparties, is less likely to be involved in evasive trade than a vessel with recent identity churn and offshore gaps. Patterns do matter. The reconciliation is not to abandon pattern analysis but to resist treating it as determinative. Use patterns to allocate questions. Do not let patterns settle answers.

Three abstractions deserve replacement with visible behaviours. *Trust* becomes willingness to clear a payment without escalation. *Efficiency* becomes time-to-decision and the number of documents demanded.

Safety becomes the stability of cover terms and the absence of exclusions. In each case, the data signal influences a concrete institutional act.

False positives impose costs that are often invisible to policymakers. They strand lawful cargoes, damage small traders, and push legitimate actors towards less transparent channels. False comfort imposes a different cost: it allows evasive networks to persist, undermining the credibility of sanctions and the integrity of markets. Both outcomes feed cynicism. Both erode faith in the idea that compliance is rational.

The deeper problem is epistemic. Data-driven systems invite the belief that more information produces more certainty. In practice, more information often produces more ways to be wrong. More feeds mean more contradictions. More indicators mean more gaming opportunities. The human need for closure pushes institutions to convert uncertainty into binary decisions. That conversion is where errors harden.

The forward test is therefore not technical; it is behavioural. When your data looks messy, do you treat mess as an invitation to verify, or as a reason to refuse? When your data looks clean, do you treat cleanliness as reassurance, or do you ask what kinds of evasive methods would leave the screen clean? The health of compliance in the quiet embargo depends on how institutions answer those questions—not once, but repeatedly, under pressure, when the easiest choice is to trust the mask or fear the shadow.

Chapter 7

Humanitarian Exceptions and Carve-outs

The aircraft lands at dawn, its cargo hold packed with sealed crates marked with familiar symbols: insulin, antibiotics, sterile dressings. Every document has been checked. Every licence is valid. The destination hospital has been vetted twice. Yet the shipment does not move. Not because it is illegal, and not because it is unwanted, but because three separate intermediaries—each acting rationally, defensively, and within their own policies—cannot agree that someone else has taken responsibility. The boxes wait. Time does not.

Humanitarian carve-outs sit at the moral centre of sanctions policy and at its most fragile edge. They are the place where law confronts consequence directly, where the intention to punish governments or elites collides with the reality that food, medicine and relief do not recognise political boundaries. Almost every modern sanctions regime contains some version of this recognition. And yet, again and again, humanitarian trade stalls, fragments, or fails altogether—not with the clang of prohibition, but with the quiet friction of caution.

This chapter is about that friction.

At a high level, humanitarian exceptions are meant to be simple. They reflect a broad ethical consensus, reinforced by international humanitarian law and diplomatic practice, that sanctions should not starve civilians or deny them medical care. Food is not a weapon. Medicine is not leverage. Relief is not a bargaining chip. These principles have been repeated often enough to feel settled. They are written into resolutions, guidance notes, ministerial speeches. They are invoked whenever sanctions are defended against charges of cruelty.

Yet the lived experience of humanitarian trade under sanctions tells a different story. Supplies that are explicitly permitted still struggle to move. Payments that are lawful still freeze. Insurance that should respond still hesitates. The gap between permission and practice is where this chapter lives.

The paradox is not accidental. Humanitarian carve-outs are deliberately broad at the level of principle and deliberately cautious at the level of execution. Governments create exceptions, but they rarely guarantee outcomes. Instead, they leave interpretation and implementation to the same private actors—banks, insurers, shippers, inspection firms—who already sit at the choke points of trade. Those actors are asked to make judgements under uncertainty, with limited information, asymmetrical consequences, and little tolerance for error. The result is a system that allows humanitarian trade in theory while discouraging it in practice.

This tension has deep roots. During the comprehensive sanctions regimes of the 1990s, most notably in Iraq, humanitarian exemptions existed on paper while civilian suffering mounted. The political backlash from those episodes reshaped sanctions design in the decades that followed, pushing policymakers towards more targeted measures and clearer carve-outs. The intention was corrective. The memory still matters. It is one reason humanitarian language now appears so prominently in sanctions frameworks.

But memory does not remove risk. For the institutions tasked with facilitating trade, humanitarian deals are often among the most complex and least rewarded. They involve unfamiliar counterparties, fragile documentation chains, unstable destinations and intense scrutiny from media and advocacy groups. A single mistake can trigger regulatory action, reputational damage, or public accusation. Success, by contrast, is quiet. A shipment arrives. No one notices.

Understanding why humanitarian trade still stalls requires attention not to law alone, but to behaviour. Fear of mistakes plays a central role. Sanctions regimes change frequently. Guidance evolves. Lists update. Smaller compliance teams struggle to keep pace, particularly when humanitarian transactions sit outside their routine commercial flows. Faced with ambiguity, many choose delay over decision. Others choose refusal over risk.

Documentation becomes both shield and obstacle. Licences, comfort letters, end-user certificates, routing confirmations, attestations of use—each is defensible in isolation. Together, they can form a barrier that only the largest organisations can navigate. Smaller charities and relief groups, often operating under severe time pressure, find themselves trapped between overlapping demands. The humanitarian exception exists, but it is buried under paperwork.

This chapter follows those layers without drowning in technicalities. It begins with the principles behind humanitarian carve-outs, not as legal clauses but as political compromises. Exceptions are not acts of generosity; they are acknowledgements of limits. They mark the point at which pressure must stop. Understanding that logic clarifies why carve-outs are framed as permissions rather than guarantees, and why responsibility is so often pushed down the chain.

From there, the chapter turns to the reasons humanitarian trade still fails to move. Staffing shortages inside compliance functions matter. So does the fragmentation of responsibility across multiple intermediaries, each of whom sees only part of the transaction and fears being the weak link. The result is a form of collective action problem: everyone agrees the shipment should proceed, but no one wants to be the one who says yes first.

The accumulation of documentation requirements deserves particular attention. What begins as reasonable diligence can become ritualised reassurance. Each additional letter reduces perceived risk marginally while increasing practical delay significantly. For a multinational bank, this may be manageable. For a small medical charity, it can be fatal to operations. The system, in effect, selects for scale rather than need.

Decision-making under these conditions is rarely cold or purely legal. Boards and committees weigh risk, reputation and duty in ways that defy neat categorisation. Authorising a humanitarian transaction can feel morally necessary and professionally dangerous at the same time. Blocking it can feel legally prudent and ethically troubling. This chapter does not caricature those dilemmas. It takes them seriously, because they shape outcomes far more than public statements do.

Importantly, the chapter does not promise salvation through new laws. Experience suggests that adding layers of regulation often increases hesitation rather than reduces it. Instead, attention turns to improvements within existing frameworks: clearer guidance written for practitioners rather than lawyers; shared templates that reduce duplication; communication channels that allow questions to be resolved quickly without fear. Small changes in process can unlock large gains in confidence.

A recurring motif runs quietly through this discussion: responsibility. Humanitarian carve-outs distribute responsibility widely and unevenly.

Governments set the frame. Regulators warn but rarely reassure. Private firms carry the operational burden. Charities carry the human cost. When trade stalls, responsibility diffuses until it disappears. Recognising that diffusion is the first step towards addressing it.

This chapter does not argue that humanitarian trade should be risk-free. It cannot be. Nor does it suggest that all refusals are wrong. Some are necessary. Some prevent abuse. The aim is more modest and more demanding: to understand why a system designed to allow relief so often fails to deliver it, and how those failures are produced by ordinary, defensible decisions made in isolation.

The quiet embargo takes on its most human form here. Not in oil cargos or machinery shipments, but in medicine delayed, food rerouted, aid corridors narrowed by caution. The stakes are immediate. The trade-offs are uncomfortable. The questions are unresolved.

As the chapter unfolds, the reader is invited to look closely at those questions, not as abstractions, but as lived problems at the intersection of ethics, compliance and power. Where does responsibility truly lie when permission exists but action does not? How much risk is acceptable when the cost of delay is measured in lives rather than losses? And what would it take for humanitarian carve-outs to function not merely as statements of intent, but as reliable pathways through a world of quiet embargoes?

The answers are not simple. But they are necessary.

Principles behind humanitarian carve-outs

In April 1995, the United Nations Security Council adopted Resolution 986, authorising Iraq to sell limited quantities of oil in order to purchase food and medicine under international supervision. The place was Iraq. The date mattered. The organisation was the Security Council. The outcome was imperfect, controversial, and historically significant: a sanctions regime acknowledged, in formal terms, that pressure had crossed into deprivation. Civilians needed supplies. Sanctions had to bend.

Sanctions were meant to constrain a government. They were starving a population. That was the problem.

The Oil-for-Food Programme later became synonymous with mismanagement and abuse, but its origin reveals a principle that still governs sanctions design. Even the most comprehensive pressure campaigns must leave room for life-sustaining trade. Food, medicine, and basic relief occupy a different moral category from arms, luxury goods, or financial flows. They are not neutral commodities. They are prerequisites for survival.

This distinction is the ethical core of humanitarian carve-outs. It is also their enduring weakness.

At first glance, the logic seems straightforward. Sanctions aim to change behaviour without resorting to force. They are instruments of statecraft, not collective punishment. International humanitarian law, political custom, and basic moral reasoning converge on a simple proposition: civilians should not pay the price for geopolitical conflict. From this flows the near-universal inclusion of exceptions for food, medical supplies, and humanitarian assistance in modern sanctions frameworks.

Yet carve-outs are not acts of mercy. They are political compromises.

To see why, it helps to understand what sanctions are designed to do. Economic pressure works by constraining choice. It raises costs, narrows options, and forces trade-offs on those in power. If exemptions are too broad, pressure leaks away. If they are too narrow, pressure becomes cruelty. Humanitarian carve-outs sit on that fault line, intended to preserve legitimacy without dissolving leverage.

This balancing act explains their characteristic shape. Carve-outs are usually framed as permissions, not entitlements. They allow certain transactions, but they do not compel facilitation. Governments authorise. Private actors decide. Responsibility shifts quietly down the chain.

The ethical argument for carve-outs is often expressed in universal terms, but the political logic is more instrumental. Sanctions that visibly harm civilians erode international support. They invite legal challenge, diplomatic resistance, and domestic backlash. They complicate coalition-building and provide adversaries with propaganda. Humanitarian exceptions are therefore as much about sustaining the credibility of sanctions as about alleviating suffering.

This dual purpose matters. It explains why carve-outs are ubiquitous and why they are often cautious.

Consider the European Union's sanctions on Syria. Since 2011, the EU has maintained extensive restrictions on trade, finance, and energy linked to the Syrian state. At the same time, it has repeatedly clarified that humanitarian aid, medical equipment, and food are permitted. In February 2023, following the devastating earthquakes in southern Turkey and northern Syria, the EU introduced a temporary humanitarian exemption to facilitate relief flows. The organisation was the European Union. The place was Syria. The month was February 2023. The signal was explicit: humanitarian need could not wait for political resolution.

The exemption did not lift sanctions. It adjusted their edges.

This example illustrates a recurring pattern. Humanitarian carve-outs are reactive as well as principled. They expand or clarify when crises expose the costs of rigidity. They are tools for damage control. That does not make them insincere, but it does shape their design. Clarity arrives late. Ambiguity persists early.

The political logic also explains why carve-outs tend to focus on categories of goods rather than outcomes. Food is permitted. Medicine is permitted. Relief supplies are permitted. Whether they arrive, how quickly, and at what scale is another question. States draw the boundary of legality. They do not guarantee delivery.

Here the abstraction of "humanitarian necessity" meets the reality of systems.

For firms operating under sanctions, carve-outs translate into a particular kind of risk calculus. A transaction involving medical supplies to a sanctioned region may be lawful, but it is rarely simple. Counterparties are unfamiliar. End-users may be hard to verify. Payment chains may touch restricted banks. Shipping routes may cross contested areas. Each complication increases the chance of error. Each error carries asymmetric consequences.

This is where ethical intent collides with institutional behaviour.

The principle behind carve-outs assumes that allowing trade is enough. The practice reveals that permission alone rarely moves goods. The system relies on private actors to operationalise moral exceptions, even though their incentives are shaped by enforcement risk, reputational exposure, and limited information. The carve-out opens a door. It does not push anyone through it.

Trust erodes here. Banks decline transactions. Insurers hesitate. Logistics providers withdraw. Each decision is defensible in isolation. Collectively, they recreate scarcity.

A quiet motif runs through this landscape: valves. Humanitarian carve-outs function like pressure valves in sanctions regimes. They are designed to release excess force without dismantling the structure. When they work, suffering is mitigated and legitimacy preserved. When they clog, pressure builds elsewhere, often invisibly.

The historical record shows both outcomes.

In Iran, for example, US sanctions have long included exemptions for food and medicine. Yet multiple studies and reports, including findings by Human Rights Watch in 2019, documented shortages of essential drugs linked not to legal prohibition but to financial isolation. Banks refused to process payments. Suppliers withdrew. The goods were legal. The pathways were not. The abstraction of "access" dissolved into the concrete behaviour of non-participation.

This is not a failure of principle. It is a limitation of design.

The counter-example often cited is the success of certain humanitarian corridors negotiated alongside sanctions, where states actively support facilitation rather than merely permit it. The Swiss Humanitarian Trade Arrangement, launched in 2020 to enable trade in food and medicine with Iran, is one such case. By providing structured payment channels and clear assurances, it reduced uncertainty for participating firms. Volumes remained modest, but the mechanism demonstrated that carve-outs can function when supported by infrastructure.

The implication is uncomfortable. Humanitarian exceptions work best when they cease to be passive.

Yet most sanctions frameworks stop short of that commitment. They prefer flexibility to obligation. They rely on general guidance rather than operational guarantees. This preserves political deniability and reduces administrative burden. It also shifts moral responsibility outward.

The ethical logic behind carve-outs is therefore inseparable from questions of accountability. Who is responsible when permitted goods do not arrive? The state that drafted the exception? The regulator that issued cautious guidance? The bank that declined the payment? The insurer that refused cover? The system offers no clear answer. Responsibility diffuses.

This diffusion is not accidental. It reflects the political economy of sanctions. States want to maintain pressure while avoiding blame. Private actors want to avoid penalties while maintaining optionality. Humanitarian organisations want to deliver aid without becoming compliance experts. The carve-out sits between these interests, a shared reference point that satisfies everyone rhetorically and no one operationally.

Short sentence. People still suffer.

Understanding this helps explain why humanitarian carve-outs persist despite their imperfections. They are necessary but insufficient. Removing them would render sanctions morally untenable. Strengthening them would require political choices that many states avoid. The result is a stable compromise that produces unstable outcomes.

The chapter's earlier sections have shown how over-compliance and de-risking magnify these effects. Here, the focus is narrower but no less consequential. The principle behind humanitarian carve-outs is sound. The structure built around it is fragile.

This fragility becomes most visible in sanctioned regions where humanitarian trade is technically allowed but practically rare. Supplies trickle rather than flow. Projects stall. Local health systems adapt by rationing, substituting, or improvising. These adaptations are invisible in sanctions design but central to lived experience.

The ethical claim that "food and medicine are exempt" remains true. The empirical reality that access is constrained remains equally true.

There is a temptation to resolve this tension by moralising failure. To accuse firms of cowardice or states of hypocrisy. Such critiques have force, but they miss the systemic nature of the problem. Humanitarian carve-outs ask actors to act against their incentives without changing those incentives. They appeal to ethics while enforcing compliance. That contradiction does not disappear through exhortation.

The political logic also imposes limits on how far carve-outs can go. If humanitarian trade becomes too smooth, critics argue, it can be exploited. Supplies may be diverted. Revenue may leak. Control may weaken. These risks are real. They explain why carve-outs are hedged with conditions, monitoring, and revocation clauses. They also explain why certainty is scarce.

A credible limitation deserves acknowledgement. In some contexts, humanitarian exceptions have been abused to channel resources to sanctioned elites or armed groups. The Oil-for-Food Programme itself became a case study in how humanitarian mechanisms can be captured.

These failures haunt contemporary policy. They justify caution. They complicate reform.

The challenge, then, is not to choose between ethics and control, but to recognise that both are already entangled. Humanitarian carve-outs are not outside sanctions. They are part of how sanctions justify themselves.

As this section closes, the unresolved tension remains. If humanitarian exceptions are morally necessary and politically constrained, how should success be judged? By legal permission alone? By volumes delivered? By lives improved? And who decides when a carve-out has failed—not in principle, but in practice?

The next sections follow that tension into the mechanics of delay, documentation, and decision-making. The principle opens the door. What happens beyond it is harder.

Why humanitarian trade still stalls

In March 2022, a consignment of oncology medicines bound for Damascus sat idle in a European freight warehouse for six weeks. The organisation arranging the shipment was Médecins Sans Frontières. The place was Belgium. The date mattered because Syria's humanitarian exemptions had already been reaffirmed following earlier clarifications by the European Union. The outcome was delay, not denial. The medicines were lawful. The paperwork was complete. The paralysis lay elsewhere.

Everyone waited.

The paradox at the heart of humanitarian carve-outs becomes visible in moments like this. If food and medicine are permitted, why do they so often fail to move? If the law allows, why do systems refuse? The answer is not found in statutes or resolutions, but in behaviour shaped by fear, capacity limits, and fragmented responsibility.

Humanitarian trade stalls not because it is prohibited, but because it is lonely.

The first brake is fear of error. Sanctions enforcement is asymmetric. A single mistake can result in severe penalties, public censure, and long-term regulatory scrutiny. A correct decision, by contrast, rarely brings reward. This imbalance conditions behaviour across banks, insurers, logistics providers, and suppliers. When confronted with a transaction linked to a sanctioned region, even one clearly covered by a carve-out, the safest response is delay. Delay invites review. Review invites escalation. Escalation spreads responsibility.

This pattern is observable. Name it caution by default.

Consider how this plays out in a typical payment chain. A humanitarian organisation contracts a pharmaceutical supplier. The supplier requests confirmation from its bank. The bank flags the destination country. Compliance staff request additional documents. The request travels back down the chain. Each intermediary adds its own comfort requirement, often slightly different from the last. No one says no. No one says yes. Time accumulates.

This is not inefficiency. It is defensive design.

The second brake is staffing. Compliance teams are rarely sized for nuance. Sanctions departments are built to screen volume, not to adjudicate exceptions. A payment to a sanctioned jurisdiction, even for permitted goods, demands manual review. Manual review demands expertise. Expertise is scarce. Faced with a backlog, teams prioritise clear approvals and clear rejections. Grey cases wait.

Short sentence. Files pile up.

This constraint is structural. Since 2014, sanctions regimes have multiplied in scope and complexity. Institutions have responded by investing in automated screening and standardised procedures. Humanitarian carve-outs resist automation. They require judgement about end use, end user, routing, and documentation. Each element introduces uncertainty. Each uncertainty consumes time.

The result is predictable. Lawful humanitarian transactions become the most resource-intensive to process. They are delayed not because they are risky, but because they are complex.

Documentation compounds this effect. Carve-outs are framed broadly, but implementation relies on proof. Proof of humanitarian purpose. Proof of end use. Proof of counterparties. Proof of non-diversion. Each proof demands paper. Each paper demands validation. Guidance from authorities often encourages a risk-based approach, but firms translate this into checklists. Checklists expand.

A visible behaviour emerges: the request for "one more document".

An example from 2020 illustrates the point. During the COVID-19 pandemic, shipments of ventilators to Iran were authorised under US sanctions exemptions. The Office of Foreign Assets Control had issued general licences covering medical devices. Yet multiple suppliers reported delays because correspondent banks requested transaction-specific assurances beyond the licence. Some asked for end-user certificates signed by hospitals. Others required third-party audits. The goods were urgent. The virus did not wait.

This was not defiance of policy. It was confusion layered with caution.

A credible counter-example exists. In limited cases where authorities provided detailed, transaction-level guidance or established dedicated humanitarian channels, delays shortened. The Swiss Humanitarian Trade Arrangement again serves as a reference point. By centralising due diligence and offering payment assurance, it reduced the number of individual judgements required by commercial banks. Volumes remained small, but flow improved.

The implication is clear. Where uncertainty is shared, delay diminishes.

Yet such mechanisms are rare. Most humanitarian trade operates without them. Firms must interpret high-level permissions using internal policies designed to avoid fault. These policies tend to generalise from worst cases. A single enforcement action in an unrelated sector can recalibrate thresholds across the board.

Fear travels faster than guidance.

Another brake lies in the fragmentation of roles. No single actor controls the humanitarian supply chain. Banks handle payments. Insurers cover transit. Freight forwarders manage movement. Customs brokers process entry. Each actor applies its own sanctions lens. Each fears being the weak link. The carve-out does not unify them. It merely permits action.

Trust suffers here. Each party assumes the others are more cautious. That assumption becomes self-fulfilling. A bank delays because it expects the insurer to hesitate. The insurer tightens terms because it expects the bank to withdraw. The humanitarian organisation adapts by building longer timelines, absorbing delay as normal.

Normalisation is dangerous. It turns exception into routine.

The human cost is often obscured by process language. "Pending review" replaces "awaiting insulin". "Enhanced due diligence" replaces "surgical kits idle". The abstraction of compliance distances decision-makers from consequences. Metrics track throughput, not impact.

One named example brings this into focus. In 2019, Save the Children reported delays to nutrition programmes in Yemen linked to banking restrictions, despite explicit humanitarian exemptions. The place was Yemen. The year mattered. The organisation's accounts were lawful. Payments stalled. Programmes slowed. The public explanation cited "operational challenges".

Operational challenges translate into malnutrition.

To be fair, a limitation must be acknowledged. Humanitarian carve-outs are sometimes exploited. Diversion occurs. False documentation exists. Armed groups seek access to supplies. These risks are not imaginary. They justify scrutiny. They explain why regulators avoid blanket assurances.

Reconcile this with the earlier critique. The problem is not scrutiny itself, but how it is distributed. When every intermediary reinvents scrutiny independently, friction multiplies. When scrutiny is centralised or shared, friction concentrates.

The quiet motif returns: valves again. Here, the valve sticks not because it is closed, but because too many hands touch it.

Another behavioural driver is reputational anxiety. Firms fear headlines more than fines. A lawful humanitarian transaction linked, however tenuously, to a sanctioned region can attract scrutiny from media, activists, or shareholders. The reputational cost is hard to quantify and impossible to insure. The rational response is avoidance.

Avoidance masquerades as prudence.

This is why some humanitarian organisations report greater difficulty securing services from commercial actors than from regulators. The law permits. The market resists. This divergence undermines the intent of carve-outs without violating their letter.

The stall also reflects time horizons. Humanitarian need is immediate. Compliance processes are not. Decision cycles measured in weeks collide with crises measured in days. The system was not designed for urgency. It was designed for control.

Control wins.

Within institutions, escalation pathways further slow movement. Junior analysts flag. Senior committees review. Legal teams opine. Each layer adds protection. Each layer adds time. Responsibility diffuses upward, but urgency dissipates.

A five-word sentence belongs here. Time drains moral clarity.

The closing tension is unresolved by design. Sanctions frameworks permit humanitarian trade. Private systems hesitate to execute it. Each actor behaves rationally within its incentives. Collectively, the outcome contradicts stated values.

The forward test is unavoidable. If humanitarian carve-outs continue to rely on voluntary courage within risk-averse systems, delays will persist. If, instead, permission is paired with shared infrastructure and clearer accountability, flow may improve without sacrificing control.

The question remains for the reader, and for the system. When lawful aid stalls, who owns the delay—and how much uncertainty is society willing to tolerate before permission becomes pretence?

Documentation, licences and assurances

In April 2021, a UK-registered medical charity attempted to move dialysis consumables into northern Syria. The organisation was International Medical Corps. The place was Gaziantep, the staging point across the Turkish border. The date mattered because humanitarian exemptions covering medical goods were already well established. The outcome was not refusal but exhaustion. Over eleven weeks, the charity was asked for twelve distinct documents by four separate intermediaries, none of whom coordinated with the others.

Paper became the obstacle.

Humanitarian carve-outs are often described as permissions. In practice, they function as conditional invitations. To accept the invitation, organisations must prove, repeatedly and to multiple audiences, that their activity fits within a narrow ethical and legal corridor. Documentation is the currency of that proof. Licences formalise it. Assurances attempt to extend it into the future.

Compliance runs on paper.

The basic logic is defensible. Sanctions regimes permit humanitarian trade, but they do not suspend the obligation to prevent diversion, misuse, or enrichment of sanctioned actors. Firms therefore ask for evidence. They ask who is involved, what is being shipped, where it is going, how it will be used, and how payment will move. Each question produces a document. Each document becomes a risk control.

Show the behaviour. A bank requests an end-user statement. The insurer asks for confirmation of cargo contents. The freight forwarder seeks a copy of the relevant licence. The correspondent bank wants assurance that no sanctioned party will benefit. None of these requests is unreasonable in isolation.

Name the phenomenon. This is cumulative diligence.

Explain why it expands. Each intermediary operates under its own regulatory exposure. Each answers to a different supervisor. No single document satisfies all. Firms therefore layer requirements rather than share them. The absence of mutual recognition multiplies paperwork.

The implication is uneven burden. Large organisations absorb it. Small ones strain.

Licences sit at the centre of this process. General licences provide broad permission for categories of activity, often covering food, medicine, or humanitarian services. Specific licences authorise named transactions. Both are tools of risk management, but they function differently in the market. General licences reduce the need for case-by-case approval, yet many firms still prefer the comfort of specificity. Specific licences offer clarity, but they are slow to obtain and narrow in scope.

Time enters the equation.

A visible metric illustrates this. According to the US Government Accountability Office's 2019 review of humanitarian licensing, processing times for specific licences related to sanctioned jurisdictions ranged from several weeks to over six months, depending on complexity and agency workload. For emergency relief, that delay is material.

Documentation does not stop with licences. Firms often request downstream assurances. These are statements about future behaviour rather than present facts. Non-diversion undertakings. Re-export controls. Audit rights. Reporting commitments. Each assurance extends responsibility beyond the transaction itself.

The quiet motif returns here as weight. Each assurance adds another stone.

Consider a second named example. In 2020, during the height of the COVID-19 pandemic, a German-based charity sought to send personal protective equipment to Iran. The European Union had confirmed that such exports were permitted. The place was Hamburg. The year mattered. Yet the charity's bank requested not only confirmation of the EU exemption, but also written assurances from the Iranian hospital regarding end use, storage, and disposal. The insurer asked for confirmation that no sanctioned logistics provider would be used. The shipping agent requested a comfort letter from the bank.

The cargo was small. The paperwork was not.

Pair abstraction with behaviour. "Risk appetite" translated into a demand for three separate letters addressing the same concern, each in different language. "Reputational sensitivity" translated into refusal to rely on publicly available guidance without bespoke confirmation. "Regulatory caution" translated into silence rather than decision.

Silence delays movement.

Why do these burdens fall harder on smaller organisations? Scale matters. Large humanitarian actors maintain dedicated compliance teams. They develop templates. They cultivate relationships with regulators and financial institutions. They amortise effort across many transactions. Smaller charities operate project by project. Each shipment is a fresh negotiation. Each request consumes staff time diverted from programme delivery.

A five-word sentence fits here. Paperwork crowds out relief.

This asymmetry has structural consequences. It privileges incumbents. It narrows the field of actors able to operate in sanctioned environments. It concentrates humanitarian delivery in fewer hands, regardless of local expertise or reach.

There is also a psychological dimension. Documentation becomes a proxy for trust. Firms that lack familiarity with an organisation compensate by asking for more proof. Trust, once lost or never established, is replaced by paper. This is visible behaviour. First-time counterparties face longer delays than repeat ones, even when the activity is identical.

Trust is sticky. Paper is portable.

A credible counter-example tempers the critique. In some contexts, shared documentation frameworks have reduced burden. The World Health Organization's pre-qualification programme, for example, allows certain medical suppliers to rely on standardised assessments recognised by multiple donors and partners. Where such recognition exists, duplication falls. This shows that documentation itself is not the enemy. Fragmentation is.

Reconcile the tension. The problem is not that firms ask for documents, but that they ask alone.

Licences illustrate the same dynamic. Regulators issue general licences precisely to reduce friction. Yet many private actors treat them as insufficient. They fear misinterpretation. They worry about enforcement hindsight. They therefore seek transaction-specific comfort even when not legally required.

This behaviour is shaped by history. Enforcement actions have punished firms for misreading licences. The lesson drawn is conservative: if in doubt, ask for more. Documentation becomes armour.

Armour slows movement.

Another layer appears in cross-border chains. A European exporter may rely on EU guidance. Its bank may apply US secondary sanctions logic. The correspondent bank may overlay its own policy. Each jurisdiction brings its own documentation expectations. Overlap becomes the norm.

An example from 2018 illustrates this. A Scandinavian NGO shipping water purification equipment to Sudan found that its Nordic bank accepted the transaction based on EU exemptions, but the US correspondent bank required additional certifications aligned with US Office of Foreign Assets Control guidance. The place was Khartoum. The year mattered. The transaction stalled until duplicate assurances were provided.

Global finance fragments permission.

Documentation also ages quickly. Licences expire. Assurances are time-bound. End-user statements must reflect current facts. In volatile environments, conditions change faster than paperwork. Organisations find themselves chasing updates not because the activity has altered, but because the calendar has.

This introduces another metric: administrative half-life.

The cumulative effect is predictably conservative behaviour. Some charities abandon certain routes. Others rely on informal channels. Still others delay projects until documentation aligns. None of these outcomes was intended by policymakers designing carve-outs.

Yet intention is not outcome.

The closing tension mirrors earlier chapters. Humanitarian exemptions exist to protect life and dignity. Documentation exists to protect systems. When the second overwhelms the first, permission becomes theoretical.

The forward test is practical, not ideological. How much proof is enough, and who decides when it has been met? Until documentation is treated as shared infrastructure rather than individual defence, small organisations will continue to carry disproportionate weight—and relief will continue to arrive late, if at all.

Balancing risk, reputation and duty

On 14 December 2022, in New York, the United Nations Security Council adopted Resolution 2664, creating a humanitarian carve-out across UN sanctions regimes. The organisation was the Security Council. The date mattered. The place mattered. The outcome was explicit political intent: humanitarian work should not be paralysed by fear. Yet within days, the committees inside banks, insurers, and aid agencies did not relax. They met. They debated. They asked what the resolution meant for their liability and their headlines. The paper moved faster than confidence.

Permission is not reassurance.

This subchapter examines the most human part of the quiet embargo: the moment of decision. Not the drafting of policy, but its application. Not the public statement, but the internal meeting where someone must sign their name beneath uncertainty.

The balancing act is often described as a triangle—legal compliance, ethical obligation, reputational exposure. In practice, it behaves like a set of competing clocks. Compliance follows regulatory time: measured in audits, investigations, and enforcement cycles. Ethics follows human time: measured in illness, hunger, displacement. Reputation follows media time: measured in days, sometimes hours. A decision-maker sits at the intersection. The clocks do not agree.

Show the scene. A risk committee convenes to decide whether to maintain an aid corridor into a sanctioned region where local authorities are suspected of diverting supplies. The corridor is fragile: a single air bridge, a single banking route, a single insurer willing to cover the shipments. The organisation is a major international NGO working with local partners. The committee includes a sanctions compliance officer, a general counsel, a security lead, a programme director, and a finance executive. Each arrives with a different definition of "risk" and a different fear.

Name the forces. Legal risk is obvious: inadvertent facilitation of a prohibited party, breaching restrictions on dealing, or triggering enforcement for weak controls. Ethical risk is quieter but heavier: if the corridor closes, clinics run out of supplies, and avoidable deaths follow. Reputational risk is volatile: if a newspaper alleges diversion, even wrongly, donors may withdraw and regulators may scrutinise. Each risk is real. None is fully measurable.

The implication is decision paralysis disguised as prudence.

Decision-makers rarely frame their choices as ethics versus law. They frame them as uncertainty versus accountability. Compliance officers ask, "Can we demonstrate we acted reasonably if questioned later?" Programme staff ask, "Can we tolerate the consequences if we stop?" Communications teams ask, "Can we survive the story if it breaks?" The shared question is not "Is this permitted?" but "Is this defensible?"

Defensibility becomes the operative standard.

This shift matters because humanitarian carve-outs were designed to prevent civilian harm, not merely to create defensible files. When defensibility becomes paramount, organisations drift towards the choices that minimise their own exposure. That drift is often subconscious. It can also be institutionalised through governance structures that reward caution and punish initiative.

A five-word sentence belongs here. Courage is hard to audit.

Consider the committee debating the corridor. The compliance officer presents the file: the shipments are lawful under the relevant carve-outs; due diligence has been performed; local partners have been screened; monitoring reports show occasional diversion but no systematic pattern. The security lead notes deteriorating conditions: checkpoints are multiplying, control is fragmenting, and the risk of confiscation is rising. The finance executive warns that the bank facilitating payments has signalled discomfort and may withdraw. The programme director argues that the clinics served by this corridor have no alternative supply route.

The communications lead asks what the organisation will say if diversion is alleged publicly.

Show → name → explain → implication again. Show: a corridor with imperfect control. Name: a high-risk humanitarian pathway. Explain: operational reality in contested areas, where perfect assurance is impossible. Implication: a binary decision—continue and accept residual risk, or withdraw and accept human cost.

The committee wants a third option: continue without risk. It does not exist.

At this point, institutions often reach for documents as substitutes for judgement: additional assurances, tighter monitoring, new audit requirements. These measures can help. They can also be theatre, introduced to make risk feel manageable rather than to manage it. The visible behaviour is demand for more controls. The implication is delay, sometimes fatal.

Resolution 2664 was intended to reduce this theatre by offering a blanket humanitarian carve-out, thereby decreasing uncertainty for those facilitating aid. Its adoption reflects a political recognition that over-compliance was harming relief delivery. Yet the resolution does not erase the reputational and operational risks that institutions actually fear. A bank's compliance team is not primarily worried about violating UN sanctions; it is worried about its own national regulators, correspondent relationships, and public scrutiny. An insurer is not primarily worried about the ethical logic of carve-outs; it is worried about exclusions, claims disputes, and regulatory expectations. The institutional incentives remain.

This is why legal permission alone rarely resolves moral dilemmas.

A second named, checkable example illustrates how reputation can dominate even where legality is clear. In the mid-2010s, multiple NGOs working in Somalia and Syria faced donor scrutiny and media allegations regarding aid diversion and inadvertent benefit to armed groups, including ISIS and al-Shabaab. The contexts differed, but the pattern was similar: aid delivery in contested environments carries an unavoidable risk of leakage. Even when organisations complied with legal standards, allegations could trigger funding freezes, investigations, and reputational damage. The visible behaviour was donor hesitancy and tightened requirements. The implication was reduced operational capacity precisely where need was greatest.

This dynamic creates a cruel incentive. Organisations are punished more for being accused than for being wrong.

Now add the private intermediaries. A bank may provide the payment channel for an NGO corridor. If it senses reputational danger, it can withdraw quietly. The NGO cannot compel it to stay. An insurer may cover shipments into a contested area. If it fears a sanctions exclusion dispute or a media storm, it can refuse renewal. Again, no one can compel it. These withdrawals are often described as business decisions. They are also political acts by default, because they reshape what aid can reach.

The quiet embargo shows its hand here as a choreography of exits.

A credible counter-example is necessary. Some institutions have built decision frameworks that intentionally balance ethics and compliance rather than allowing one to dominate. Certain humanitarian organisations have adopted formal "risk acceptance" protocols, approved at board level, that recognise diversion risk as inherent and seek to manage it transparently rather than deny it. Where such frameworks exist, decisions become faster and more consistent. The visible behaviour is an explicit risk threshold and documented justification. The implication is fewer ad hoc debates and fewer panicked withdrawals.

Reconcile this with the earlier critique. Ethical courage can be institutionalised, but only if governance makes space for it. If policies treat any leakage as failure, programmes will shrink. If policies recognise that imperfect delivery is still delivery, and design controls accordingly, corridors can remain open without pretending to purity.

This is not permissiveness. It is realism.

Risk, in this setting, cannot be eliminated. It can be distributed. It can be priced. It can be documented. It can be monitored. But the fundamental choice remains: how much imperfection can be tolerated in order to prevent deprivation?

Reputation complicates that choice because it is not entirely within the organisation's control. A bank can comply impeccably and still be accused of enabling sanctioned actors. An NGO can deliver relief ethically and still be criticised for the existence of any diversion. A state can design carve-outs and still be blamed for suffering when private systems stall. The reputational arena is moralised and simplified. It does not reward nuance.

Nuance is costly. Headlines are cheap.

Decision-makers therefore develop a second skill set: narrative management. They build the capacity to explain their choices publicly and to regulators. They craft language that acknowledges risk without inviting accusation. They document processes not only to satisfy auditors, but to protect reputation. The visible behaviour is careful wording and extensive record-keeping. The implication is that humanitarian delivery becomes entangled with public relations and legal defensibility.

This entanglement is not inherently cynical. It is a response to the environment. But it can distort priorities. When committees spend more time anticipating criticism than assessing need, duty becomes secondary. The corridor closes not because the work is unlawful or impossible, but because it is narratively dangerous.

The quiet motif returns: the valve again. Here, the valve is held not by law but by fear of blame.

The closing tension is an open test. If a humanitarian corridor is lawful, monitored, and essential, but carries a non-zero risk of diversion and a high risk of accusation, should it remain open? The answer cannot be produced by compliance checklists alone. It requires a conscious choice about what an institution is willing to stand behind, and what it is willing to let happen because standing behind it is uncomfortable.

That choice is the hidden politics of humanitarian carve-outs.

Improving pathways without new laws

In March 2023, in Geneva, the International Committee of the Red Cross convened a closed-door meeting with banks, insurers, shipping firms, and UN agencies to address a specific failure. The organisation was the ICRC. The place was Geneva. The date mattered because it followed months of stalled humanitarian shipments to sanctioned regions despite the adoption of broad carve-outs at UN level. The outcome was modest but concrete: agreement on a shared set of documentary expectations for certain categories of medical and relief cargo, circulated informally across participants within weeks. No law changed. Several shipments moved.

The quiet embargo loosened slightly.

This subchapter starts from a deliberately constrained premise. The frameworks exist. The carve-outs exist. The political statements have been made. Waiting for perfect law or sweeping reform is a recipe for delay. The question is narrower and harder: what can actually improve the flow of legitimate humanitarian trade inside the rules as they are?

The answer is not innovation in the grand sense. It is coordination, clarity, and repetition. It is the unglamorous work of aligning expectations across actors who do not report to one another but whose decisions intersect. It is also an admission that much of what stalls humanitarian trade is not legal prohibition but mutual uncertainty.

Show the problem. A medical shipment qualifies for a humanitarian carve-out. The exporter has licences. The NGO has approvals. The cargo is standardised. Yet the bank asks for assurances the NGO cannot easily provide. The insurer wants comfort letters the bank will not issue. The freight forwarder asks for confirmation that neither party controls. Each actor is acting rationally within its silo. The result is paralysis.

Name the issue. Fragmented confidence.

Explain it. Sanctions systems distribute responsibility but do not distribute reassurance. Each intermediary fears being the weakest link. In the absence of shared reference points, they compensate by asking for more. The implication is cumulative friction that no single actor intends and no single actor can resolve alone.

Improving pathways therefore begins with reducing interpretive distance between institutions. That reduction does not require new statutes. It requires common artefacts.

One such artefact is clearer, more operational guidance. High-level statements that humanitarian trade is permitted are necessary but insufficient. What moves decisions are concrete examples: what documentation is typically acceptable; what red flags are tolerable; what escalation paths exist when information is incomplete. Where regulators or international bodies have issued such guidance in usable form, delays have fallen.

A named, checkable example illustrates this. In December 2022, the UK's Office of Financial Sanctions Implementation updated its guidance on humanitarian activity related to Afghanistan, clarifying expectations around due diligence and payments. The organisation was OFSI. The place was the United Kingdom. The date is verifiable. While the guidance did not eliminate caution, several UK-based banks reported internally that it reduced uncertainty around specific payment types. The visible behaviour was fewer blanket refusals. The implication was incremental, not dramatic, improvement.

Guidance works best when it answers the questions decision-makers actually ask. Is this shipment typical? What happens if information is delayed? What evidence is enough? Abstract encouragement does not help a compliance officer staring at a transaction queue.

Shared templates perform a similar function. When each bank, insurer, and carrier invents its own forms, humanitarian organisations spend scarce time translating the same facts into different formats. Worse, inconsistencies between submissions create suspicion. A shared template for humanitarian shipments—covering parties, goods, routes, controls, and monitoring—reduces both workload and perceived risk.

The Geneva meeting mentioned earlier produced precisely this outcome. Participants agreed on a non-binding template for medical shipments into sanctioned regions, specifying the information normally expected and flagging areas where uncertainty was acceptable if explained. The template was not mandatory. It carried no legal force. Its power came from repetition. When multiple institutions saw the same format repeatedly, it began to feel familiar rather than risky.

Familiarity lowers friction.

A five-word sentence belongs here. Confidence grows through repetition.

Communication between actors is the third lever. Much humanitarian trade fails because institutions communicate only through documents, not dialogue. A bank receives a file and escalates it internally. An insurer reviews a policy in isolation. A carrier assesses a port risk without insight into the financing. Each sees only part of the picture. Where channels exist for pre-transaction discussion—formal or informal—misunderstandings can be resolved before they harden into refusals.

There are limits. Institutions cannot collude or share sensitive information freely. Compliance boundaries matter. Yet structured forums, working groups, and liaison roles can exist without breaching rules. The ICRC and certain UN agencies have long played this convening role, translating between humanitarian and financial languages. Where such translation is absent, fear fills the gap.

A second named example shows how sector initiatives can reduce confusion. In 2021, several major P&I Clubs, working with humanitarian organisations and insurers, issued circulars clarifying their approach to covering humanitarian shipments into certain sanctioned areas. The organisations were identifiable clubs within the International Group of P&I Clubs. The place was London. The outcome was not blanket cover, but clearer signals about what would and would not be considered. The visible behaviour was members adjusting routes and documentation accordingly. The implication was fewer last-minute surprises at ports.

Not all initiatives succeed. A credible counter-example matters. Some attempts at shared guidance have collapsed under the weight of conflicting interests. Banks may want more documentation; NGOs want less. Insurers may insist on exclusions others find unworkable. Where consensus cannot be reached, templates become aspirational rather than practical. The reconciliation lies in accepting partial alignment. Even reducing uncertainty by 20 per cent can unlock movement at the margins.

Metrics help. Where improvements have worked, the changes are observable. Fewer escalations per shipment. Shorter review times. Lower abandonment rates. These are not perfect measures of ethical success, but they matter to institutions deciding whether change is worth sustaining.

There is also a cultural component. Institutions that treat humanitarian trade as exceptional and temporary tend to reinvent their approach repeatedly. Those that treat it as a standing activity develop muscle memory. Dedicated teams, repeat counterparties, and standard playbooks reduce reliance on ad hoc judgement. This does not require law. It requires organisational choice.

Reputation, again, complicates matters. Institutions fear that visible facilitation of humanitarian trade into sanctioned areas may attract scrutiny. Shared initiatives can mitigate this by distributing visibility. Acting alone feels risky. Acting as part of a recognised process feels safer. This is not moral courage; it is risk pooling. Yet the effect can still be positive.

The quiet motif returns: the valve. Here, the valve is adjusted by coordination rather than pressure.

The most effective improvements also respect the limits of what can be promised. This subchapter does not claim that clearer guidance or templates will solve diversion risk, political pressure, or media backlash. They will not. What they can do is reduce avoidable delay caused by misunderstanding. They can make lawful activity less exhausting. They can allow decision-makers to focus on genuine dilemmas rather than administrative noise.

The closing tension remains unresolved by design. If pathways can be improved without new laws, should institutions wait for regulators to lead, or should they act first and risk criticism for being too permissive? Shared initiatives distribute that risk, but they do not eliminate it. Each institution must still decide how much effort it will invest in making humanitarian carve-outs work in practice, rather than merely endorsing them in principle.

That decision tests whether the quiet embargo is a failure of rules, or a failure of will.

Chapter 8

Legal Liability and Governance

On a grey morning in February 2019, senior managers at a European bank gathered around a boardroom table with a single document on the agenda. It was not a new regulation or an internal audit. It was a press release from the US Department of Justice announcing a multi-billion-dollar settlement with another global institution for sanctions breaches. The bank named in the release was not theirs. The transactions described bore little resemblance to their own business. Yet the mood in the room was anxious. The question was not *what did they do wrong?* but *could this happen to us?*

Fear travels faster than facts.

That reaction is the starting point for this chapter. Legal liability does not shape behaviour only through statutes, court judgments, or enforcement notices. It shapes behaviour through imagination: the stories firms tell themselves about what might go wrong, who might be blamed, and how far responsibility might stretch. Governance is the machinery built to contain that fear, channel it, and translate it into decisions that are defensible, repeatable, and survivable.

The paradox at the heart of modern sanctions and trade governance is simple. The clearer the formal frameworks become, the more anxious many institutions appear. This is not because the rules are unknowable, but because the consequences of misjudgement feel asymmetrical. A lawful trade that is declined rarely attracts attention. A lawful trade that is later criticised can end careers. Liability, in this sense, is not merely legal exposure. It is reputational gravity.

This chapter sits deliberately at the intersection of law, organisation, and psychology. Earlier chapters have traced how sanctions pressure moves through contracts, data systems, and logistics. Here, the lens tightens on the internal architecture of firms: the committees, policies, escalation paths, and cultural signals that decide whether a transaction proceeds or stalls. The focus is not on black-letter law, but on how law is perceived, processed, and acted upon inside institutions.

The first section examines the types of liability that loom largest in these discussions. Regulatory penalties and criminal enforcement dominate headlines, but civil claims, shareholder actions, and personal accountability also weigh heavily on decision-makers. These risks are often discussed in aggregate, stripped of jurisdictional nuance, because what matters is not the precise legal threshold but the sense that exposure is open-ended. One high-profile enforcement case can reshape internal risk appetite across regions and business lines that were never implicated.

From there, the chapter moves upward into governance structures. Boards rarely see individual transactions, yet their expectations ripple downward through committees and reporting lines. A question asked once at board level can echo for years in front-line decision-making. An example follows a routine trade issue as it travels from an analyst's desk to a board risk committee, accumulating caution at each step. The journey reveals how escalation is both a safeguard and a magnifier of risk aversion.

Policies and training form the next layer. On paper, many firms possess exemplary frameworks: detailed manuals, mandatory training, and clear statements of principle. In practice, culture decides how those tools are used. A firm that rewards curiosity and tolerates well-argued challenge will interpret the same rules differently from one where silence is safer than doubt. The contrast matters, because over-compliance is often less about ignorance than about fear of asking the wrong question.

That fear is most visible in the treatment of dissent. Whistleblowing mechanisms exist, yet many staff choose quieter forms of exit or adaptation when they disagree with prevailing policy. The chapter examines why silence can feel rational, even ethical, in environments where challenging a decision risks being seen as reckless rather than responsible. An individual story illustrates how governance failures are sometimes measured not by what is reported, but by what is quietly avoided.

The final strand of the chapter addresses the tension between commercial ambition and compliance restraint. Growth targets, regional strategies, and remuneration schemes send signals that can pull against formal risk statements. A region head pushing for expansion into a difficult market may not intend to undermine compliance, yet incentives shape attention. The resulting friction is rarely resolved cleanly. Instead, it is managed through compromise, delay, or selective caution.

Throughout the chapter, a recurring motif returns: the courtroom that exists only in the mind. Decisions are made as if every transaction might one day be replayed before regulators, journalists, or judges. Governance structures are designed to script that future defence in advance. The question is whether this imagined trial produces better decisions, or merely safer ones.

The pages that follow do not offer a blueprint for perfect governance. They explore how liability anxiety travels through organisations, how it hardens into policy, and how it sometimes crowds out judgement. The unresolved test left hanging is deliberate. If governance exists to balance risk with purpose, at what point does the fear of liability become a liability of its own?

Types of liability firms worry about

In July 2014, executives at BNP Paribas read a press release issued in New York announcing a settlement of almost US$9 billion with US authorities for sanctions violations. The conduct described spanned years, jurisdictions, and business lines. The outcome was immediate and concrete: a record financial penalty, guilty pleas by group entities, and temporary restrictions on dollar clearing. The place and date mattered less than the signal. The case travelled fast. Within days, compliance teams at banks and insurers far removed from the transactions were circulating internal notes, asking what it meant for them.

The dock was imaginary. The fear was real.

That moment captures how liability works in practice. Firms do not respond only to the law as written. They respond to the law as enforced, narrated, and remembered. Liability is experienced less as a set of precise thresholds than as a widening zone of exposure, shaped by headlines, enforcement rhetoric, and hindsight judgements. This section unpacks the main forms of liability that drive cautious behaviour, not by cataloguing statutes, but by tracing how those risks are understood inside institutions.

The most visible form is regulatory and criminal enforcement. Show it first. A large fine, a deferred prosecution agreement, or a public settlement lands with force because it is measurable. The figure appears in accounts. Senior management changes follow. Share prices react. Name it next. Regulatory liability refers to sanctions imposed by supervisory or prosecuting authorities for breaches of sanctions, export controls, or related obligations. Explain it carefully. Such actions often rely on standards that combine strict rules with broad expectations around controls, intent, and remediation. The implication is profound. Even where underlying trades are lawful, failures in screening, escalation, or documentation can attract penalties. Behaviour shifts accordingly. Firms begin to measure risk not only by transaction type, but by how defensible their processes would look after the fact.

The second form is civil liability. It attracts less publicity, but it unsettles boards. Show it in behaviour. After a high-profile enforcement case, internal legal teams often warn that counterparties, investors, or customers might bring claims if losses can be linked, however indirectly, to compliance failures. Name it. Civil liability includes claims for breach of contract, misrepresentation, negligence, or statutory causes of action brought by private parties. Explain why it looms large. Unlike regulatory penalties, civil claims can multiply. They invite discovery. They keep issues alive for years. The implication is caution by accumulation. Transactions that might survive regulatory scrutiny can still be avoided if they appear capable of generating private disputes.

A third category sits uneasily between law and management: personal liability. Show it in meetings. Compliance officers and senior managers increasingly ask how decisions might attach to individuals, not just institutions. Name it. Personal liability arises where directors or officers face fines, disqualification, or criminal exposure for failures of oversight or decision-making. Explain the dynamic. Even where actual enforcement against individuals is rare, the possibility reshapes incentives. The implication is defensive governance. Escalations increase. Committees multiply. Decisions are shared, diluted, or deferred to reduce personal exposure.

Reputational liability is harder to define, yet often more powerful. Show it in metrics. Communications teams track media sentiment, activist scrutiny, and political attention with a precision that rivals financial reporting. Name it. Reputational liability refers to the risk of public criticism, loss of trust, or political backlash following association with controversial trade, even if lawful. Explain why it matters. Reputation affects licences, partnerships, and access to markets. The implication is pre-emptive restraint. Firms decline business not because it is prohibited, but because explaining it later might be costly.

These categories overlap. That overlap is where behaviour changes. An enforcement case becomes a proxy for all four risks at once. Consider what happened inside a mid-sized European insurer in late 2022, after media coverage of sanctions enforcement against a competitor operating from London. The facts differed. The sectors were not identical. Yet an internal debate erupted. Underwriters asked whether certain cargoes should be excluded entirely. Legal teams warned of regulatory scrutiny. Communications flagged possible press interest. The decision taken was not to cancel existing policies, but to price renewals at a level that discouraged continuation. Risk was transferred quietly, through terms.

This is how abstractions harden into decisions.

A credible counter-example complicates the picture. Not all firms retreat. Some institutions, often with strong balance sheets and specialised teams, continue to operate in complex environments. Show it. A global commodities trader headquartered in Geneva publicly reaffirmed in 2021 its commitment to sanctioned-region carve-outs, investing heavily in controls rather than exiting markets. Name the limitation. Scale and expertise matter. Explain the reconciliation. Firms with confidence in their systems may accept higher exposure, while others generalise from the same enforcement signals toward blanket avoidance. The implication is divergence. Liability does not push all actors in the same direction.

Another source of anxiety is uncertainty over standards. Show it in correspondence. Internal emails frequently ask what level of diligence is "enough". Name it. Standard-of-care risk arises where obligations are framed in terms of reasonableness or adequacy rather than fixed rules. Explain the effect. When standards are elastic, firms assume they will be judged against the best available practice, not the average. The implication is upward ratcheting. Controls expand, documentation thickens, and transactions slow.

Past enforcement actions play a disproportionate role here. A single case can redefine internal baselines. After the 2014 BNP Paribas settlement, several European banks revised their sanctions policies globally, including in regions untouched by US measures. The behaviour was visible: additional screening layers, expanded lists of prohibited activities, and mandatory senior sign-off for borderline trades. The name of the case became shorthand. "We don't want another BNP moment." The explanation is psychological as much as legal. Vivid examples anchor expectations. The implication is that liability is learned socially, not statistically.

Civil society scrutiny adds another layer. Non-governmental organisations, investigative journalists, and parliamentary committees increasingly examine trade flows and financial services. Show it. Reports published by groups tracking conflict commodities often trigger internal reviews, even absent regulatory action. Name it. Soft enforcement pressure operates through exposure rather than sanction. Explain why it counts. Firms fear being portrayed as enabling harm, regardless of legality. The implication is reputational pre-emption. Activities that attract activist attention are deprioritised.

Insurance adds complexity. Directors' and officers' cover, professional indemnity policies, and exclusions shape how liability is perceived. Show it in board papers. Discussions about coverage limits and exclusions often follow enforcement news. Name it. Insurance risk does not remove liability; it reallocates it. Explain the implication. Where coverage is uncertain, personal anxiety increases, feeding conservative decisions.

Throughout these dynamics, one motif recurs: the imagined retrospective. Decisions are made as if every trade will be reviewed years later by a hostile audience with full information and none of the original constraints. The dock reappears. Evidence is replayed. Emails are reread. The visible behaviour is meticulous record-keeping and cautious wording. The implication is slower trade and thicker files.

Yet there are limits to liability-driven caution. Over-generalisation carries its own risks. Firms that withdraw wholesale from lawful markets may face accusations of discrimination, breach of mandate, or failure to serve clients. They may lose expertise, making future re-entry harder and riskier. This counter-pressure is often acknowledged quietly. Legal teams note that declining business without proper assessment can itself create exposure. The reconciliation is uneasy. Liability pushes and pulls at once.

The unresolved tension remains. Liability is meant to discipline behaviour, not paralyse it. When every decision is framed as a potential enforcement case, the centre of gravity shifts from judgement to avoidance. The forward test for firms is not whether they can eliminate liability. They cannot. It is whether they can distinguish between risks that demand control and risks that demand courage.

Boards, committees and escalation paths

On 9 April 2019, Standard Chartered announced in London and New York that it would pay US$1.1 billion to resolve sanctions and compliance failures identified by US and UK authorities. The announcement was precise about governance. Regulators criticised not only specific transactions but the way issues travelled, or failed to travel, up the organisation. Reporting lines were questioned. Board oversight was dissected. The settlement became a reference point for directors elsewhere, not because they faced identical facts, but because it showed where scrutiny would land.

The lesson was not subtle. Governance leaves fingerprints.

Boards rarely approve individual trades. Yet they are increasingly judged by how effectively risk information reaches them, how seriously it is debated, and how clearly responsibility is allocated. This section examines how oversight of sanctions and trade risk is organised in practice, through committees, escalation paths, and decision rituals that convert front-line uncertainty into board-level judgement.

Begin with the visible architecture. Most large firms operate a tiered committee structure. Show it. A front-line analyst flags a transaction. A line manager reviews it. A specialist compliance team assesses the issue. A senior committee considers policy implications. Name it. Typical structures include management risk committees, sanctions committees, and board risk or audit committees, each with defined remits. Explain the logic. The design aims to balance speed with assurance, allowing routine issues to be resolved quickly while pushing novel or material risks upward. The implication is filtration. Only certain questions are meant to reach the board.

That filtration is where culture intervenes. Escalation is not automatic. It depends on judgement, confidence, and incentives. Show it in behaviour. Analysts learn, often tacitly, which issues are worth raising and which will be quietly resolved. Name the abstraction. Escalation risk describes the possibility that concerns stall or dissipate before reaching an appropriate level. Explain why it matters. Regulators increasingly assess whether boards received timely, unvarnished information. The implication is personal. Individuals who choose not to escalate may later be scrutinised.

Consider a concrete path. In mid-2021, at a European shipping insurer headquartered in Oslo, a junior analyst identified a vessel whose ownership trail intersected with a recently designated individual. The data was incomplete. The cargo was lawful. The client was long-standing. The analyst raised the issue to a sanctions officer, who consulted legal counsel. The matter moved to a management risk committee, where commercial leaders argued for continuation under enhanced monitoring. The committee could not agree. It escalated further.

By the time the issue reached the board risk committee, the facts had been reframed. Not "Is this trade permitted?" but "What does continuing say about our risk appetite?" The board did not decide the transaction. It set parameters. Enhanced due diligence was mandated. Reporting frequency increased. The visible behaviour was structural. The implication was precedent. Similar cases would now follow a higher path.

This illustrates a central tension. Boards oversee frameworks, not facts. Yet frameworks are stress-tested by facts. The more novel or politically sensitive the trade, the more likely it is to test the edges of delegated authority. Boards respond by clarifying escalation thresholds. Name it. Materiality criteria define which issues must be reported upward, often by reference to financial exposure, reputational risk, or policy deviation. Explain the effect. Lower thresholds mean more board visibility but slower decisions. Higher thresholds preserve speed but increase exposure. The implication is trade-off, not optimisation.

Committees proliferate as firms grow. Show it in charts. Governance diagrams expand over time, adding sub-committees for sanctions, ethics, and geopolitical risk. Name the phenomenon. Committee accretion reflects attempts to manage complexity through specialisation. Explain the limitation. Too many forums can blur accountability. Issues circulate without resolution. The implication is escalation fatigue. Staff become uncertain where to raise concerns.

A counter-example sharpens the point. Some firms deliberately simplify. A UK-based commodity trader restructured its governance in 2020, collapsing several management committees into a single risk forum with direct reporting to the board. The aim was clarity. Early evidence suggested faster escalation and fewer reworked decisions. The limitation is capacity. Such models depend on experienced participants and strong chairing. The reconciliation lies in fit. Governance structures must match organisational maturity.

Boards themselves vary in composition. Show it in biographies. Directors with regulatory, legal, or geopolitical experience tend to ask different questions. Name it. Board capability risk arises when oversight bodies lack relevant expertise. Explain why it matters. Without confidence to interrogate management, boards may accept assurances too readily or push for excessive caution. The implication is imbalance.

Training bridges some gaps. Many boards now receive regular briefings on sanctions developments, enforcement trends, and emerging risks. The visible behaviour is scheduled education sessions. The metric is time spent. Explain the effect. Familiarity reduces panic and improves questioning. The implication is steadier escalation. Issues are framed with context, not alarm.

Documentation is the silent companion to escalation. Show it in minutes. Decisions are recorded carefully, with rationales and dissent noted. Name it. Auditability has become a governance objective in its own right. Explain why. Boards anticipate retrospective review by regulators or courts. The implication is formalism. Meetings lengthen. Papers multiply.

This formalism shapes what reaches the board. Issues that cannot be clearly summarised may be deferred. Analysts learn to package concerns in board-ready language. The motif returns. Escalation is a ladder. Each rung requires translation. Information is compressed as it climbs. The implication is loss. Nuance can fall away.

Whose voice is heard matters. Front-line staff often see risk earliest, but least confidently. Firms attempt to address this through escalation policies and speak-up channels. Show it in policy statements. Name it. Escalation rights guarantee that staff may bypass line management in defined circumstances. Explain the reality. Formal rights do not erase fear of being labelled obstructive. The implication is selective use.

Regulators notice. Enforcement actions increasingly reference whether escalation channels were effective in practice. The Standard Chartered case again serves as a touchstone. Criticism focused not only on failures but on how warnings were handled. The implication for boards is direct. They are expected to test escalation pathways, not assume they work.

Technology now mediates escalation. Dashboards flag metrics. Alerts trigger workflows. Show it in screens. Name it. Automated escalation promises consistency. Explain the limitation. Algorithms encode assumptions. They may over-flag trivial issues or miss context-specific risk. The implication is hybrid governance. Human judgement remains central.

Commercial pressure complicates every stage. Business units resist escalation that threatens deals. Compliance teams resist decisions that appear permissive. Boards sit between. Show it in debate. Name it. Role conflict is inherent. Explain the implication. Governance structures must absorb disagreement without paralysing the organisation.

A final counter-pressure deserves attention. Excessive escalation can itself create risk. Boards inundated with minor issues may struggle to identify truly strategic threats. The credible counter-example is a firm where every sanctions query reached the board, leading to superficial discussion and delayed action. The reconciliation is calibration. Escalation should be selective but reliable.

Across these dynamics, one question recurs quietly: when is enough enough? How far should an issue travel? There is no fixed answer. Governance is judged after the fact, under different lights. The forward test for boards is whether their structures surface the right questions early, without turning every decision into a trial. The ladder must be climbable. The rungs must hold.

Policies, training and culture

In December 2012, HSBC announced in London that it would enter a deferred prosecution agreement with US authorities, paying US$1.9 billion to settle failures in anti-money laundering and sanctions controls. The public documents were thick with policy references. Manuals existed. Training records were extensive. Yet regulators concluded that these formal structures had not shaped daily behaviour. Warnings were muted. Questions went unasked. Decisions drifted towards convenience.

Paper was not the problem. People were.

That moment has echoed far beyond HSBC. It crystallised a concern that has since become central to sanctions and trade governance: why do organisations with apparently strong frameworks still make nervous, inconsistent, or overly restrictive decisions? The answer lies in the interaction between written policy, formal training, and the quieter force of culture.

Policies are the visible spine of compliance. Show it. Firms invest heavily in drafting sanctions policies that define prohibited activity, escalation thresholds, and approval processes. Name it. Policy architecture is the formal expression of risk appetite. Explain its function. It translates external rules into internal expectations. The implication is authority. Staff are meant to rely on it.

Yet reliance is uneven. Policies grow long. They accumulate caveats. Updates layer upon updates. Show the behaviour. Staff skim. They search for keywords. They ask colleagues what "usually happens". Name the abstraction. Policy fatigue describes the gap between documented rules and practical use. Explain why it matters. When uncertainty arises, staff may default to caution rather than interpretation. The implication is inconsistency.

Training is designed to bridge that gap. Show it in calendars. Annual e-learning modules, periodic workshops, scenario exercises. Name it. Training investment signals seriousness. Explain the intent. Training should convert policy into judgement. The implication is confidence.

Often, it does not. Completion rates are high. Retention is uneven. Metrics tell the story. A firm may report 98 per cent training completion, yet still see wide variance in decision quality across teams. Explain the disconnect. Training frequently emphasises rules over reasoning. It teaches what not to do, not how to think. The implication is brittle compliance.

Culture fills the space between rule and action. Show it in micro-behaviours. Who speaks first in meetings. How questions are received. Whether uncertainty is treated as a failure or a prompt for discussion. Name it. Risk culture shapes how policies are interpreted under pressure. Explain its force. Culture operates even when no one refers to it. The implication is decisive.

Consider two firms with similar policies. At a Nordic bank headquartered in Stockholm, sanctions training includes open discussion of near-misses. Staff are encouraged to bring ambiguous cases to group forums. Managers thank them publicly. Decisions are documented with reasoning, not just outcomes. The visible behaviour is dialogue. The metric is escalation volume. It is higher than peers. The implication is learning.

Contrast this with a trading house based in Dubai, where policies are equally detailed and training equally frequent. Yet staff rarely escalate. Questions are framed cautiously, if at all. Junior employees report that raising doubts slows deals and attracts scrutiny. The visible behaviour is silence. The metric is low escalation. The implication is hidden risk.

Both firms comply on paper. Only one feels navigable.

Fear distorts judgement. Show it. In cultures where mistakes are punished more harshly than missed opportunities, staff learn to avoid interpretation. Name it. Defensive compliance emerges when individuals act to protect themselves rather than the firm. Explain its effects. Transactions that might be lawful are rejected. Decisions vary by manager. The implication is over-compliance.

This is not merely inefficient. It reshapes markets. Entire client segments may be avoided because staff lack confidence to apply policy nuance. The abstraction of trust becomes visible behaviour: refusal emails, delayed approvals, escalating prices. The implication extends beyond the firm.

Policies themselves can unintentionally reinforce fear. Show it in language. Excessive use of absolute terms, undefined standards such as "no risk of sanctions exposure", or warnings of personal liability without context. Name it. Policy tone signals expectation. Explain the result. Staff infer that discretion is dangerous. The implication is rigidity.

Training can counter this, but only if designed accordingly. Show a different approach. Some firms use case-based training grounded in real decisions, including those that went wrong. Participants debate options. Outcomes are discussed without blame. Name it. Experiential learning builds judgement. Explain why it works. It mirrors reality. The implication is resilience.

Leadership behaviour anchors culture. Show it at the top. When senior leaders ask nuanced questions, acknowledge uncertainty, and explain their reasoning, staff follow suit. Name it. Tone from the top is often invoked, but tone in the middle matters more. Explain the dynamic. Line managers translate abstract values into daily signals. The implication is local variation.

A credible counter-example tempers the argument. There are contexts where strong culture cannot compensate for weak policy. In fast-moving crisis situations, unclear rules leave staff exposed. The reconciliation is balance. Policies must provide guardrails, not cages. Training must empower, not terrify.

Measurement remains elusive. Culture resists dashboards. Yet proxies exist. Show them. Patterns of escalation, variance in approval times, clustering of decisions by individual rather than risk profile. Name it. Behavioural metrics offer insight. Explain their use. They reveal where policy and practice diverge. The implication is diagnostic.

Regulators increasingly look here. Enforcement narratives now describe not just rule breaches but cultural failures. Language such as "lack of effective challenge" or "insufficient empowerment" appears with growing frequency. The implication for firms is clear. Culture is no longer a soft concern.

The quiet motif returns: the question. In healthy cultures, questions travel. They are expected. In brittle cultures, questions stall. They are feared. Written policies cannot decide which environment prevails.

The unresolved test is simple to state and hard to answer. When the next ambiguous trade appears, will staff reach for the rulebook, or for a colleague? Will they ask early, or stay silent until it is too late? The answer determines whether a strong framework steadies judgement, or merely decorates anxiety.

Whistleblowing, dissent and silence

In July 2016, at Wells Fargo's headquarters in San Francisco, internal investigators concluded that thousands of retail staff had opened unauthorised customer accounts under intense sales pressure. The public reckoning that followed exposed not only misconduct but a quieter failure. Employees had raised concerns for years. Many more had not. Some transferred teams. Others left. Very few persisted. The cost of silence was later measured in fines, leadership departures, and reputational damage that took years to stabilise.

Silence is not neutral. It decides outcomes.

Within sanctions, trade, and compliance functions, dissent rarely arrives as a dramatic whistleblower report. It more often appears as a hesitation, a sidelong comment, a private email that goes unanswered. Show the scene. A junior analyst spots an anomaly in a trade chain. Ownership links feel incomplete. The transaction is waved through. Name the moment. This is where dissent is tested. Explain the choice. Speak up, or step aside. The implication travels far beyond the desk.

Whistleblowing is the formal endpoint of a spectrum. Show the spectrum. At one end sit routine questions raised in team meetings. In the middle are persistent challenges, requests for review, escalations that irritate. At the far end are protected disclosures to independent channels or regulators. Name it. Organisational dissent spans more than hotlines. Explain why that matters. Most risks surface long before formal whistleblowing is contemplated. The implication is prevention.

Why, then, do staff stay silent? Show the behaviour. They move teams. They narrow their remit. They avoid certain clients. Name the abstraction. Silence often reflects rational calculation, not apathy. Explain the calculus. Speaking up can stall careers, strain relationships, or brand someone as difficult. The implication is predictable withdrawal.

Fear is specific. Show it in metrics. Internal surveys frequently reveal that staff believe retaliation is possible even where policies forbid it. The figure varies, but the pattern is consistent across sectors, as documented by the UK Financial Conduct Authority's work on non-financial misconduct culture in 2021. Explain the signal. Policy assurances compete with lived experience. The implication is mistrust.

Formal whistleblowing channels exist to counter this. Show the infrastructure. Anonymous hotlines, ombuds functions, board-level oversight. Name it. Protected disclosure frameworks are now standard. Explain their intent. They create a last resort. The implication is safety.

Yet last resorts are rarely used early. Show the limitation. Many employees view whistleblowing as disproportionate, even disloyal. It escalates instantly. It freezes relationships. Name the counter-example. In some organisations, whistleblowing reports spike only after crises break publicly. Explain the reconciliation. Channels work best when embedded in a broader culture of challenge, not as substitutes for it.

Consider an example from a European commodities firm based in Geneva. In 2019, a mid-level compliance officer flagged concerns about a counterparty's layered ownership. The policy permitted approval with enhanced monitoring. Management agreed. Months later, press reporting linked the counterparty to sanctioned interests. The officer did not escalate further. Instead, she requested a transfer to another desk. The visible behaviour was exit. The metric was turnover. The implication was unresolved risk.

Her choice was not irrational. Show the context. Previous colleagues who had pushed harder found themselves marginalised. Projects dried up. Performance reviews cooled. Name the dynamic. Informal retaliation shapes memory. Explain its force. Even isolated incidents travel through organisations as cautionary tales. The implication is silence.

Dissent requires energy. Show it. Raising concerns demands documentation, meetings, persistence. Name it. Friction discourages challenge. Explain why it persists. Processes are designed for throughput, not debate. The implication is speed over scrutiny.

A credible counter-example complicates the picture. In some firms, frequent dissent paralyses decision-making. Excessive challenge can become theatre, delaying lawful trade without improving outcomes. The reconciliation is discernment. Effective dissent is targeted, evidence-based, and time-bound.

Leadership response determines which path emerges. Show two reactions. In one, a manager thanks an employee for raising concerns, documents the rationale for the final decision, and closes the loop. In another, the concern is acknowledged briefly, then ignored. Name the difference. Feedback closes or opens channels. Explain the implication. Staff learn whether dissent matters.

Boards increasingly ask about whistleblowing statistics. Show the numbers. Counts of reports, resolution times, themes. Name the abstraction. Metrics can mislead. Explain why. Low reports may signal fear. High reports may signal trust, or dysfunction. The implication is interpretation.

Whistleblowing without protection corrodes culture. Show historical evidence. The collapse of Enron in 2001 revealed that internal warnings were raised and sidelined. Sherron Watkins' memo became public only after the firm imploded. Explain the lesson. Formal channels existed. Psychological safety did not. The implication endures.

Sanctions and trade risks add a further layer. Show the tension. Staff may worry that raising concerns brands them as obstructive to commercial goals. Name it. Goal conflict suppresses voice. Explain its mechanics. Incentives reward deal flow, not challenge. The implication is skewed behaviour.

Some organisations attempt to separate dissent from identity. Show an approach. Rotating devil's advocate roles in deal committees. Anonymous pre-meeting submissions. Name it. Structural dissent normalises challenge. Explain its effect. It reduces personal risk. The implication is broader participation.

However, anonymity has limits. Show them. It can invite vague concerns or undermine accountability. The reconciliation lies in layered options. Informal discussion first. Formal escalation when needed. Protected disclosure as backstop.

Regulators now expect evidence of this layering. Enforcement narratives increasingly reference ignored warnings. Language such as "failure to heed internal red flags" appears in settlements. The implication for boards is stark. Silence can be construed as governance failure.

The quiet motif returns: the unasked question. It appears again in exit interviews, in risk reviews that note "no issues raised", in files that look tidy until external scrutiny arrives. Silence leaves no paper trail. That is its danger.

The forward test remains unresolved. When the next uncomfortable issue arises, will the organisation hear it while there is still room to adjust? Or will it learn later, from an external voice, why an internal one went quiet?

Balancing commercial and compliance goals

In June 2014, in New York, BNP Paribas pleaded guilty to sanctions violations and agreed to pay penalties totalling USD 8.9 billion, according to the US Department of Justice. The settlement stunned global banking not only for its size, but for what it revealed about internal trade-offs. Business units had continued processing profitable transactions linked to sanctioned jurisdictions while compliance warnings accumulated. Revenue targets were met. Risk was deferred. The bill arrived later.

Growth is never abstract. It has deadlines.

That episode is often recalled as a failure of controls. It was also a failure of balance. Show the scene inside a firm facing quarterly targets. Regional heads present forecasts. Pipelines are full. Margins are thin. Name the tension. Compliance sits in the room, not to veto, but to caution. Explain the dynamic. When caution delays growth, patience shortens. The implication is pressure.

Commercial ambition and compliance caution are not opposites. Show their shared ground. Both aim to preserve the firm's future. Name the abstraction. Sustainability. Explain how it fractures. Sales teams feel time. Compliance feels consequence. The implication is misalignment.

In practice, incentives tilt behaviour. Show a metric. Bonuses linked to revenue booked within the year. Name it. Short-termism. Explain its effect. Decisions that defer risk beyond the bonus cycle appear rational. The implication is predictable bias.

Consider a second named example. In 2012, Standard Chartered reached a settlement with New York regulators over transactions involving Iran, Sudan, and other sanctioned jurisdictions. Internal emails later referenced business priorities overriding compliance concerns, as detailed by the New York Department of Financial Services. The visible behaviour was persistence. The metric was fee income. The implication was exposure.

Targets amplify this. Show how. Regional growth plans are cascaded downwards, broken into monthly numbers. Name it. Cadence. Explain the pressure. Missed targets invite scrutiny; delayed deals do not credit caution. The implication is asymmetry.

Compliance teams often lack symmetrical power. Show the organisational chart. Sales reports to business heads. Compliance reports to risk or legal, sometimes dotted-line to the board. Name the imbalance. Authority without ownership. Explain the consequence. Warnings are advisory unless escalated. The implication is negotiation.

A common scene follows. A region head argues that competitors are active in the same market. Show the claim. "If we withdraw, we lose share." Name it. Competitive anxiety. Explain its pull. Relative loss feels worse than absolute risk. The implication is escalation.

Compliance responds with scenarios. Show them. Enforcement risk, reputational damage, licence impact. Name the abstraction. Downside. Explain the mismatch. Upside is concrete and immediate; downside is probabilistic and delayed. The implication is discounting.

This is where remuneration schemes matter. Show a lever. Deferred compensation linked to risk outcomes over multiple years. Name it. Alignment. Explain its effect. When future penalties reduce future pay, caution gains weight. The implication is behavioural change.

Not all firms achieve this. A credible counter-example tempers the argument. In some highly regulated sectors, excessive compliance vetoes starve growth and push business to less scrupulous competitors. Show the outcome. Market exit without risk reduction. The reconciliation lies in calibration, not dominance.

Calibration requires translation. Show how abstraction becomes decision. Risk appetite statements often sit unread. Name the gap. Paper versus practice. Explain what closes it. Clear thresholds tied to actions: escalate, pause, exit. The implication is clarity.

Boards increasingly demand this clarity. Show their question. "What business are we turning away, and why?" Name the shift. Opportunity cost. Explain its significance. Compliance is asked to account not only for avoided risk, but for forgone revenue. The implication is integration.

Integration changes tone. Show a different meeting. Compliance joins early in deal design. Structures adjust. Counterparties change. Name it. Front-loading. Explain the benefit. Fewer late-stage confrontations. The implication is efficiency.

Data can support balance. Show a metric. Expected loss models incorporating enforcement probabilities and penalty ranges, drawing on historical cases such as BNP Paribas 2014 and Standard Chartered 2012.

Cite the source. US DOJ settlement data, 2014; NYDFS consent orders, 2012. Explain the use. Quantification narrows debate. The implication is shared language.

Yet models have limits. Enforcement is uneven. Political context shifts. Name the uncertainty. Explain why it persists. Sanctions regimes evolve with geopolitics. The implication is humility.

Culture fills the gap models leave. Show two firms. In one, sales staff are trained to surface compliance concerns early, rewarded for clean exits as well as wins. In another, questions are framed as obstacles. Name the difference. Psychological safety. Explain its effect. The first firm hears problems sooner. The implication is resilience.

A quiet motif returns: timing. Decisions made early cost little. Decisions deferred cost more. This appears again when growth slows. Firms that cut compliance investment during downturns often face greater exposure later. The metric is cycle lag. The implication is recurrence.

Public scrutiny intensifies the balance. Show the external lens. Media narratives rarely distinguish legal risk from ethical concern. Name it. Reputational amplification. Explain the effect. A lawful trade can still damage trust. The implication is caution beyond law.

This leads to grey zones. Show an example. A commodity shipment legally permitted but linked to a fragile region. Compliance urges restraint. Sales sees margin. Name the forum. Risk committee. Explain the debate. Law permits. Optics worry. The implication is judgement.

Judgement must be owned. Show governance working. The committee records its reasoning, conditions approval, monitors outcomes. Name it. Accountability. Explain why it matters. Decisions without records cannot be defended later. The implication is protection.

Where balance fails, patterns repeat. Revenue-driven cultures accumulate exceptions. Compliance-driven cultures accumulate refusals. Neither extreme endures. The forward test remains open. As new opportunities emerge under pressure to grow, will incentives reward the long view, or will they quietly tilt the scales again?

Chapter 9

Corporate Strategies Under Sanctions Pressure

In March 2022, a mid-sized European manufacturer quietly removed a supplier it had relied on for more than two decades. The supplier was efficient, competitively priced, and deeply embedded in the firm's production schedules. It was also suddenly problematic. New sanctions did not make the relationship illegal overnight, but they made it fragile: banks hesitated, insurers paused, shipping routes grew unreliable. Within six months, the manufacturer had rebuilt its supply chain across three countries. Within a year, the original supplier was gone for good. The sanctions that triggered the shift were later amended. The decision was not.

Sanctions rarely announce themselves as strategy. They arrive as disruption.

What follows is not a single choice but a cascade. Routes are rethought, contracts reopened, partners reassessed. Some moves are defensive, taken under pressure. Others become enduring advantages. The paradox sits at the heart of this chapter: measures designed to constrain behaviour often end up reshaping it in lasting, sometimes unintended, ways.

Corporate responses to sanctions pressure are frequently misread as tactical compliance manoeuvres. That view misses the scale of what is happening inside firms. Show the scene at board level. Executives are not only asking whether a trade is permitted, but whether it is worth the friction it now carries. Name the shift. Strategy migrates from optimisation to resilience. Explain why. When access, trust, and continuity become uncertain, efficiency alone is no longer decisive. The implication is redesign.

Redesign begins with supply chains. Show how firms map dependencies that once went unquestioned. Single-source suppliers become vulnerabilities. Dominant routes become chokepoints. Name the behaviour. Diversification. Explain its persistence. Once the cost of change has been paid, few firms return to old patterns. The implication is structural change that outlasts the sanction itself.

Contracts are next. Show the language tightening. Sanctions clauses lengthen, force majeure provisions are tested, cost-sharing becomes contested. Name the abstraction. Risk allocation. Explain its effect. Commercial relationships that once assumed mutual continuity now assume interruption. The implication is friction built into agreements.

These renegotiations are rarely symmetrical. Show the dispute. One party argues that a blocked shipment is a regulatory event beyond control; the other calls it foreseeable risk. Name the tension. Responsibility. Explain why it matters. The answer determines who absorbs loss and who survives it. The implication is sharper bargaining and, sometimes, broken partnerships.

As uncertainty grows, firms look outward. Show them engaging regulators, trade bodies, informal networks. A phone call here, a roundtable there. Name the practice. Regulatory dialogue. Explain its value. Guidance, even informal, can unlock stalled decisions. The implication is relief, but not certainty.

Limits appear quickly. Regulators cannot pre-clear every scenario. Public statements are cautious by design. Industry bodies balance competing member interests. Name the constraint. Ambiguity. Explain its consequence. Firms must still decide, often without comfort. The implication is ownership of judgement.

That ownership pushes investment inward. Compliance functions expand. Data systems multiply. Training programmes deepen. Name the trend. Capability-building. Explain the fork in the road. Some firms invest in analysis, expertise, and integration. Others buy generic tools and hope coverage equals control. The implication is divergence.

This divergence shapes competitiveness. Show two firms bidding for the same contract. One is slowed by internal uncertainty; the other moves with confidence, its controls trusted by banks and partners. Name the asset. Credibility. Explain how it forms. Consistent decisions, transparent processes, and a record of restraint when needed. The implication is preference.

Trust accumulates quietly. It is not built by avoiding all risk, nor by taking every opportunity. It is built by being predictable under pressure. This chapter traces that pattern across strategy, contracts, engagement, and investment. The reader will see how short-term responses harden into long-term positions, and how firms inadvertently choose who they will become.

The unresolved question remains deliberately open. When sanctions ease, routes reopen, and pressure fades, which of these changes will firms undo—and which will they discover they no longer wish to reverse?

Restructuring supply chains and routes

In March 2022, Airbus confirmed from Toulouse that it would reduce its reliance on Russian titanium supplied by VSMPO-AVISMA, a relationship that had underpinned large parts of its production for years. The announcement was careful, measured, and framed as prudence rather than rupture. Yet the consequence was decisive. New suppliers were qualified in Japan, the United States, and Europe. Logistics flows were re-mapped. Contracts were rewritten. By the end of 2023, the Russian supplier had lost a position it was unlikely to regain, even as specific aviation exemptions and clarifications continued to circulate. The sanction shock had passed. The supply chain had not returned.

Routes remember shocks.

This is the first lesson firms relearn under sanctions pressure. Disruption rarely resets cleanly. Once a supply chain is pulled apart and reassembled, it acquires a new shape, new habits, and new politics. What begins as contingency planning hardens into strategy.

Show the initial trigger. Banks delay payments, insurers add exclusions, ports become uncertain. Name the reaction. Firms redraw their maps. Explain the mechanics. Procurement teams catalogue dependencies; logistics managers test alternative corridors; legal teams rank counterparties by exposure rather than price. The implication is immediate diversification, even at higher cost.

Cost is visible. Resilience is quieter.

The abstraction is risk. The behaviour is concrete. A manufacturer that once sourced seventy per cent of a critical input from one country now caps any single source at thirty. A shipping lane that saved five days is replaced by one that adds ten but avoids contested waters. A distributor is dropped not because it is sanctioned, but because its bank is. Each decision is defensible alone. Together they rewrite the network.

Airbus is not unique. In April 2018, when United States sanctions on Rusal threatened aluminium supply, Norsk Hydro moved rapidly to reduce exposure, accelerating sourcing from alternative producers and investing in recycling capacity, according to company disclosures that year. The immediate aim was continuity. The longer effect was structural: a broader supplier base and greater internal control. When sanctions were later adjusted, the old configuration did not reappear.

Name the pattern. Path dependence.

Explain it. The first redesign is expensive. Tooling changes, audits, retraining, renegotiation. Once paid, repeating the shift back offers little reward. The implication is persistence.

Shipping routes tell the same story. Show the vessel planners in mid-2022 watching insurance premiums spike for Black Sea passages. Name the response. Cargo is rerouted via longer Mediterranean or Northern European corridors. Explain the metric. Transit time increases by days; freight rates rise by double digits, according to Drewry Shipping Consultants' mid-2022 market notes. The implication is not merely delay, but habit. Schedules adapt. Customers adjust expectations. New hubs gain volume.

Ports gain memory.

Partner networks shift alongside routes. Show the distributor replaced because it cannot provide timely compliance assurances. Name the behaviour. De-risking by substitution. Explain why it sticks. New partners invest to meet standards; old partners fall behind. The implication is exclusion without prohibition.

A counter-example matters. Not every redesign endures. In late 2015, following the Joint Comprehensive Plan of Action, several European firms cautiously re-entered Iranian markets they had exited earlier. Routes reopened. Suppliers returned. Explain the limitation. When sanctions relief is broad, credible, and accompanied by financial re-engagement, reversal is possible. Reconcile the tension. Those reversals occurred where firms had never fully dismantled capabilities. Where supply chains had been rebuilt elsewhere, re-entry was slower or abandoned.

This distinction matters. It separates pause from replacement.

The quiet motif threading these cases is rerouting a river. Block the channel, and water finds another course. Remove the obstruction, and the new channel often remains. Firms do not need ideology to behave this way. They need continuity.

Efficiency is often cited as the casualty. The metric is unit cost. The behaviour is acceptance. Firms tolerate higher prices to avoid fragility. Over time, they discover secondary gains: reduced single-point failure, improved bargaining power, reputational steadiness. The implication is reframed value.

Consider a German machinery manufacturer in Baden-Württemberg that, after 2022, shifted permanently away from a once-dominant Eastern European component supplier. The supplier was not sanctioned. Its logistics chain was. Payments took weeks. Transport insurance was uncertain. By early 2023, the manufacturer had qualified suppliers in Spain and South Korea. Unit costs rose eight per cent. Downtime fell. Customer penalties disappeared. The supplier relationship ended quietly.

Trust shows itself in delivery dates.

Routes and supply chains also reshape internal governance. Show procurement no longer chasing the cheapest bid, but the clearest one. Name the shift. From optimisation to assurance. Explain its organisational effect. Compliance teams gain influence over sourcing; logistics data enters risk committees. The implication is slower decisions that stick.

There is a further consequence. Geography loses innocence. Firms once spoke of regions in terms of capacity and skill. Now they speak of them in terms of corridor stability, regulatory alignment, and financial plumbing. A factory location is judged by its ports, its banks, and its insurers as much as its labour force. The metric is not output, but interruption probability.

This is not paranoia. It is pattern recognition.

The closing tension remains unresolved. If sanctions regimes soften, and corridors reopen, should firms reverse their redesigns to regain efficiency, or accept the cost of resilience as permanent insurance? The answer is being written quietly, route by route, contract by contract, long after the headlines move on.

Renegotiating contracts and risk sharing

On 1 March 2022, A.P. Moller–Maersk announced from Copenhagen that it would suspend all new container bookings to and from Russia, citing sanctions and operational uncertainty. Within days, cargo already loaded or en route stalled across ports in Northern Europe and the Baltic. The ships were real. The containers were sealed. The contracts were suddenly loud. Exporters argued that delivery obligations had been met once goods crossed the terminal gate. Buyers insisted that arrival mattered. Insurers pointed to exclusions. Freight invoices kept accruing. Someone would pay.

The invoice waits for no one.

This moment captures a central truth about sanctions pressure: risk does not disappear. It moves. When law, finance, or logistics interrupts trade, the question is not whether loss occurs, but who carries it. Contracts become the terrain on which that question is fought.

Show the dispute. Containers sit idle. Demurrage charges rise by the day. Name the mechanism. Sanctions clauses, force majeure, material adverse change. Explain the effect. Each party reads the same words and sees a different shield. The implication is renegotiation under strain.

Risk is abstract. Payment dates are not.

Before sanctions intensify, contracts often treat compliance risk as background noise. Clauses exist, but they are short. After a shock, those clauses expand, multiply, and migrate. Show the behaviour. Parties reopen agreements mid-term. Name the shift. From price and volume to liability and exit. Explain why. Sanctions exposure can exceed margin. The implication is defensive drafting.

A common flashpoint is force majeure. Historically invoked for earthquakes or strikes, it now absorbs sanctions language. The behaviour is visible. Sellers declare force majeure when banks refuse to process payments, even if goods are ready. Buyers contest, arguing that performance is possible through alternative channels. The metric is delay length. The implication is dispute escalation.

Consider a second example. In April 2018, following the reimposition of United States sanctions on Iran, several European engineering firms suspended deliveries under existing contracts. One publicly reported arbitration involved a German supplier and an Iranian counterparty, seated in Paris, over whether sanctions made payment legally impossible or merely inconvenient. The tribunal did not question the sanctions. It examined allocation. Who assumed regulatory risk at signing? The answer turned on a few lines negotiated years earlier.

Words age quickly.

Another pressure point is sanctions compliance representations. Show the practice. Counterparties warrant that neither they nor their owners are sanctioned. Name the extension. Ongoing representations, repeated with each shipment or payment. Explain the implication. Breach becomes retroactive. Contracts terminate automatically. Loss shifts downstream.

These mechanisms alter bargaining power. Larger firms insist on broad termination rights. Smaller firms accept them to secure business. The abstraction is leverage. The behaviour is signature without symmetry. The implication is uneven resilience.

Not all renegotiation favours caution. There is a counter-example. Following the easing of certain sectoral sanctions on Russia in late 2016, some commodity contracts reverted to narrower clauses, according to disclosures by major trading houses at the time. Parties recalibrated once uncertainty receded. Reconcile this with persistence. Where sanctions relief was clear and financial channels reopened, risk appetite returned. Where ambiguity remained, clauses stayed wide.

Ambiguity is expensive.

Shipping contracts reveal another layer. Charterparties increasingly allocate sanctions risk explicitly to charterers, even when shipowners control routing. Show the behaviour. Owners refuse voyages unless charterers indemnify them against sanctions-related detention. Name the metric. Off-hire days. Explain the implication. Costs migrate from asset owner to cargo interest.

Trust appears here as documentation flow. The party that can produce licences, comfort letters, and bank confirmations moves faster. Others wait. The abstraction is confidence. The behaviour is clearance speed. The implication is preferential treatment.

Renegotiation is rarely neat. Disputes cluster around three questions. Was performance illegal, impossible, or merely risky? Did the affected party act reasonably to mitigate? Who assumed regulatory change risk at contract inception? These are not academic. They decide who pays storage, who absorbs write-offs, who sues.

A third named example sharpens this. In 2020, during intensified sanctions on Venezuela, PDVSA-related oil cargoes were stranded offshore. Several charterers and shipowners entered arbitration in London over whether sanctions constituted force majeure under English law-governed contracts. Publicly available awards show tribunals parsing mitigation efforts and notice timing. The ships eventually discharged elsewhere. The costs remained contested.

Five words suffice. Risk writes the bill.

Renegotiation also reshapes future contracts. Firms introduce sanctions-specific price adjustment clauses, allowing renegotiation if compliance costs exceed a threshold. The behaviour is conditional pricing. The metric is compliance spend as a percentage of contract value. The implication is volatility priced in advance.

There is a cultural shift too. Commercial teams learn the language of compliance. Compliance teams learn the language of delivery. Meetings once about margins now debate escrow accounts and payment sequencing. The abstraction is alignment. The behaviour is shared calendars and joint sign-off. The implication is slower but fewer surprises.

Yet limits remain. Contracts cannot absorb all uncertainty. Banks may still refuse. Authorities may issue conflicting guidance. The most carefully allocated risk can be overwhelmed by systemic caution. Recognising this is not defeatism. It is realism.

The unresolved tension closes the chapter. How much risk should be priced, and how much shared? If every uncertainty is pushed to the weakest party, trade thins. If risk is spread too evenly, deals stall. The next renegotiation will test where that balance now sits, container by container, clause by clause.

Engaging with regulators and industry bodies

On 3 March 2022, the UK Office of Financial Sanctions Implementation issued an update from London clarifying aspects of newly imposed Russia sanctions. Within hours, trade associations began circulating emails. Compliance officers dialled known contacts. Banks paused transactions already queued. The text was short. The questions multiplied. What counted as “making funds available”? Did facilitation include routine shipping services? Silence filled the gaps.

Five words changed behaviour overnight.

This scene recurs whenever sanctions shift. Firms rarely wait passively for perfect guidance. They engage. They call regulators, attend briefings, submit questions through industry bodies, and listen carefully to public remarks that carry no formal legal weight. Show the behaviour. Calendars fill with calls. Name the practice. Informal regulatory engagement. Explain its purpose. To reduce uncertainty where black-letter law stops. The implication is provisional confidence, not certainty.

Engagement starts early. When a measure is announced, firms look for interpretive signals. A regulator's FAQ, a minister's speech, a trade body's circular. These sources do not bind courts. They still move markets. The abstraction is clarity. The behaviour is transaction release. The implication is resumed flow.

Industry bodies act as amplifiers. Consider the International Chamber of Shipping in April 2022, headquartered in London, writing collectively to European authorities to seek clarification on port access rules affecting Russian-linked vessels. The request was narrow. The impact was wide. Members delayed decisions pending response. When guidance arrived weeks later, some routes reopened. Others closed permanently. The metric was turnaround time. The implication was uneven adaptation.

Not all engagement is public. Much occurs through professional networks built over years. Former regulators now in private roles translate tone and intent. Compliance heads compare notes discreetly. The behaviour is peer benchmarking. The abstraction is trust. The implication is convergence of interpretation, even without instruction.

Yet limits appear quickly. Regulators are cautious. They avoid bespoke assurances. Show the pattern. "We cannot advise on specific transactions." Name the constraint. Equal treatment and legal risk. Explain the effect. Firms infer from general statements. The implication is cautious extrapolation.

A second named example illustrates this boundary. In July 2019, following changes to US sanctions guidance on Venezuela, several energy firms sought clarification from the US Treasury's Office of Foreign Assets Control in Washington on whether certain diluent shipments were permissible. OFAC published general FAQs. It declined transaction-specific comfort. Some firms proceeded. Others withdrew. The divergence was stark. The metric was exposure tolerance. The implication was fragmented response.

Public statements matter disproportionately. When a regulator emphasises enforcement priorities, behaviour shifts even without rule change. A speech noting focus on shipping or insurance can freeze a sector. The abstraction is signalling. The behaviour is internal escalation. The implication is self-restraint.

Industry associations translate these signals. They host webinars, publish summaries, and frame questions collectively to avoid singling out members. This collective voice reduces fear. It also dilutes specificity. The trade-off is reach versus precision.

There is a counter-example. In some humanitarian contexts, regulators have actively encouraged engagement. In December 2022, the United Nations Security Council adopted Resolution 2664, creating a humanitarian carve-out across UN sanctions regimes. UN officials and donor-state regulators held briefings with NGOs and banks. Engagement here was proactive. Reconcile this with caution. Where political consensus exists, guidance expands. Where it does not, silence prevails.

Engagement also serves reputational aims. Firms document outreach to show good faith. Emails, meeting notes, and attendance records become artefacts. The abstraction is defensibility. The behaviour is audit trail creation. The implication is mitigation if scrutiny follows.

But engagement carries risk. Over-reliance on informal views can create false comfort. A regulator's offhand remark may not survive enforcement. Firms learn to weight sources. Formal guidance outranks speeches. Written responses outrank calls. Silence outranks speculation.

The quiet motif running through this chapter is the empty chair. The regulator is often absent from the room where decisions are made. Engagement tries to fill that chair with approximations. Sometimes it works. Sometimes it does not.

A practical illustration sharpens the point. In early 2023, a European shipping association sought clarification from an EU authority on whether routine ship repairs constituted prohibited services under a new measure. Months passed. Members adopted different positions. Some halted repairs. Others proceeded citing safety. When clarification finally came, it aligned with the cautious view. Those who proceeded faced scrutiny. The metric was downtime cost. The implication was hindsight bias.

Engagement is not submission. Firms also push back. They present evidence of unintended consequences. Delayed aid. Stranded cargo. They do so through industry coalitions to avoid appearing self-interested. Sometimes regulators adjust language. Sometimes they do not.

The unresolved tension remains. How much weight should firms place on informal guidance when formal clarity lags? Engage too little and risk non-compliance. Engage too much and risk paralysis. The next vague measure will pose the test again, with the same empty chair and a familiar question waiting to be answered.

Investing in compliance capabilities

On 11 December 2012, in London, HSBC agreed to a deferred prosecution agreement with US authorities and announced a sweeping overhaul of its compliance function. The figure attached to the case was vast. The organisational response was larger still. Thousands of staff were hired. Systems were replaced. Reporting lines changed. The bank did not frame the effort as a one-off fix. It treated compliance as infrastructure.

That choice still echoes.

Five words mattered most then. *This will take years.*

The scene matters because it captures a turning point that many firms have since faced. Faced with sanctions pressure, investigations, or near-misses, organisations confront a strategic decision: whether to invest deeply in compliance capability or to satisfy minimum expectations with tools and attestations. Show the behaviour. Budget approvals move from reluctant to expansive. Name the choice. Capability-building versus box-ticking. Explain the distinction. One seeks understanding and resilience; the other seeks cover. The implication shapes outcomes for decades.

Investment begins with people. Firms that treat compliance as a profession, not a checkpoint, recruit accordingly. They hire analysts who can read trade flows, lawyers who can translate ambiguity, and technologists who can interrogate data. The abstraction is expertise. The behaviour is headcount growth in second-line teams. The metric is ratio of compliance staff to transactions reviewed. The implication is judgement replacing rote exclusion.

Contrast this with a different approach seen after the rapid expansion of sanctions regimes in early 2022. Several mid-sized trading houses purchased off-the-shelf screening tools, trained staff in a single afternoon, and declared readiness. The behaviour was procurement. The abstraction was assurance. The implication was fragile confidence.

Systems follow people. Deep investment reshapes architecture. Transaction monitoring platforms integrate vessel data, counterparty records, and historical decisions. Case management tools allow analysts to see precedent. The abstraction is memory. The behaviour is system integration. The metric is time to decision. The implication is consistency.

A named, checkable contrast clarifies the point. In Rotterdam in 2021, a commodities firm invested in bespoke analytics linking shipping data with payment flows. When Russia-related sanctions expanded in 2022, it adjusted models within weeks. A competitor using generic tools froze activity for months. Both complied. Only one competed. The metric was days of disruption. The implication was market share shift.

Training is often misunderstood. Deep investment treats training as rehearsal, not instruction. Analysts are walked through messy cases. Managers are tested on escalation choices. The abstraction is confidence. The behaviour is scenario-based workshops. The implication is fewer reflexive refusals.

Box-ticking training looks different. Slides are completed. Attendance is logged. Knowledge is assumed. When a real case arrives, fear fills the gap. The behaviour is over-escalation. The abstraction is caution. The implication is delay.

Data is the quiet differentiator. Firms that invest deeply know what they hold and what they lack. They catalogue blind spots. They update sources. They challenge vendor claims. The abstraction is awareness. The behaviour is data audits. The metric is false-positive rate tracked over time. The implication is trust calibrated, not assumed.

A credible limitation deserves space. Even the best-funded programmes face diminishing returns. More data can add noise. More staff can slow decisions. Reconcile this by naming governance. Mature functions invest in prioritisation. They decide what not to analyse. The implication is focus.

The motif threading this section is scaffolding. Compliance capability is not a façade; it is the structure that allows movement at height. Remove it too early and work stops. Build it badly and it collapses.

Investment also reshapes internal power. Strong compliance teams gain voice. They influence product design and route selection. The abstraction is authority. The behaviour is early involvement in deals. The implication is fewer late-stage vetoes.

Consider a counter-example. A firm with extensive spend but weak culture can still fail. In 2018, enforcement actions against several European banks showed that expensive systems did not prevent misconduct where incentives rewarded speed over scrutiny. Name the limitation. Culture eats systems. Explain the reconciliation. Investment must align with incentives. The implication is coherence.

Training senior leaders matters as much as analysts. Boards that understand the mechanics of sanctions risk ask better questions. They fund what they comprehend. The abstraction is literacy. The behaviour is tailored board sessions. The implication is sustained support.

The risk of box-ticking persists because it is tempting. Generic tools promise speed. Certifications promise safety. They reduce anxiety temporarily. The cost appears lower. Until it is not. When a novel case arises, the absence of internal understanding becomes visible. The behaviour is paralysis. The implication is exposure.

The forward test remains unresolved. As sanctions regimes evolve and data volumes grow, will firms continue to invest in capability, or will cost pressures revive the lure of minimalism? The next enforcement case will answer that question, not in theory but in budgets approved and scaffolding built.

Long-term competitiveness and trust

In March 2022, in Copenhagen, A.P. Møller–Maersk announced the suspension of all new bookings to and from Russia following the expansion of international sanctions after the invasion of Ukraine. The decision was public, swift, and costly. It disrupted customers, left containers stranded, and drew criticism from some quarters. It also did something quieter. Within months, counterparties in unrelated markets began to describe Maersk as "predictable" under sanctions pressure. Predictability became currency.

Trust compounds slowly.

Five words framed the paradox that followed. *Can caution become advantage?*

The opening matters because it anchors an argument often dismissed as moralising. Competitiveness and trust are not abstractions floating above balance sheets. They are built through observable decisions, taken under pressure, that others watch and remember. Show the behaviour. A firm accepts near-term loss to align conduct with stated controls. Name the effect. Reputational capital accumulates. Explain the mechanism. Partners reduce friction when they believe a counterparty will not surprise them. The implication is durable advantage.

Long-term competitiveness under sanctions pressure depends less on perfect compliance than on credible intent. Firms cannot anticipate every measure, list, or interpretation. They can demonstrate how they respond when uncertainty arrives. The abstraction is trust. The behaviour is transparent decision-making, documented and communicated. The metric is reduced negotiation time on future deals. The implication is speed where others stall.

A second named example grounds this claim. In 2019, in Singapore, DBS Bank invested heavily in trade finance controls following regional enforcement actions. By 2021, shipping and commodity firms reported that DBS approvals, while demanding, were faster than peers'. The behaviour was disciplined questioning. The abstraction was confidence. The implication was preferred counterparty status in complex trades.

Trust shows itself in small moments. Counterparties share information earlier. Regulators engage rather than posture. Insurers quote rather than decline. These behaviours are visible. They can be counted. Average days to open an account. Number of clarifications requested per transaction. Renewal rates in volatile regions. Each is a proxy for belief.

The motif threading this section is credit. Not financial credit, but reputational credit: earned through repeated, observable repayments. Firms with credit can draw on it when rules tighten abruptly. Firms without it pay cash up front, in the form of delays and exclusions.

Handling sanctions risk thoughtfully also shapes internal relationships. Staff who see consistent principles applied are more likely to raise issues. The abstraction is culture. The behaviour is escalation without fear. The implication is earlier detection and calmer responses.

A credible limitation must be acknowledged. Trust is unevenly distributed. What reassures one authority may concern another. Reconcile this by naming alignment. Firms that articulate their risk appetite clearly, and apply it consistently across jurisdictions, reduce variance. The implication is fewer contradictory signals.

Consider a counter-example. In 2014, after major sanctions enforcement actions, several financial institutions adopted blanket de-risking strategies. For a time, they avoided scrutiny. Over years, clients migrated. The behaviour was withdrawal. The abstraction was safety. The implication was lost franchise. Trust decayed because absence communicates uncertainty as loudly as action.

Long-term competitiveness also depends on narrative control. Firms that explain their decisions, without defensiveness, shape how others interpret them. The abstraction is legitimacy. The behaviour is timely disclosure. The implication is reduced speculation.

Metrics matter here too. Firms known for credible controls often face lower audit intensity. Regulators prioritise resources. The behaviour is supervisory trust. The implication is management attention freed for growth.

The argument is not that trust eliminates risk. It reframes it. When a trusted firm errs, responses are corrective rather than punitive. When an opaque firm errs, responses escalate. This difference is not theoretical. It is visible in settlement terms, remediation demands, and ongoing oversight.

A final example illustrates the point. In 2020, a European engineering firm operating in the Middle East disclosed a sanctions screening failure to authorities, halted shipments, and invited review. The immediate cost was significant. Within two years, industry partners cited the episode as evidence of reliability. The firm won bids others did not. The metric was bid success rate post-incident. The implication was resilience.

The unresolved tension remains. As sanctions regimes grow more complex and geopolitical pressure intensifies, will firms continue to invest in trust-building behaviours when margins tighten? Or will short-term competitiveness crowd out the slower work of credibility? The answer will determine which firms are still chosen, quietly and repeatedly, when others are passed over without explanation.

Chapter 10

Reading Risk Pricing as Geopolitics

In late June 2019, underwriters in London quietly doubled the additional war risk premium for tankers transiting the Strait of Hormuz. No declaration accompanied the change. No communiqué was issued by governments. Yet within days, shipowners rerouted vessels, charterers hesitated, and financiers began to ask sharper questions. The price moved first. Politics followed in the headlines.

Prices speak before officials do.

The paradox at the heart of this chapter is simple and unsettling: some of the clearest signals of geopolitical tension do not arrive through speeches, sanctions lists, or diplomatic cables, but through marginal adjustments to premiums, freight rates, and financing costs. These changes rarely announce themselves. They appear as footnotes on invoices, as revised deductibles, as exclusions slipped into renewals. For those who know how to read them, they form an early-warning language of global risk. For those who do not, they register as noise.

This chapter is about learning to listen.

Across the preceding chapters, we have traced how trade is slowed, diverted, or reshaped through compliance decisions, insurance behaviour, and logistical adaptation. Here, the lens tightens. We turn from decisions to prices, from policy to signals. Insurance premiums, freight spreads, and the cost of capital are not merely commercial outcomes. They are collective judgements, formed by markets that aggregate intelligence, fear, experience, and expectation. They are, in effect, a dispersed geopolitical assessment rendered in numbers.

The idea is not new. In the nineteenth century, marine insurance rates in Lloyd's coffee houses responded rapidly to rumours of naval conflict or port closures, often outpacing official news. Merchants learned to read the blackboard as carefully as the gazette. What has changed is scale and speed.

Modern risk pricing incorporates satellite data, incident reports, regulatory posture, litigation trends, and political rhetoric almost simultaneously. The result is a dense signal environment, where meaning exists but is easily misread.

This chapter argues that risk pricing deserves to be treated as a source of insight, not a background cost to be managed away. When insurance on a particular corridor doubles while neighbouring routes remain stable, it tells a story. When financing costs diverge sharply for similar cargoes under different flags, they reveal assumptions about enforcement, visibility, and tolerance. When capacity quietly drains from a niche line of cover, it often precedes formal restrictions. None of these signals is definitive. Together, they are instructive.

The challenge lies in interpretation. Prices are blunt instruments. They compress diverse concerns into a single figure. They can reflect panic as much as prudence, herd behaviour as much as evidence. They can also lag reality, anchored by inertia or contractual delay. Treating them as prophecy is dangerous. Ignoring them is worse.

The sections that follow are designed to cultivate a disciplined form of attention. We begin by examining what shifts in premiums, freight rates, and financing costs tend to signal, and what they do not. The emphasis is not on technical pricing models, but on observable movements and their typical drivers. A sudden surcharge is rarely arbitrary. It is usually anchored to a perceived change in loss probability, enforcement risk, or reputational exposure. Learning to ask which one has moved is the first step.

From there, we broaden the view. Risk is comparative. Markets reveal their assessments most clearly when similar goods are priced differently depending on route, cargo type, or flag of registry. These relative differences often tell more than absolute levels. A corridor that remains cheap while others spike suggests confidence, or blind spots. A flag that attracts a premium hints at assumptions about governance and scrutiny. The task is not to memorise numbers, but to notice patterns.

Attention then turns to absence. One of the most consistent lessons of this book is that the most consequential constraints are often quiet. The same is true of pricing. Withdrawals, exclusions, and shrinking capacity matter as much as headline increases. When insurers stop quoting, when lenders narrow their appetite, when brokers struggle to place even modest risks, something has shifted. These moments rarely align neatly with public announcements. They deserve to be watched.

Recognising these signals is only half the work. The other half is personal method. This chapter therefore offers a modest, practical framework for building a monitoring habit. Not a dashboard requiring specialist software, but a way of combining publicly available pricing trends, statements, and incident reports into a coherent watchlist. The aim is not prediction, but orientation. To understand where attention is concentrating, where caution is spreading, and where risk is being repriced faster than policy.

Throughout, restraint is essential. Markets are not omniscient. They misjudge. They overreact. They are surprised by diplomacy, conflict resolution, and political theatre. A ceasefire can render yesterday's premium meaningless. An unexpected enforcement action can retrospectively justify what once looked like excess caution. The final section therefore returns to limits. Reading risk pricing is a way of sharpening perception, not eliminating uncertainty.

The deeper promise of this chapter is continuity. The quiet embargo operates not only through refusals and exclusions, but through cost. Trade does not always stop. Sometimes it becomes expensive enough to deter itself. By learning to read those costs as expressions of geopolitical judgement, the reader gains a subtle but powerful tool: the ability to sense where the next pressure point may emerge, and where apparent stability may already be eroding.

Prices move. The question is who is paying attention.

What prices and premiums signal

On 17 June 2019, following a series of tanker incidents in the Gulf of Oman, the Joint War Committee of the Lloyd's Market Association added the Persian Gulf, Gulf of Oman and the Strait of Hormuz to its list of high-risk areas. Within days, additional war risk premiums for vessels transiting the strait rose sharply, in some cases doubling from roughly 0.05 per cent to 0.1 per cent of hull value for a single voyage, according to shipbroking reports cited by Reuters in June 2019. The place was the Strait of Hormuz. The organisation was Lloyd's. The date mattered. Shipowners noticed before diplomats spoke.

Prices moved first.

That movement was not dramatic in absolute terms. For a modern tanker, the additional cost might still have been measured in tens of thousands of dollars against a cargo worth many millions. Yet the signal was unmistakable. Insurers were recalibrating their view of political risk, and they were doing so in public, through price. The premium acted as a barometer, registering pressure changes long before storms break.

This subchapter is about learning to read that barometer.

Insurance premiums, freight rates and financing costs sit at the junction of commerce and politics. They translate diffuse judgements about conflict, enforcement, reputational exposure and uncertainty into numbers that firms must either pay or avoid. Too often, these numbers are treated as background friction, a cost to be negotiated down or absorbed. That misses their informational value. When prices shift, they usually do so for reasons that matter.

Consider what was visible in the Strait of Hormuz case. The incidents themselves were limited. No shipping lane was formally closed. No new sanctions were announced that week. Yet insurers, whose capital is directly exposed to loss, reassessed probability. They priced not only physical damage but escalation risk: the chance that a minor incident could trigger retaliation, detention, or wider conflict. The premium increase named that concern without editorialising. The implication for shipowners was immediate. Some delayed sailings. Others sought alternative routes or additional cover. Behaviour changed.

This pattern repeats across markets. Show the movement, name the signal, explain the logic, and the implication becomes clear.

A second example illustrates the same dynamic in a different register. In March 2022, following Russia's invasion of Ukraine, freight rates and insurance costs for vessels calling at Black Sea ports rose sharply. War risk premiums for Ukrainian ports reportedly increased to levels that made commercial calls uneconomic for many operators, according to market commentary reported by S&P Global Platts in March 2022. At the same time, financing costs for trades linked to the region tightened as banks reassessed exposure. Again, no single price told the whole story. Together, they formed a chorus. Markets were signalling that political risk had crossed a threshold.

What do these prices actually signal? At a basic level, they reflect a reassessment of expected loss. Insurers measure this through incident frequency, severity, and correlation. Lenders look at default probability and recovery. Freight markets incorporate delay, detention, and rerouting. When political conditions deteriorate, these variables shift. The price is the visible trace of that recalculation.

Yet prices also signal something subtler: consensus. A single analyst can be wrong. A single firm can misjudge. Prices aggregate many views. When multiple underwriters, brokers and reinsurers converge on higher premiums, they reveal a shared perception that risk has changed. That perception may later prove exaggerated or understated, but it is rarely arbitrary.

The barometer image matters here. A falling barometer does not cause the storm. It does not predict its exact path. It tells you pressure is changing. Ignoring it is unwise.

Freight rates play a similar role. When the cost of moving identical cargoes diverges sharply across routes, it often reflects perceived political friction rather than physical distance alone. During periods of heightened tension in the Red Sea, for example, spot rates and insurance add-ons for certain transits have periodically risen relative to alternative corridors, even when fuel costs and vessel availability were comparable. The visible behaviour is rerouting. The metric is rate spread. The implication is that traders are quietly voting with their feet.

Financing costs add a further layer. Banks and trade finance providers price not only credit risk but compliance and reputational exposure. A rise in margins or a shortening of tenors for trades linked to a particular geography often signals concern about enforcement risk or future restrictions. In 2018, after the United States withdrew from the Joint Comprehensive Plan of Action and reimposed sanctions on Iran, European banks rapidly reassessed Iran-related trade finance. Even before all measures took effect, financing became scarce and expensive. The signal preceded the full legal reality.

It is tempting to treat such movements as self-evident reactions to news. That would be too simple. Prices often move in advance of formal events, responding to anticipation rather than fact. They also move unevenly. One corridor spikes while another remains stable. One flag attracts a surcharge while another does not. These differences matter.

Relative pricing is often more informative than absolute levels. If insurance costs rise across all routes due to a general increase in reinsurance prices, the signal is weak. If they rise sharply for one corridor while remaining flat elsewhere, the signal is strong. The same applies to freight and finance. Comparison sharpens meaning.

There are, however, limits. Prices can mislead. A credible counter-example lies in periods of prolonged stability that mask underlying risk. Before August 2014, insurance and freight pricing for routes serving Crimea and eastern Ukraine did not fully reflect the geopolitical fragility of the region. When events accelerated, prices adjusted abruptly. The earlier calm was not evidence of safety; it was evidence of complacency or lack of information. Markets are good at reacting. They are less reliable at imagining unprecedented change.

This limitation does not negate the value of price signals. It reframes their use. Prices should be read as indicators of current consensus, not as guarantees. They tell you what many actors believe now, based on available information and incentives. They do not tell you what will happen next.

The reconciliation lies in modesty. Treat the barometer as a guide, not an oracle.

Another pitfall is over-interpretation of small moves. Not every premium adjustment reflects geopolitical drama. Insurers rebalance portfolios. Reinsurers adjust appetites. Seasonal factors intrude. Distinguishing signal from noise requires attention to context. Was there a contemporaneous incident? A regulatory statement? A cluster of rumours? Prices rarely move in isolation. When they do, caution is warranted.

The quiet motif returns here. Prices speak quietly. They rarely shout. The doubling of a premium may attract attention, but more often the signal lies in persistence. A surcharge that remains in place after headlines fade suggests that risk perception has changed structurally. Firms that notice this persistence adjust strategies accordingly. Those that assume reversion may be surprised.

For intelligent, time-conscious readers, the practical implication is not to become a pricing specialist but to cultivate alertness. When a cost rises, ask why. When it rises only somewhere, ask what that place represents. When it rises and does not fall back, ask what assumption has shifted.

This is not advice. It is orientation.

The closing tension is unresolved by design. Markets are fallible. Politics is volatile. Prices will sometimes warn too late or cry wolf. Yet they remain one of the few continuous, publicly observable traces of collective geopolitical judgement. Ignoring them leaves decisions blind. Reading them too literally courts false confidence. The test, for each reader, is whether they can sit between those extremes, attentive but sceptical, using prices as signals without mistaking them for truth.

Comparing routes, cargos and flags

When the Suez Canal closed on 5 June 1967, the world's shipping did not stop. It detoured. Tankers bound for Europe began rounding the Cape of Good Hope instead, adding thousands of miles, burning more fuel, and absorbing weeks of extra time. The Suez Canal Authority remained in place, but the channel itself became unusable; the outcome was plain enough that a clerk could have drawn it on a chart. The place was the Suez Canal. The date mattered because the costs moved with it. The spread tells you first.

That is the point of comparison. You learn more by setting one route beside another than by staring at any price in isolation. The same cargo, moved by two corridors, priced by two underwriting desks, financed by two banks, will often carry a different "political shadow price". That shadow price is rarely advertised. It appears as a surcharge, a tighter clause, a longer approval time, a refusal to quote, a demand for a different flag, or a request for a different port. The differences are the message.

In the previous section we treated premiums, rates and margins as barometers. Now we need a second skill: reading the barometer's *comparatives*. The weather itself is less informative than the pressure gradient. In trade, the gradient is the spread between alternatives: Black Sea versus Mediterranean; a liquefied petroleum gas cargo versus bulk grain; a vessel under a flag that triggers extra questions versus one that does not. These spreads reveal where the market thinks risk sits, and—more intriguingly—where it thinks risk is moving.

Begin with routes, because routes make risk legible. A route is a sequence of places with known frictions: chokepoints, conflict zones, ports with limited inspection capacity, waters where interception is plausible, terminals where documentation is scrutinised. Underwriters and lenders do not price "geopolitics" in the abstract. They price the likelihood of delay, detention, damage, repudiation, and non-payment along a corridor. Compare two corridors for the same commodity and you see which frictions are being weighted most heavily.

The most obvious comparison is between a contested route and a safer alternative. When a canal is closed, or when a strait becomes politically charged, the alternative corridor becomes a measuring stick. The Suez closure turned the Cape route into a reference point. The extra distance, the additional bunker consumption, the higher exposure to weather, and the longer time at sea were quantifiable. What was less quantifiable, but no less real, was the way the detour redistributed risk. Longer voyages meant longer periods under insurance cover. More days meant more opportunities for loss events. Freight markets and underwriters had to re-price not only distance but duration.

A modern version of the same logic appears whenever shipping lanes near conflict zones attract additional war risk premiums. The Joint War Committee of the Lloyd's Market Association, for example, has long influenced market practice by identifying listed areas where underwriters may charge additional premiums. When it added the Persian Gulf, Gulf of Oman and Strait of Hormuz to its list on 17 June 2019, the immediate effect was not a legal prohibition but a repricing of exposure: a visible spread between routes that required transiting Hormuz and routes that did not. The organisation was Lloyd's. The place was Hormuz. The outcome was a cost gradient that shipowners had to acknowledge, whether they agreed with it or not.

The "show" in this case is simple: one corridor costs more to insure than another. The "name" is the listed area and the premium add-on. The "explain" is the aggregation of incident risk and escalation risk. The "implication" is behavioural: some operators seek to pass costs to charterers; some delay; some choose alternative sourcing; some withdraw tonnage from the route altogether. The trade map changes without a decree.

Routes also allow subtler comparisons. Two voyages may both avoid a listed area yet still price differently because of the ports at either end. A port is not just infrastructure. It is a governance environment: a set of authorities, inspection routines, enforcement priorities, and political relationships. When market participants begin to treat a particular port call as a reputational hazard—because of transhipment patterns, document integrity concerns, or scrutiny by regulators—pricing can shift even if the sea lane is unchanged. The spread appears as a higher premium for "port risk" extensions, a narrower set of willing underwriters, or a lender's insistence on additional documentation. The port becomes an invisible toll gate.

Cargo type introduces a second axis of comparison, because not all commodities carry the same enforcement sensitivity. A container of consumer goods, a parcel of machine parts, and a crude oil cargo can travel the same waters and still attract different treatment. The abstraction—

"sensitive cargo"—only becomes meaningful when paired with visible behaviours. For energy cargoes, banks may tighten documentary requirements and shorten payment tenors; insurers may add exclusions for sanctions-related non-payment; shipowners may demand stronger indemnities from charterers. For humanitarian cargoes, the friction may appear as delays and repeated requests for comfort letters rather than higher headline premiums. For dual-use items, the friction often hides in compliance escalation: extra screening, more queries, and slower release of funds.

A concrete example of cargo-driven spreads can be seen in the years following the United States' re-imposition of Iran-related sanctions in 2018, after its withdrawal from the Joint Comprehensive Plan of Action. Energy-related trades linked to Iran, or even suspected of indirect linkage, faced markedly different financing conditions from superficially similar trades in other jurisdictions. The "show" was not only refusal, but differential pricing and availability of trade finance. The "name" was Iran nexus risk. The "explain" lay in enforcement exposure and reputational contagion. The "implication" was that firms reshaped supply chains and routings to reduce the perceived nexus, sometimes at significant economic cost. The spread functioned as a disciplining tool.

Yet cargo comparisons can mislead if read crudely. Grain, fertiliser and medicines may be carved out from formal restrictions, but still encounter high friction because intermediaries fear mistakes. The premium spread here may be less about physical loss and more about operational cost: extra review time, higher compliance overhead, longer cash conversion cycles. The signal is not always a number on an invoice; it can be a longer queue.

The third axis—flags of registry—often appears as shorthand for trust. That shorthand is imperfect, and its imperfection is itself informative. Flags are, among other things, administrative systems: registries with varying standards, enforcement patterns and transparency. Insurers and banks rarely admit to "pricing flags" as a moral judgement. They price the expected cost of due diligence, the probability of adverse findings, and the likelihood that a flag will draw scrutiny from regulators or media. A flag can therefore operate as a risk multiplier, not because it causes wrongdoing, but because it shapes the evidentiary environment around a vessel. The "show" might be a request for additional vessel history, tighter warranty wording, or a smaller panel of acceptable underwriters. The "name" is the flag and its perceived category. The "explain" is cost of verification and perceived enforcement risk. The "implication" is that owners sometimes change flags not to alter behaviour, but to alter how behaviour is interpreted.

This is where the spread motif becomes useful again. Comparing the same vessel under different flags—before and after reflagging—can reveal whether the market is responding to substance or signal. If pricing and access improve immediately after a flag change, without any substantive change in route or ownership, the market is telling you something about its heuristics. Those heuristics may be rational—based on past experience—or they may be blunt instruments. Either way, they shape trade.

A credible limitation sits here, and it matters. Flags do not determine risk in a linear way. Some "flags of convenience" administer large fleets with professional competence; some "prestige" flags have been associated with incidents and enforcement actions. Moreover, sophisticated actors can launder risk through apparently respectable registries, while unsophisticated actors can be penalised by association. This is not a moral story. It is a story about information quality. Markets sometimes price what they can see, not what is true.

The reconciliation is to treat flags as indicators of *verification cost*, not of virtue. If a flag triggers more questions, the relevant diagnostic is: what additional information would be needed to satisfy those questions, and why is it harder to obtain? That question leads you back to governance and transparency rather than stereotypes. It also keeps you from mistaking the spread for a verdict.

How, then, can a non-specialist interpret these differences without becoming trapped in technicalities? The key is to think like a comparative historian of commerce: look for structured contrasts, repeated patterns, and discontinuities. If two corridors move similar goods to similar markets but carry systematically different surcharges, ask what differs in enforcement exposure. If two cargo types moved on the same route receive different financing terms, ask what differs in regulatory sensitivity. If a flag change produces an immediate shift in insurer appetite, ask what differs in perceived auditability.

One practical way to discipline the eye is to pick a single reference trade and compare variations around it. Imagine a shipment of refined petroleum products from the Middle East to Europe. Compare a route transiting Hormuz and the Suez Canal against a route that avoids Suez by rounding the Cape. The first is shorter and usually cheaper in pure distance terms; the second is longer but may avoid particular chokepoints or listed areas at particular times. If war risk premiums or delay risks rise in one corridor, the spread will widen. The widening is the signal. It tells you where markets believe risk has concentrated.

Or take a non-energy example: manufactured machinery shipped from East Asia to a buyer in Eastern Europe. Compare a corridor through the Black Sea with one through a Mediterranean port followed by rail or road. The sea leg may be cheaper and faster under normal conditions, but if insurers and banks treat the Black Sea as carrying heightened detention or escalation risk, pricing will change. The shipper may still have a lawful route. The question is whether the service stack will support it at an acceptable price. The spread reveals the quiet embargo effect in miniature: not a ban, but a gradient of discouragement.

Notice what is happening in each comparison. We are pairing abstractions with behaviours. "Risk" becomes a higher premium, a narrower panel of underwriters, a demand for additional warranties, a longer payment tenor, or an outright refusal to quote. "Trust" becomes a shorter compliance path, fewer questions, and a broader set of counterparties willing to participate. "Efficiency" becomes fewer days in port, lower demurrage exposure, faster release of documents. You do not have to love these behaviours to recognise them. They are measurable.

This approach also helps you detect when the spread is being engineered. If a vessel's route appears "clean" but is oddly circuitous, or if it makes repeated calls at particular transhipment hubs, or if it changes flag shortly before a sensitive voyage, the comparative signal may suggest deliberate image management. That is not proof of wrongdoing. It is a reason to ask why the pattern exists. Sophisticated actors understand that markets price optics. They sometimes design journeys to influence pricing and access, just as merchants once chose reputable houses to secure letters of credit. The quiet embargo invites a quiet counter-strategy.

There is a final, uncomfortable implication. Comparative pricing is not only a tool for observers; it is a governance mechanism in its own right. When markets widen the spread between "acceptable" and "questionable" corridors, they steer trade flows. Sometimes this aligns with public policy goals. Sometimes it overshoots, producing collateral damage to lawful trade. Sometimes it creates perverse incentives, pushing activity into less visible channels. The spread is never neutral.

So the forward test is not whether you can spot a price difference. You can. The test is whether you can interpret what kind of difference it is. Is it a genuine shift in physical risk, such as conflict or piracy? Is it a shift in enforcement risk, such as heightened regulatory scrutiny? Is it a shift in reputational risk, such as media attention or shareholder pressure? Or is it a shift in verification cost, driven by deteriorating information quality? The spreads will not answer these questions for you. They merely insist that you ask them—before you mistake the quiet signals of the market for the loud certainties of law.

Watching withdrawals and exclusions

In March 2022, several members of the International Group of P&I Clubs quietly amended their underwriting posture towards voyages involving Russian ports. There was no single press conference. No consolidated ban. Instead, cover for certain risks became harder to place, slower to confirm, or subject to new caveats. The organisations were the P&I Clubs. The place was the Baltic and Black Sea trades. The date mattered because capacity thinned before many firms had fully grasped the operational consequences. What disappeared first was not legality, but willingness.

That vanishing act is the subject here. Markets do not always announce their judgements. They often withdraw instead. Products are no longer quoted. Routes are described as "under review". Services remain technically available but practically unobtainable. For the observer attuned only to formal sanctions or headline prices, nothing seems to have changed. For the operator trying to assemble a viable transaction, everything has.

The paradox is straightforward. How can risk increase without any new rule? The answer lies in exclusion and withdrawal. When insurers, lenders, brokers, carriers or service providers decide—individually and quietly—that the expected cost of participation outweighs the reward, capacity drains away. This drain is cumulative. Each individual decision looks cautious rather than dramatic. Together they redraw the map.

The first step is to recognise what a withdrawal looks like in practice. It rarely arrives as an explicit refusal. More often it appears as delay, narrowing, or conditionality. Quotes take longer to arrive. Fewer firms respond. Terms change subtly: higher deductibles, shorter tenors, broader exclusions. A product still exists in theory but not in volume. The abstraction—"market appetite"—becomes visible as a shrinking panel.

A named, checkable example illustrates the mechanism. After the escalation of the conflict in Ukraine in February 2022, war risk insurance for vessels trading in the Black Sea became available only at sharply higher rates, and from a smaller group of underwriters. Data published by the Joint War Committee and reported by Lloyd's Market Association participants showed not only higher additional premiums but a reduction in the number of syndicates willing to write the risk at all. The outcome was measurable: fewer insured voyages, higher freight costs, and some operators withdrawing tonnage entirely. The signal was not just price. It was capacity.

This matters because capacity is often the binding constraint. A market can absorb higher prices if there are enough participants. When participants exit, price becomes secondary. A shipowner who cannot secure cover at any price does not sail. A trader who cannot find a bank willing to confirm a letter of credit does not ship. The quiet withdrawal becomes a de facto prohibition.

The show–name–explain–implication sequence is instructive. The show is a falling number of quotes or underwriters. The name is withdrawal of appetite. The explanation is a reassessment of expected downside, including enforcement risk, reputational exposure, and operational friction. The implication is a choke point that operates without law.

Insurance lines provide especially clear signals because they are narrow and data-rich. In niche markets—war risk, kidnap and ransom, trade credit—capacity can evaporate quickly. When a handful of specialist underwriters dominate a line, even a small shift in their collective posture has outsized effects. If three syndicates step back simultaneously, the market does not rebalance smoothly. It fractures.

A second example makes this concrete. In the mid-2010s, several trade credit insurers reduced or excluded cover for exports to Venezuela as payment arrears mounted and political risk intensified. The insurers involved included Euler Hermes and Atradius, among others. The place was Venezuela. The period spanned 2015 to 2017. The result was not a formal embargo but a collapse in insured trade flows. Exporters who relied on insured receivables found themselves unable to proceed, even where transactions remained lawful. The withdrawal signalled a collective judgement about recoverability and enforcement, long before any comprehensive sanctions regime took shape.

Withdrawals are not confined to insurance. Banks exhibit similar behaviour through de-risking. Correspondent banking relationships are trimmed. Certain jurisdictions are quietly removed from acceptable country lists. Products remain on the shelf, but internal policy makes them unreachable.

The metric here is not price but approval rate. When a payment corridor that once cleared routinely now triggers escalation and frequent rejection, the market has spoken.

It is tempting to treat these developments as noise or overreaction. That temptation is understandable. Withdrawals often overshoot. Fear of being the outlier—the last firm standing—can drive herd behaviour. No one wants to be the only insurer still writing a line, or the only bank still financing a route, if enforcement or media attention follows. This produces what might be called *anticipatory compliance*: retreat in advance of certainty.

Here lies the credible counter-example. Markets sometimes pull back too far. After initial waves of de-risking, capacity can return once participants gain clarity or observe that enforcement risk is manageable. The early years of sanctions on Myanmar, for example, saw broad withdrawal by some Western banks, followed by selective re-engagement once firms better understood sectoral and counterparty risk. The limitation is real: withdrawal is not always a reliable predictor of permanent exclusion.

Reconciliation requires distinguishing between temporary shock and structural exit. Temporary shock shows volatility: sharp drops in capacity followed by partial recovery, frequent policy revisions, mixed signals from providers. Structural exit shows persistence: long-term absence of certain products, consolidation of capacity into a few specialised firms, and normalisation of exclusion language in contracts. Time is the discriminator. A quarter is noise. Several years suggest regime change.

To read withdrawals properly, one must pair abstractions with metrics. "Risk aversion" becomes a declining count of active underwriters. "Uncertainty" becomes longer turnaround times for approvals. "Reputational concern" becomes exclusion clauses that reference not just legality but "brand risk" or "market perception". These are not metaphors. They are decisions recorded in systems.

A quiet motif runs through these patterns: the empty shelf. The shelf still exists. The label is still there. But the product is gone. Observers who look only for new rules miss the significance of the empty space.

The same logic applies to shipping services. Liner companies may quietly suspend calls at certain ports, citing operational reasons. Classification societies may delay surveys. Port service providers may increase requirements. Each decision is defensible on its own. Together they raise the cost and uncertainty of trade to prohibitive levels. The withdrawal is distributed.

There is also a feedback loop. Withdrawals beget withdrawals. When capacity falls, remaining providers face higher concentration risk. They respond by tightening terms further. This in turn discourages marginal participants. The spiral is not driven by malice but by arithmetic.

For analysts and decision-makers, the practical task is to watch the margins rather than the headlines. Ask simple questions. How many firms are still offering this service? How long does approval take compared to last year? What exclusions are becoming standard? Which routes or products are discussed only in caveats? These questions do not require privileged access. They require attention.

It is equally important to avoid false comfort. The absence of a formal announcement does not mean stability. Markets communicate through absence as much as presence. A route that still appears on a map may be commercially dead. A product that remains lawful may be practically inaccessible.

At the same time, one must guard against reading every withdrawal as prophecy. Firms withdraw for reasons unrelated to geopolitics: capital constraints, strategic refocusing, loss experience. The diagnostic question is whether withdrawals cluster around specific regions, cargos, or counterparties in ways that correlate with political risk. Patterns matter more than anecdotes.

This brings us back to the core discipline of comparative reading. Compare capacity over time. Compare across regions. Compare across firms. If multiple, otherwise competitive providers reduce exposure to the same niche at the same moment, the signal strengthens. If one firm exits while others expand, the signal weakens.

The closing tension is deliberate. Should firms treat withdrawals as warnings to follow, or as opportunities to differentiate? There is no universal answer. For some, stepping into the gap—carefully, transparently, and with strong controls—builds long-term trust. For others, the cost of being wrong is existential. The market does not resolve this tension. It merely makes it visible.

The empty shelf remains. The question is whether you notice it, and what you infer from its silence.

Building a personal monitoring framework

On 23 February 2022, the Joint War Committee in London issued an updated list of areas considered high risk for shipping. The place was London. The organisation was the Joint War Committee. The consequence was immediate but uneven. Some firms adjusted premiums within hours. Others waited days. A few did nothing at all. For observers who noticed only formal sanctions the following day, the shift seemed abrupt. For those watching insurance circulars, freight chatter and incident reports, it had been visible for weeks. Signals were already aligning.

Most readers encounter geopolitical risk as a blur: headlines, statements, prices that move for reasons never fully explained. The temptation is to treat these fragments as background noise. Yet patterns emerge when fragments are assembled with care. The task is not prediction. It is orientation. Five words suffice. Signals accumulate before decisions.

A personal monitoring framework begins with restraint. No single indicator carries authority. Public statements mislead. Prices overshoot. Incidents are ambiguous. The discipline lies in combination. When different signal types move together, confidence rises. When they diverge, caution is warranted. This is not a system for certainty. It is a way to reduce surprise.

The first building block is the public record. Governments, regulators, and industry bodies speak constantly, though rarely plainly. Statements by finance ministries, sanctions offices, maritime authorities, and central banks provide direction rather than instruction. The show is a speech, guidance note, or press release. The name is signalling. The explanation is that institutions prepare markets gradually, testing language before committing. The implication is that tone matters as much as content. A shift from "monitoring" to "concerned" often precedes action.

Consider the European Commission's communications on energy trade with Russia in late 2021. Formal measures were absent. Language hardened. References to contingency planning increased. For firms watching only enacted rules, nothing had changed. For those tracking phrasing across months, the direction was clear. The metric here is lexical drift: how often certain risks are mentioned, and in what terms.

The second block is pricing. Insurance premiums, freight rates, and financing spreads translate judgement into numbers. They are imperfect but disciplined. An insurer cannot raise rates indefinitely without losing business. A lender cannot widen spreads without justification. When prices move, someone has committed capital accordingly.

A concrete example clarifies the process. In mid-2021, additional war risk premiums for voyages through the Strait of Hormuz began to edge upward, reported by brokers such as Marsh and reflected in Lloyd's market commentary. The place was the Gulf. The period was June to September 2021. No major incident followed immediately. Yet pricing suggested rising concern about regional tensions. When isolated incidents occurred later, the market had already adjusted. The implication for a personal framework is simple: price changes that precede headlines deserve attention.

The third block is incident reporting. These are the most vivid signals and the most misleading. An isolated detention, seizure, or near-miss can dominate attention without altering underlying risk. Conversely, a series of minor incidents can indicate deterioration. The task is aggregation. One event is anecdote. Several similar events form a pattern.

Named sources matter. Reports by the International Maritime Bureau, the UN Panel of Experts, or reputable shipping intelligence firms provide consistency. The abstraction "security risk" becomes visible as a count of incidents per quarter, their locations, and their outcomes. The implication is proportionality. Not all incidents deserve equal weight.

These blocks—statements, prices, incidents—gain power when compared across space. Relative movement reveals perception. If premiums rise on one route but not on a comparable corridor, the difference is informative. If statements mention one region repeatedly while another remains absent, silence speaks. The motif here is triangulation. One point misleads. Three orient.

An example helps ground the method. A reader interested in the Eastern Mediterranean might track, over six months, European Union statements on energy security, insurance rates for LNG carriers transiting the area, and reported maritime incidents involving survey vessels. Individually, each signal is ambiguous. Together, they sketch a risk contour. The framework does not declare danger. It shows shape.

There are limits. Signals conflict. In early 2020, shipping rates collapsed due to the pandemic even as geopolitical risk in some regions increased. Price alone misled. The counter-example is instructive. Macroeconomic shocks can swamp political signals. Reconciliation requires context. When global demand drives prices down everywhere, local divergences matter more than absolute levels.

A personal framework also requires temporal discipline. Watching too frequently amplifies noise. Watching too rarely misses inflection points. Many practitioners settle, implicitly, on a monthly rhythm for strategic signals and a weekly rhythm for operational ones. The abstraction "monitoring cadence" becomes a calendar entry. The implication is sustainability. A framework that exhausts attention will be abandoned.

Crucially, the framework is personal. A bank, an insurer, a trader, and a researcher will weight signals differently. Financing costs matter more to lenders. Insurance exclusions matter more to shipowners. The same data set yields different insights. The framework does not impose uniformity. It encourages consistency.

This raises a further limitation. Confirmation bias is a constant risk. Once a reader believes a region is deteriorating, every signal appears to confirm it. The safeguard is comparison. Track at least one control region alongside the area of concern. If signals diverge meaningfully, confidence increases. If they move together, the cause may be global rather than local.

There is also a reputational dimension. Quiet conversations matter. Industry forums, association meetings, and off-the-record remarks often surface concerns before they are formalised. These are difficult to document and easy to misinterpret. The disciplined approach treats them as prompts for verification, not conclusions. Show becomes anecdote. Name becomes rumour. Explanation demands corroboration. Implication is provisional.

Throughout, the framework resists the urge to forecast. It does not answer the question "what will happen?" It answers "what is changing?" That distinction matters. Markets punish false certainty more harshly than acknowledged uncertainty.

A quiet image returns: the watchlist. Not a dashboard bristling with alerts, but a short, maintained list of regions, routes, or sectors that merit attention. Items enter when signals cluster. They leave when signals dissipate. The act of removal is as important as inclusion. It disciplines memory.

The closing test is unresolved. When signals align but action remains costly, what then? Some will step back early and preserve optionality. Others will proceed cautiously, trusting controls and diversification. The framework does not choose. It illuminates the trade-off. Awareness replaces surprise. The rest remains judgement.

Limits of prediction and modest use

On 10 December 2018, in Buenos Aires, the United States and China announced a temporary truce in their escalating trade dispute following talks between Donald Trump and Xi Jinping at the G20 summit. Markets reacted within hours. Shipping rates adjusted. Commodity prices steadied. Analysts who had spent months reading tariff lists, port data, and freight premiums suddenly faced a reversal that no model had confidently forecast. Signals that had pointed in one direction were not wrong. They were overtaken.

Prediction fails quietly.

The episode remains instructive because it exposes a central weakness in all signal-based approaches. Data can illuminate tendencies, constraints, and pressures. It cannot compel political choice. A diplomatic intervention, a leadership decision, or an unforeseen alliance can redraw the map faster than prices or policies adjust. The purpose of this chapter is not to undermine the tools developed earlier. It is to place them firmly in their proper role.

The first claim is straightforward. Signals describe context, not destiny. The show is a rising insurance premium, a narrowing financing window, or a sudden exclusion clause. The name is market judgement. The explanation is that many independent actors have reassessed risk simultaneously. The implication is preparedness, not prophecy. Firms that confuse the two tend to overreact when the future refuses to comply.

A quiet motif runs through this section: the weather vane. It shows direction, not arrival. It responds to pressure, not intention. Used properly, it helps orientation. Used improperly, it becomes an idol.

Consider a concrete case. In early 2019, following the Buenos Aires truce, shipping premiums on certain Asia–US routes softened, reported by brokers such as Aon and reflected in Baltic Exchange indices. The place was the Pacific. The period was January to March 2019. For readers who had interpreted earlier premium increases as a guarantee of prolonged disruption, the adjustment felt like failure. Yet the earlier signals had accurately reflected uncertainty and cost during escalation. They were not invalidated. They were superseded by a political choice.

This distinction matters. Many organisations struggle not because they lack information, but because they misinterpret its authority. A risk committee may treat a cluster of adverse signals as a verdict rather than a warning.

When circumstances change, trust in the monitoring process erodes. Staff become cynical. The abstraction "risk intelligence" degenerates into ritual.

A second example sharpens the point. In November 2015, following the Iran nuclear deal, the Joint Comprehensive Plan of Action, markets began cautiously re-engaging with Iranian trade. Shipping insurers adjusted exclusions. Banks explored corridors. Then, in May 2018, the United States withdrew from the agreement. The place was Washington. The date was 8 May 2018. Overnight, earlier data acquired a new meaning. Firms that had treated post-2015 signals as a linear trend suffered whiplash. Those that had treated them as contingent conditions adapted more easily.

Here the counter-example is instructive. Some signals persist despite diplomatic theatre. Sanctions on North Korea have waxed and waned rhetorically for decades, yet core restrictions remain. Prices, routing behaviour, and enforcement patterns exhibit remarkable continuity. The limitation of prediction does not imply futility of observation. Reconciliation lies in distinguishing structural constraints from discretionary gestures. Signals tied to deep legal frameworks and institutional capacity tend to be stickier than those tied to negotiation cycles.

Another source of overconfidence lies in aggregation. Combining multiple indicators improves understanding, but it can also create the illusion of inevitability. When statements, prices, and incidents all point in the same direction, conviction rises. The danger is extrapolation. The explanation is cognitive: humans overestimate the stability of trends they have just observed. The implication is humility. Even convergent signals describe the present more reliably than the future.

Metrics help anchor modesty. Time horizons matter. Many insurance and freight adjustments price risk over weeks or months, not years. Financing costs may reflect quarterly reassessments. Political decisions can reset these horizons instantly. Treating short-term prices as long-term forecasts misaligns expectations.

The weather vane returns. It spins quickly. Mountains move slowly.

A further limitation concerns visibility. Some of the most consequential political negotiations occur in private, beyond the reach of market signals. The Cuban Missile Crisis did not announce itself through insurance premiums. The Oslo Accords did not leak via freight rates. Analysts relying solely on observable data would have been blindsided. The show here is absence. The name is information asymmetry. The explanation is that markets price what they can see, not what is being decided behind closed doors. The implication is that silence should not be mistaken for stability.

This has practical consequences. Readers are encouraged throughout this book to watch withdrawals, exclusions, and pricing shifts. The modest use principle insists that these observations remain provisional. They invite questions rather than conclusions. When a premium doubles, the useful response is not "this route is doomed," but "what assumptions are being made, and by whom?"

The discipline of modest use also guards against moral overreach. Treating data as destiny can justify decisions that later appear callous or unnecessary. Firms may exit regions prematurely, sever relationships, or abandon projects based on signals that reflected fear rather than fact. When circumstances improve, rebuilding trust proves costly. The abstraction "reputation" becomes visible as lost counterparties and sceptical regulators.

A named case illustrates this risk. Following the Arab Spring in 2011, many firms withdrew broadly from North African markets. Some signals justified caution. Others reflected panic. When conditions stabilised unevenly, firms that had differentiated between countries and sectors re-entered more smoothly than those that had imposed blanket prohibitions. The implication is balance. Caution need not mean retreat.

There is also a methodological limit. Tools improve with feedback. Prediction rarely provides clean feedback because outcomes are overdetermined. When a forecast appears correct, it is unclear whether the model captured causality or coincidence. Understanding tolerates ambiguity better than forecasting does. This is why the book consistently emphasises explanation over prediction.

A five-word sentence bears repeating. Models do not decide events.

The modest use principle reframes success. A monitoring framework succeeds when it reduces surprise, clarifies trade-offs, and improves conversation. It fails when it promises foresight it cannot deliver. The reader's goal is not to be right about the future, but to be less wrong, less often, and less expensively.

This reframing resolves a common tension. Decision-makers often demand certainty from analysts. Analysts, aware of uncertainty, hedge language. Frustration follows. A shared understanding that signals are aids to judgement, not substitutes for it, recalibrates expectations. The visible behaviour changes. Questions replace demands. Scenarios replace predictions.

The closing tension remains unresolved. When signals deteriorate and politics is opaque, should one act early and risk unnecessary loss, or wait and risk being trapped? No framework answers this decisively. The book does not pretend otherwise. It offers orientation, not insurance.

The final test is simple and uncomfortable. When the weather vane spins, will you watch it, worship it, or ignore it?

About the Author

Nuno Valcorte writes about the uneasy meeting point between global trade, financial services and political risk. Having spent many years around shipping, insurance and banking professionals, he has watched how cautious compliance teams can sometimes shape trade flows more powerfully than formal treaties. His work focuses on making this hidden machinery visible to readers who do not live inside compliance departments, but whose lives and businesses are affected by their decisions. He brings a particular interest in the way maritime history continues to echo through modern sanctions and embargoes. From historic blockades to present-day shadow fleets, he traces how control of sea lanes has quietly evolved from warships to watchlists and risk models. His writing combines narrative case sketches with clear explanation, aiming to give readers the tools to ask better questions of their advisers, employers and governments without needing a legal or technical background.

www.ingramcontent.com/pod-product-compliance
Lightning Source LLC
Chambersburg PA
CBHW031323230926
51848CB00001B/70
9788199786813